Dynamics of
Presentation Graphics

About the Author

Dona Z. Meilach has been at the forefront of the presentation graphics market since charts were first generated on personal computers. She is a dynamic presenter whose seminars and workshops on the use of effective graphics are in great demand by industry and educators. She is a popular speaker at business and computer conferences.

Dona is the author of more than 65 books and hundreds of articles on art, design, and computer topics. Her byline appears in *Computer Graphics Today*, *AudioVisual Communications*, *PC Magazine*, *MacWeek*, and nationally and internationally syndicated columns. She is on the staff of the University of California, San Diego, where she teaches a course in Marketing with Visuals.

This second edition of *Dynamics of Presentation Graphics* was developed using an IBM AT with a VGA board and a Princeton Graphics UltraSync monitor. Author-generated graphics were done with Draw Applause, Applause II, Freelance Plus 3, 35mm Express, and ImageBuilder on the IBM. Examples from the Macintosh were produced with More II, Aldus Persuasion, and Microsoft PowerPoint. Slides were imaged by MAGICorp and Brilliant Image. Black and white output was generated on the LaserPro Silver Express (Oasys) and the Apple LaserWriter II.

In addition to using WordPerfect 5.0 for writing, the author relied heavily on two additional programs, PRD+ and Grammatik.

Contact CompuWrite, 2018 Saliente Way, Carlsbad CA, 02009 (619 436-4395) to schedule a presentation.

Other computer books by Dona Z. Meilach

Better Business Presentations
Before You Buy a Used Computer
Before You Buy Word Processing Software
Before You Buy a Computer
Perfect Guide to Perfect Writer
The Illustrated Computer Dictionary

Also

Decorative and Sculptural Ironwork
Creating Modern Furniture
Woodworking: The New Wave
Creating Small Wood Objects as Functional Sculpture
Contemporary Stone Sculpture
Sculpture Casting (with Dennis Kowal)
How to Create Your Own Designs (with Bill and Jay Hinz)

. . . and more

Dynamics of Presentation Graphics

13

Second Edition

Dona Z. Meilach

BUSINESS ONE IRWIN
Homewood, Illinois 60430

*Dedicated to artists everywhere who are
tackling the computer as an expressive and
practical art medium.*

This publication is designed to provide accurate and
authoritative information in regard to the subject matter
covered. It is sold with the understanding that neither the
author nor the publisher is engaged in rendering legal, accounting,
or other professional service. If legal advice or other expert
assistance is required, the services of a competent
professional person should be sought.

*From a Declaration of Principles jointly adopted by a Committee
of the American Bar Association and a Committee of Publishers.*

Sponsoring editor: Susan Glinert Stevens, Ph.D.
Project editor: Karen Smith
Production manager: Carma W. Fazio
Cover Designer: Michael S. Finkelman
Compositor: Arcata Graphics/Kingsport
Typeface: 10/12 Souvenir
Printer: R. R. Donnelley & Sons Company

Library of Congress Cataloging-in Publication Data

Meilach, Dona Z.
    Dynamics of presentation graphics / Dona Z. Meilach.—2nd ed.
      p.   cm.
    ISBN 1-55623-229-2
    1. Computer graphics.   2. Computer art.   I. Title.
T385.M43   1990
006.6—dc20   89–28997
                                           CIP

Printed in the United States of America

3 4 5 6 7 8 9 0 DO 6 5 4 3

Preface

This source and resource volume emphasizing the esthetic aspects of computer images for presenters emerged as a result of divergent interests and experiences. As the author of over 60 books dealing with art, computers, and other subjects, I have been invited to speak as a lecturer, panelist, and seminar leader, and to be on radio and appear on television in many countries. Magazine assignments have frequently required covering conferences and listening to speakers whose presentations ranged from awful to fantastic.

During computer conferences, I observed that the new do-it-yourself graphics software available at every businessman's desk was plummeting slide quality from what formerly was merely dull to terrible. The presenter's attitude was "Look, I did it myself with my own PC." Visuals too often lacked flair, imagination, and knowledge of elements required to pour impact into an image. The presenter was enticed by the new artistic power at hand and attempted to throw everything at the canvas until it became a hodgepodge. Often visuals violated elementary principles of the subject and how to make good slides. The medium eclipsed, and often killed, the message.

Other factors emerged. Those who must request visuals do not know how to communicate needs to a graphic artist or a slide service. Many presenters, who often had no visuals, were unaware that professional services were available as an adjunct to the computers on their desks.

Dynamics of Presentation Graphics is the result of countless contacts with graphics artists, presenters, computer graphics hardware and software companies, slide services, and production companies, and interviews with conference directors and leaders of effective management seminars. Notes were taken at NCGA (National Computer Graphics Association), SIGGRAPH (Special Interest Group Graphics), Comdex, NCC, Autofact, and meetings for telecommunications, CAD/CAM, and scores of others, detailing the not-so-good, good, and superb presentations, and analyzing the presenters and their graphics support. As chairperson of technical sessions for the San Diego Computer Society's conferences, finding a lineup for dynamic presenters posed a problem that helped hone my conviction that a book like this was needed. My role as a teacher and a consultant to industry provided a proving ground.

As you use the book, please note photo credits to companies that supply software and hardware. Each company address and phone number is listed in the appendix or the chapter in which the credit appears. Write or phone for additional information about the latest software, hardware, or service available. Please mention that you saw the listing in this book.

Also note that the captions of many of the slides and photographs that appear in this book are marked with a C. This means they are reproduced in **color** elsewhere in the book, on special inserts. I hope these will heighten your appreciation for the use of color in your own presentations.

Acknowledgments

I particularly want to thank Apple Computer Inc., Santa Clara, California, for the use of a Macintosh II loaded with memory and a hard disk, and for a laser printer; CDI, Tigard, Oregon, and Larry Jacobson for the unexpected VGA board; and Office Automation Systems (OASYS), San Diego, California, for the use of a LaserPro Silver Express Laser Printer to generate the manuscript and test printing capabilities of many programs.

I am indebted to the cooperation of presidents, marketing managers, communication managers, public relations representatives, and technical support people from the following hardware, software, and photo imaging companies. They were all eager to provide help.

3 M Corp.	Eastman Kodak Corp.
Advanced Graphics Software	Electrohome
Agfa Matrix Division	Electronic Arts
Aldus Corp.	Epson America, Inc.
Ashton-Tate	Genigraphics Corp.
Autodesk, Inc.	General Electric Co.
Autographix	General Parametrics
Brightbill-Roberts	Hartford Insurance Co.
Brilliant Image	Hewlett-Packard Co.
Business & Professional	Hill & Knowlton, Inc.
Software	IBM Corp.
Calcomp	Inset Systems
CDI (Computer Dynamics	Jones Photocolor
Inc.)	Kurta Corp.
Computer Accessories	Lasergraphics
Computer Associates, Intl.	Lotus Corp.
Computer Support Corp.	MAGICorp
Corel Systems Corp.	Management Graphics,
Digital Equipment Corp.	Canada

Management Graphics,
  Minneapolis
Micrografx, Inc.
Microsoft Corp.
Mistubishi Electronics
Moniterm Corp.
National Computer Graphics
  Assn.
New England Software
Numonics, Corp.
Pansophic Systems
Pix Productions

Polaroid Corp.
Presentation Technologies
Software Clearing House
Software Publishing Corp.
SummaGraphics Corp.
Symsoft, Inc.
Symantec Corp.
Tektronix Corp.
Visual Business Systems, Inc.
WordPerfect Corp
Xerox Corp.
Zenographics, Inc.

My thanks to the editors of these magazines, whose assignments led me into this fascinating market: *Associated Features, Audio Visual Communications, Computer Graphics Today, Design Graphics World, Lotus Magazine, MacWeek, PC Week, PC Magazine, Singer Syndicate, Step-by-Step Graphics,* . . . and others.

To conference directors who have invited me to speak: Sandy Krueger, AEC Expo; Richard Dym and Andy Hatkoff, Ashton-Tate; David Small, Computer Graphics New York; Katherine Alesandrini, National Computer Graphics Association; Dr. Howard Qvarnstrom, San Diego TEC Centers; Dr. John Peak, University of California– San Diego; . . . and others.

Specific artists are credited with their artwork. Names were not always provided with submitted slides, so for those anonymous artists whose work appears as a courtesy of a company, my deepest appreciation for your time and talents.

A special acknowledgment to my husband, Dr. Melvin M. Meilach, for his understanding, patience, encouragement, and assistance—photographic and all around—during the months required to prepare this book.

Dona Z. Meilach

Note: Every effort has been made to present all information correctly. Because of the nature of the industry, its rapid changes, and constantly updated equipment and software, no guarantee or warranty is implied by the author or the publisher regarding software, hardware, prices, distributors, addresses, and telephone numbers.

All data examples are fictional and used for demonstration only. They do not necessarily reflect true statistics.

Contents

1 Graphics—Painting a Picture of Your Future   2

The Wharton Study. The Need for Multimedia Graphic Support. Every Company Can Justify Savings and Efficiency. Making Tools and Techniques Available. The Message and the Medium.

2 Planning—The Priority Procedure   10

Planning Is the Key: *WHO? Target Your Audience. WHAT Do You Want to Accomplish? HOW WILL You Accomplish It? WHEN Must You Have the Entire Presentation Ready? WHERE Will the Presentation Be Given?* Theories for Organizing Visuals: *Analyzing Audience Reaction. Beginning, Middle, and End.* Budgets. Plan Visuals for More than One Use. Security. Know Do's and Don'ts for Professional Results. Your Planning Checklist. Products and Software Mentioned in This Chapter.

3 Stage Set for Success   24

Assurance—Reassurance. Survey Your Surroundings. Meeting Room Guidelines: *Overhead Transparency Projection Considerations. Slide Projection Considerations.*

4 Words Can Work Visual Wonders   32

Types of Text Slides: *How Much to Put on One Slide? Type Styles. Color. Layout. Emphasis Using Reveal or Build-up Slides.* Interpreting Text into Drawings. The Text Becomes the Image. Printed and Plotted Text Handouts.

5 Getting a Grasp on Business Graphs   50

Why Some Charts Miss the Mark. Poorly Designed Software Compounds the Presentation Problem. There Are Excellent Software Packages. Twelve Rules for Creating Analytical Graphs: *Simplicity. Emphasis. Unity. Balance. Spacing. Scale. Shade and Color. Texture and Pattern. Grid Line Use. Line Thickness. Data and Tic Mark Placement. Placement of Numbers and Labels. A Note about Titles and Legends.* Chart Style Is the First Consideration.

Which Chart to Use When? Bar Charts: Vertical and Horizontal: *Horizontal Bar Charts.* Pie Charts: *Design Considerations.* Line and Surface Charts: *Other Types of Comparison Charts.* Table, Or Tabular, Charts. Maps as Charts. Diagram Charts.

6 Showing How Things Work 104

How Arrows Depict Movement. Illustrating Size in Physical Space.

7 Picture Libraries Speed Presentation Preparation 114

Create Your Own Library of Images. Stock Slides.

8 Special Effects—Electronically 124

Combining the Effects. Glow or Eclipse. Zoom. Mirrors—Vibrations—Neon Lighting. Starburst, Starbeam, and Laser Highlights. Swirl, Spin, or Pinwheel. The Effect of Movement in Lettering. Animation. Superimposed Photography. Digitizing and Superimposing.

9 Presentations—Clear and Perfect 138

Slide Service Overheads. Color Printers and Plotters: *Black and White Transparencies. Adding Color to Black and White.* Software Simplifies and Improves the Process. Mini-Transparencies. Overhead Projector Considerations. Transparencies Have Their Rules, Too: *Color Schemes. Reveal and Build Techniques. Preparing the Frames.* Readability and Projection Tests. Your Interaction with a Projector. Sources for Information.

10 Making Points with Desktop Slide Shows 158

Animated Presentations. The Origin of Disk Shows: *Software Choices.* How Are Shows Used Effectively? Making the Point. Screen Show Design Suggestions. Special Effects Tools. LCD Units—The Ultimate Transparent Transparency. Designing for LCD Projection. Sources for Information.

11 A Gallery of Art and Advertising Designs 172

12 Software that Generates Presentation Visuals 188

Purchasing Problems: *Protecting Your Purchase. Support.* Programs for Different Purposes. Feature Leapfrog. Macintosh Software Is Stunning. MS DOS Software Takes on Mac Characteristics. General Programs Begin to Tout Presentation Capability. Choices—Choices—Choices. Keystroke Testing. How to Assess Your Needs. Evaluating Software: *Software Information. Hardware Requirements. User Conveniences. Chart Types. Drawing Tools/Free-Form Graphics. Data*

Import/Export. Miscellaneous. Output Devices. Slide Services. Documentation. Worksheet.

13   Capturing the Image with a Camera   216

Film Recorders: *How Do Film Recorders Work? Analog Film Recorders. Digital Film Recorders.* Resolution and Slide Quality: *How to Detect Differences in Slide Quality.* Software Compatibility. Wide Range of Film Recorders: *The BRAVO! Instant Slides from Hard Copy.* When Is an In-House System Practical? Slides from Front of Screen: *Hood Devices.* Slides From Hard Copy. Sorting Out Film Types. Products and Distributors/Manufacturers.

14   Tapping Slide Service Resources   242

Turnaround Time. Slide Prices Vary. Services Support Different Software. Sending Slides by Modem. Workstations. Other Hard Copy and Services. What to Expect from a Slide Service. Full-Production Companies. Stock Slides. Slide Service Bureau Checklist. Directory of Services.

15   Hardware: The Hard Choice   256

Personal Computers. Graphics Workstations. Input Devices: *Mouse. Joystick. Trackball. Light Pen. Graphics Tablet. Image Scanners. Video Capture Systems. Screen Capture Utilities.* Output Devices: *Monitors. Printers and Plotters. Color Printers. Laser Printers. Plotters.* Products and Companies.

16   The Big Picture: Projecting the Image   276

Small-Screen CRT and Video Projectors: *VideoShow. PC Emcee. VIP. Showmate 4.* Large Screen Projectors: *35 mm Slide Projectors. LCD Flat Panel Display Units. Stand-Alone Monochrome Projectors. Kodak Video Projectors for Large-Screen Presentations. Computer/Video Projectors.* What to Consider in Computer/Video Displays: *Resolution, Scan Rate, and Brightness.* Projection Screens. Products and Distributors/ Manufacturers.

Appendix A: Glossary   291

Appendix B: Software, Sources, and Company Lists   296

Appendix C: Selected Bibliography   315

Appendix D: Graphics Publications and Organizations   317

Appendix E: Trademarks   320

Index   323

Dynamics of
Presentation Graphics

1 Graphics—Painting a Picture of Your Future

It's hard to imagine what most people mentally conjure when the term *computer graphics* is mentioned. Something futuristic? Games? Film and television production? However you picture it now, if you're in business—any kind of business—computer graphics will have an impact on your future: not the arcade game graphics variety, or the superslick television and movie displays, but business graphics in a broad brushstroke of applications. Computers will be used to produce visuals quickly for use in and out of the office, for every conceivable type of presentation.

Image processing is the associated term: this is a sister to data and word processing. Instead of numbers and letters being moved about, it's pictures: squares, rectangles, circles, ovals, triangles, parabolas, and so on. These are the building blocks for business charts, mechanical drawings, advertising design, and more.

The usual image of a graphic arts department is one of people bending over drawing boards creating sketches, pasting infinite headlines and bits of copy, drawing pictures, having layouts OK'd, resketching. They send roughs to a photographer and typesetter, proofread galleys, and order printing. Weeks pass between inception of idea and final copy.

There is also the mind's-eye image of the harried executive standing over the art director's desk and wondering why his slides or transparencies aren't ready NOW!

Picture it all again. Computers are replacing these drawing boards, paste pots, brushes, and paints. They are speeding up all processes.

Every employee who needs visuals (not only an executive) can now stand over the art director's desk with slides and transparencies in hand only a short time after they were requested. In many offices employees can create and process the graphics.

State-of-the-art technology is rapidly changing the graphics production department of the past with results that will make a corporate financial officer grateful. A few of these results are savings in time, money, and frustration. When it is used properly, the graphics department can generate money.

Courtesy, Applicon, Inc.

The office of the future is here already in Applicon's BRAVO! CAD/CAM systems.

Graphics processing is escalating, with predictions that someday it will rival, and possibly eclipse, its sister processing procedures. Those responsible for decision making are beginning to understand that there is more to graphics than meets the eye. Within the next few years the exploding computer graphics industry is expected to double, then triple in sales; all future projections expect increases after that.

Why the current excitement about computerized picture making? Several factors are:

1. The Wharton Business School Study citing the impact of graphics on business meeting outcomes.
2. Industry's growing sophistication, with requirements in multimedia visuals available only via computerization.
3. Lower-priced computer graphics equipment with overall cost savings when used.
4. Improved efficiency and a faster turnaround time for finished visuals.

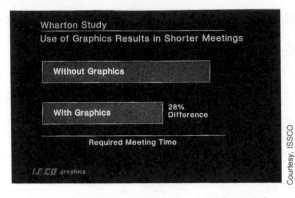

The results of the Wharton Study show that graphics shorten meetings and save time.

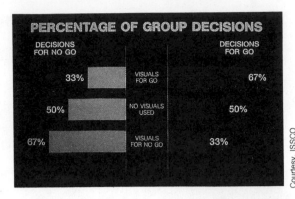

The Wharton Study: The effect of visuals on group decision making.

The Wharton Study

The importance of visuals was brought into sharp focus in 1982 in a study made by the Wharton Business School's Applied Research Center, under a grant from the Audiovisual Division of 3M Company. The conclusions were that visual communications (overhead transparencies and slides) significantly influence how decisions are reached, how the presenter is perceived by the audience, and how much time is required to reach a decision.

During the six-month study, several role-playing situations were tested, with students giving the presentations. Presenters using overhead transparencies won their point 67 percent of the time and were perceived as more professional by group members. Consensus of the group regarding a decision was reached in a 28 percent shorter meeting time.

One aspect of the study involved role players whose goal was to convince an audience of the validity of their argument. When the presenter used visuals, 67 percent agreed with a "go" decision. When the presenter used visuals and argued for a "no go" decision, the same percentage agreed. When no visuals were used, there was a 50–50 deadlock.

Presenters were rated on 11 key characteristics, using a seven-point scale; the presenter with visuals was rated as "significantly better prepared, more professional, more persuasive, more credible, and more interesting." Similar overwhelming favor was given in every category to the presenter with visuals, compared to the presenter with the same topic and outline but no visuals.

The Need for Multimedia Graphic Support

Raymond J. Lasky, technical director of Audiovisual Services, The Hartford Insurance Group, says, "Effectively explaining new products, new marketing strategies, and corporate goals and directions often requires audiovisual support. The nature of that support can vary from the production of one piece of conventional graphic art to a multimedia extravaganza designed to dazzle as well as to inform."

Lasky says that in the past, Hartford presentations consisted mostly of speakers and 35 mm slides. Design work was done in-house but actual production was contracted outside. Costs were high and the production time required was long. "The final presentation was often good, but rigid," says Lasky. "If we wanted to change data or use the material in another form, there were frequent delays and difficulties. Often we had to scrap what had been done before and recreate visuals from scratch."

So Lasky designed a system for The Hartford Group that gave them control, faster turnaround time, and flexibility. It was planned to integrate a variety of media. It could take input from video cameras, videotape recorders, 35 mm slides, print photographs, or 16 mm film. It could then take this input and transform it into 35 mm color slides, overhead transparencies, color prints, magazine separations, video, or videotape animation. It could also store this input for eventual access to videodisk recorders.

Initially, the proposed equipment was rented. With it the in-house production of slides, staging, and presentation for a national seminar was done at a fraction of the cost quoted by an outside vendor. Total overall cost for the seminar was $52,000, compared to the $100,000 fees involved when working with outside sources.

Courtesy, Management Graphics, Inc., Minneapolis MN

A typical graphics computer station is the TTS/PLUS, which includes (from left to right) a video film recorder, a black and white CRT with keyboard, a color video monitor, and a digitizing tablet (drawing tablet) with a puck for input. Hard copy peripherals, not shown, may be a printer or a plotter.

Courtesy, Scarlett Letters

The program MacPaint on the Macintosh computer can integrate graphics with text or be used to create graphics only.

As that first production was used by salespeople, within three months accounts jumped over 600 percent; more than $3.2 million of new business revenues were generated. The company realized that by investing $100,000 to buy the necessary equipment, they would save more than $640,000 over a 10-year span. In essence, investing in the system not only saved money but also held promise of an invaluable tool that would earn money.

Yet there is more to the story than dollar figures. The AV department can produce a complete slide in minutes, or a visual presentation in a matter of hours, compared to the weeks required previously. The department is flexible in scheduling and developing new directions.

Every Company Can Justify Savings and Efficiency

It is logical that every company cannot justify, and does not require, equipment in the $100,000 category of The Hartford's Chyron System; perhaps, not even in the $20,000 category. Not every company is ready for multimedia productions. But is there a company that is not interested in saving money, or making money, or that does not require some presentation material (whether overhead projections, 35 mm slides, or distributed hard copy)?

Anyone who has not considered computers for generating graphics has the proverbial "head buried in the sand" syndrome.

The reality of more sophisticated and improved graphics on the microcomputer is here, and the applications are spiraling upward. A graphics-capable microcomputer such as an IBM PC, Epson, Leading Edge, Compaq, Apple II series, Macintosh, Commodore, or NCR can generate valuable basic business and report graphics. Equipment in the hands of people with design knowledge and artistic talent can generate exciting and dynamic graphics.

When graphics equipment is intelligently installed and integrated with appropriate peripherals, it can reduce substantially the time required to create visuals for everyone, from the chief executive officer to the salesperson calling on customers. It can eliminate bottlenecks in an existing graphics department and enable people to meet their own needs at the right time.

Making Tools and Techniques Available

Placing computer graphics in the hands of an executive, a secretary, or an art department does not automatically spell success. The computer, graphics programs, and peripherals are only tools. The person who uses them provides the brains and talent.

In many corporate offices, top management doesn't think its executives should spend their time "playing" with paint and draw

Graphics output as hard copy on paper or as overhead transparencies is clear and crisp as it comes from Enter Computer's Sweet-P Six-Shooter six-pen plotter (see Chapter 14).

Courtesy, Enter Computer, Inc.

software. That doesn't mean no one in the office should do so. If massaging meaningful data into well-designed charts and graphs that can explain concepts more quickly than rows of numbers is essential, then someone should do it. In the office of the present, and most likely the future, the computer graphics designer promises to be as essential as the accountant and the office manager.

Today, a 36-picture presentation can be generated from final data to finished slides, and placed in a carousel for projection, in less than an hour, with readily available equipment and film. Slides can be produced at the desk; it isn't necessary to send film out to a lab for processing. Those slides can be colorful, conform to the rules of good visuals, and convey the intended message.

The Message and the Medium

The message is of prime importance, but the medium that targets that message must be a subtle accompaniment. Ideas for images, culled from the best examples available from companies and services around the world, are shown and explained to help you add punch to the contents of your presentations.

A new family of software has made it easy to display numbers and concepts visually with bar and line graphs, pie and other types of charts, and to underscore thoughts with text and pictures.

But having these new, enticing tools is only the first step. Business slides, no matter how they are produced, can be as boring as the travel photographer who stands his wife in front of every monument.

They can also be as snappy and memorable as a pro's view of the Mediterranean at sunset.

The purpose of visuals is to help make you an impressive, lively presenter with a meaningful message. To work properly, they should look professional and contain titles, concepts, viewpoints, true representation of data, correct colors—and be restrained. They have to be easy to read and command attention.

The difference between "ordinary" and "dynamic" presentation graphics can be discerned by an audience, felt by a presenter, and reflected in sales figures.

Those who must listen to a sales pitch or a report are becoming more demanding and discriminating in what they expect to see. Those who present must catch and hold attention with quality, carefully planned slides, overhead transparencies, or hard copy handouts. If presentations are dull and visuals are sloppy, an intricately developed, costly campaign could be undermined.

How does one use the new software to create dynamic presentations?

The first step is to recognize what "dynamic" is. That means heightening your awareness of elements used to translate an idea into an exciting visual that supports, but does not eclipse, the point. It means analyzing presentation media, understanding why and what makes some punchier and more successful than others.

For those who create presentations, the information and examples offered in this book will spark ideas, offer suggestions, and show how and how not to develop ·a sales pitch, lecture, training session, and report for any type of business and one appropriate for the specific audience. There are do's and don'ts regarding the presentation environment. You will become aware of how your positive approach can enhance the total picture. You'll find checklists to help you avoid possible disasters resulting from not being totally in command.

Each chapter offers approaches that may help you plan an impressive presentation in a few hours, instead of days or even weeks (time spans that are too often the norm in many companies). Thirty-five mm slides may not even be required now that slides can be presented directly on, or projected from, the computer screen (also referred to as "on-line" slides).

The book emphasizes images, esthetics, and subtle artistry. These must be incorporated into a presentation of professional quality that will help you keep on top of today's fast-paced, constantly changing business environment, with its requirements and competition.

You will find information about programs for text and chart slides used in business graphics, CAD/CAM (Computer-Aided Design/Computer-Aided Manufacturing) for drawing and painting to enhance visuals; equipment for presentation, commercial slide services, image-producing cameras; and more. There's a gallery of picture elements and a gallery of finished art used for every facet of illustrations.

Presentations, whether by slide, overhead projection, hard copy, or video, can be dynamic in any environment when the elements that comprise the design are known and applied. These are not esoteric, hard-to-understand concepts. They are apparent once they are pointed out.

How can this book help the person who must be a dynamic presenter yet lacks the time or inclination to create visuals? When that person knows what can be achieved, he can communicate his needs intelligently to a graphic artist or a slide-making service. He knows what is possible, what the limitations are, what to request, and how to get it without wasting time, editing sessions, and expense.

The reader will find a wealth of stimulating ideas, visual images, and procedures that can be applied in planning, creating, and using any of the presentation media before an audience of 1 or 1,000.

Courtesy, Tymlabs Corp.

Today, almost any computer with enough memory and hard disk space will run popular presentation, charting, painting, drawing, design, and CAD software. Shown are the Hewlett-Packard Vectra (left) and the Apple Macintosh II (right), with software from Tymlabs Corp.

Planning—The Priority Procedure

You know you have to present something to someone. Probably no one is more familiar with the subject than you. You know exactly what you want to say and how to say it. But do you know the most effective methods for accomplishing the task quickly, effectively, and economically?

There is an art, a methodical approach, to creating hard-hitting, succinct presentations guaranteed to hold an audience's attention. Once you've given a presentation that clicked, you'll know it. If you've given one that failed, you'll know that, too. Will you know why?

There can be sundry reasons for failing, and unexpected exigencies. It's not always possible to control every aspect of a presentation. You should be prepared for anything that can go awry.

The best presentation for any purpose, whether it's to sell one person or to convince an audience of hundreds, needs perfect planning and organization *before* you face your audience.

Planning Is the Key

Often the most obvious factors are skipped over casually, but if you note each item in order, and write it on a planning sheet, you will know what requires attention. It's the tried and true, who, what, why, how, when, and where approach.

WHO is your audience?
WHAT do you have to tell them?
WHY are you telling them?
HOW will you do it?
WHEN is it needed?
WHERE will it be given?

A convenient checklist that includes points you should consider within each of the above is at the end of the chapter.

Courtesy, Visual Horizons

A visual image of a key is more dynamic than words only. A commercially available stock slide can be used where applicable.

WHO? Target Your Audience

Who will be listening to your presentation? Audiences fall into three categories: personal, peer, and public. A short synopsis of this week's business goals to 4 people in your department requires a completely different approach from that of a paper presented to 20 people at your management level. Both differ from a multiple projector hoopla, aimed at motivating a sales force, before an audience of 500.

The same business report you give extemporaneously to the people in your department using an overhead projector requires more polishing before being given to the board of directors or the company's shareholders.

The first question asked by a company that creates graphics is "Who is your audience and how many people will your message reach?"

The knowledge and experience of the audience are factors to consider when visuals are planned. What is the best way to reach them using words and images? Why do they want to listen to you? How can you make it worth their time? What can they hope to learn?

Studies of audiences indicate that each person experiences the world through three perceptual systems: visual or sight, auditory or sound, and kinesthetic or feeling. Most people, perhaps 60 percent, think in terms of pictures; they remember how people look, what they wear, how they perform. About 30 percent think in terms of sounds; they remember what was said, how it was said, and the tone. Kinesthetic people comprise about 10 percent of the population; they feel and remember the warmth of a touch, the comfort of a chair.

Using that same breakdown, people who plan slide presentations professionally advise placing the greatest emphasis on the visual aspect and lesser emphasis on verbal communication; both should include words and images that suggest feelings.

WHAT Do You Want to Accomplish?

A presentation designed to attract venture capital is aimed differently from one designed to sell a product. A sales pitch to an individual prospect targets a person's specific needs and response to the product or service; it has a goal different from that of a presentation made to a committee or large group. Write down the exact goals for each presentation you must give, and keep them on file.

Be specific: What do you have to tell them? How informed are they already about the subject? What level—beginning, advanced, or peer group—should you address? What are your objectives, and

A target image in the computer's memory can be updated with a new figure as needed and a new photo taken; the picture does not have to be redrawn.

Artist: Diane K. O'Malley. Courtesy, Autographix, Inc.

what do you want to accomplish? Does the audience have precon- ceived ideas you're trying to change or sway? How forceful can you be? Must you use a soft-sell or a hard-sell approach? Will your talk help them do something better? How much can you hope to accomplish in the time you have?

HOW Will You Accomplish It?

After you analyze your audience and their objectives, design a plan that accomplishes your goals. What medium will you need? Here are the six most often used.

A Flip Chart or Write-On Board. This medium works well for a small audience in a lighted room. The surface may be chalk- board or an erasable white surface used with a felt-tip pen. These media invite audience interaction. The information may be drawn on the surface. The sheets of paper from a flip chart can be torn off and hung across the front of the room for a review of points covered.

Overhead Transparencies. These are recommended for a small audience in a small room that is lit. This method encourages audience interaction and gives the presenter control over the timing of prepared graphics. Although the graphics are prepared in ad- vance, additional points can be made spontaneously by writing on the medium as you talk. Transparencies are excellent during training seminars because they can be instantly updated (see Chapter 9).

Flip charts or boards for writing with chalk or erasable felt-tip pen may be suspended on specially designed tracks in the front of the room; this is a more efficient arrangement than putting them on flimsy tripod stands.

Courtesy, Charles Mayer Studios, Inc.

35 mm Slides.   Use these for any size audience but usually one where interaction is not encouraged because the room is dark. A 35 mm slide presentation may range from a single slide at a time on the screen to a multimedia presentation of as many as 16 projectors. The amount of planning depends on the complexity of the presentation. Still pictures can be dynamically enhanced by many visual special effects so they appear to zoom, move, twist, and dance across the screen.

Direct Computer Terminal (On-Line) Viewing.   The computer screen may be used to show a series of slides without requiring any other graphics medium. The generated "slides," as they are called, are not the traditional 2 × 2 inch, 35 mm slides that you physically hold in your hand. They are the data on disk that become images on your terminal's screen. New units on the market enable you to project these images from the computer onto a projection screen as you would with 35 mm slides (see Chapters 9 and 16). You can achieve effects as dramatic as those of 35 mm and video presentations. The computer is capable of animation and of speeding up and slowing down a presentation. These computer-generated images may be made into 35 mm slides (see Chapters 13–14).

Videotape.   Slides made on a computer or by traditional photographic methods can be placed on a videotape with a sound track added. The presenter does not interact with the presentation as the tape is being shown; the tape carries the message. The presenter may be available for questions afterward. Videotape may eliminate the presence of a person and allow the audience to view the tape at its leisure.

Hard Copy Printouts.   You may wish to supplement information you present on transparencies or slides with a printed sheet summarizing your topic. When detailed reports are required showing figures that must be studied, the slides should summarize the resulting general trends; amplification should be accomplished with handouts. The logos and graphics design used in slides should be carried over to the format of the handout.

Regardless of the medium, the general design principles offered throughout the book prevail. Ideas from examples in one chapter are applicable to those in another.

WHEN Must You Have the Entire Presentation Ready?

Here's a major bottleneck and bugaboo in developing the presentation. Last-minute preparations for a presentation usually appear as slapdash as they are. Be aware of the time requirements and constraints for preparing the material you need, and allow extra time for unexpected delays. Whether you are preparing the slides yourself, working with your in-house art department, or working with a slide service, allow ample time to create and edit the material to perfection. Then add a buffer period for anything that may go wrong.

A Gantt chart or production schedule for creating a presentation could be as helpful for scheduling slide presentations, as it is in other project management applications.

WHERE Will the Presentation Be Given?

Know in advance, if possible, the physical environment for the presentation: the room size, seating arrangement, time of day, lighting, lectern and screen placement (see Chapter 3 for a further discussion of the presentation environment).

Theories for Organizing Visuals

When all planning problems have been identified and dealt with, the next step is to organize the material. Planning a scenario for visuals requires that you organize your thoughts and the order in which they will be presented. Then you begin to create the visuals that "support" your talk.

Support is the main word here. A slide or overhead transparency should be designed to prod the audience along as you talk; it should not be a readout of what you are saying. If the visual did that, it would have too much on it; the audience would be too busy reading to give you the necessary attention.

Analyzing Audience Reaction

Psychologists have probed audience reaction for years, and those who study the phenomenon are acutely aware of the findings. Ridgie Barton, president of Pix Productions, explains that a visual must be designed to keep the viewer's attention where you want it. Each time a slide appears, the viewer turns his mind to that slide and focuses on it—not on the speaker. That thought process switch requires only a few milliseconds, and then the mind returns to the speaker. However, if the slide has too much information on it, the mind's processing time takes longer and the message begins to interfere with the speaker. Therefore, visuals must be kept short and simple and must act like a quick poke in the side. Says Barton,

> Each time a slide comes up, the mind must stop, read, and process the information. If you poke the viewer too much he will turn off as if to say "I can't take this," and stop trying. It's an information

overload. If you poke too slowly the viewer will fade away; his mind will wander and possibly the head will begin to nod. The trick is to poke at the right rate. About two to four slides per minute average is a practical goal with some slides remaining on screen longer than others.

Beginning, Middle, and End

Beginning, middle, and end are three essentials of every presentation. It's the journalist's old trick of

> Tell 'em what you're going to tell 'em.
> Tell 'em.
> Tell 'em what you told 'em.

A prepared presentation precludes an off-the-cuff, extemporaneous speech which, in turn, avoids rambling. With practice, one can eventually sound as though one is not reading a presentation and appear to be presenting it extemporaneously. Presenters who can carry off that effect are experienced, at ease, and familiar with their subject. It's the result of planning, organizing thoughts beforehand, and rehearsing.

"Pacing should be planned initially, also," emphasizes Barton. "It means changing the speed of the images, the thoughts, and even the cadence of the sentences during the beginning, middle, and end of a speech." It's a build-up effect that avoids monotony and keeps the audience tuned in. The plan is:

> Begin with a punch, slow down to show an overview of
>   what you plan to say for the beginning;
> Build up for the middle and emphasize each point;
> End quickly with a summary.

The beginning should use up about one fourth of the time period; the middle, five eighths; the end punching out the summary in the remaining one eighth time allotment.

Organizing a presentation with visuals may be approached in several ways, from rough chicken scratches on yellow legal pads to elaborate storyboards. Slide services may have forms to help a client organize a presentation. When working with an artist or a slide service, people learn to work with one another and understand what each expects.

There is no substitute for outlining your thoughts carefully and editing each to one short sentence or phrase. There are certain limitations for the slide and overhead transparency formats outlined and explained throughout the book.

Aids suggested by companies and art directors interviewed include the following.

Courtesy, Reactive Systems, Inc.

A computerized response system lets each audience member respond immediately and simultaneously to multiple-choice questions. The system may be used during sales and marketing meetings, training sessions, boardroom decision making, testing, and at exhibits. The responses, either by group or individual, can be instantly tabulated and shown on a video display or printout. Each response pad is equipped with 10 response buttons.

Several programs offer outlining capabilities. When the outline is complete, you select the format you want and the outline automatically becomes a bullet chart, outline chart, text chart, or other. You still have control over the final appearance by editing and revising templates. Word processing programs with outline capability can also be used to generate slides and overhead transparencies.

Photo: Author

Index Cards. Write each topic heading on an index card and each subhead on a separate card. You can move these about and easily change one in relation to another. The technique of revealing only one line at a time as the speaker moves through a subject can be developed more easily from an outline form. [This is called a "reveal" or "build up" (see Chapter 4)]. Rearrange the cards until you are absolutely sure of the wording and the order in which each line is to be highlighted or revealed. When the slides are produced, there is a separate slide for each line as it is discussed. Don't telegraph all your ideas to the audience instantly by leaving one slide on-screen during the entire portion of the talk. The audience tends to focus ahead of what you are saying; you may lose the attention you're trying hard to retain.

Thought Processing and Outlining Software. Software that automatically generates outlines helps to organize thoughts and rearrange their order. Now, several presentation packages will automatically generate a slide to the chart format you select, perhaps a bullet chart or an organization chart. Often, a change you make in the slide on-screen will also update the original outline. Aldus Persuasion, MORE II, and Cricket Presents do this on the Macintosh. HOTSHOT Presents does it on the PC.

It's also possible to create your outline in a word processing file in a program such as WordPerfect, WordStar, or Word, then export it to a presentation program. The presentation program must have ASCII import capabilities. Word processing files can also be made into boardroom quality visuals by a slide service

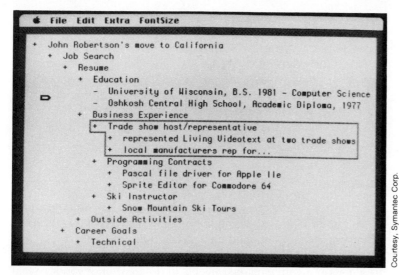

An outline on-screen from ThinkTank on the Apple Macintosh. Any line or group of lines can be selected and moved to a new location. When used in MORE II for slide output, each main head will become the title of a new chart. The sublevels will be formatted according to the template.

bureau. You don't need a presentation, graphics, or slide making program (see Chapters 9 and 14).

Generally, people who create visuals fall into two types: those who like to work from outlines and those who prefer to create as they go.

Storyboards. A storyboard represents the sequence of visuals with roughly drawn sketches or pictures and accompanying narra-

Storyboarding can be accomplished on paper or light cardboard; it is a tool to aid planning visuals and the text that accompanies them.

tion. Storyboarding (a procedure taken from filmmakers) gives a clear overview of the progression and interaction of each visual. For example, a "reveal" series (where only one idea at a time is shown as the talk progresses) may require four slides: one for each point to be made, plus a special effect slide for the beginning or end. Storyboarding a presentation helps the presenter and the person creating visuals to understand one another. It can reduce and possibly eliminate the time, expense, and frustration involved in excessive editing.

Budgets

The costs for visuals can vary tremendously. Slides can range from $3.50 to $20.00 if you design them, $25.00 to $125.00 and more if they are custom designed by a slide service.

But spending megabucks on slides does not guarantee a dynamic presentation. Learn what is available in different price ranges, what you would like, what you can afford, and where and how you can get it. You can take slides with simple equipment or with image cameras (see Chapter 14).

Equipment is a major investment. After that is amortized, the cost per graphic drops considerably. Multiimage productions can run into the tens of thousands of dollars; they are usually scheduled for major promotions, television, and video displays. Well-planned presentations can pay for themselves in sales and income generated.

Planning Visuals for More Than One Use

A presentation, depending on its scope and sophistication, may be considered an "investment" in time and energy. If it is carefully conceived, it may be applied to more than one use, and some or all of the images may be used again at different times. Logos, title slides, and images that generalize about your company or its services can be stored in a slide holder so that others in the company can reuse them for their talks and not duplicate efforts and costs. Presenters can work with slides already in-house and fill these in with the new slides for a particular presentation.

In many companies, there are established parameters for slides, such as colors for backgrounds and placement, and color for logos, font and type size, and style. "General" slides may then be reused. There is a continuity in their appearance, an essential design approach further discussed at the end of the chapter and in chapters dealing with specific types of slides.

Most software for generating slides requires that a format be established for the slide; this includes size and style of font, placement of text, colors, and so on, so that new slides will have the same look.

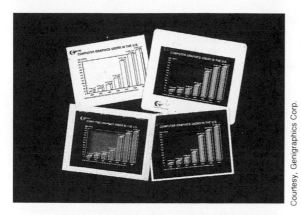

Courtesy, Genigraphics Corp.

Courtesy, Multiplex

Well-designed visuals can be applied to more than one medium. Shown are a black and white print, a color transparency, a black and white proof, and a color print.

When a standardized design format is used and the slides are stored and filed for easy access, they may be reused for various presentations. The Visulite II Console viewer and cabinet helps organize visuals for quick access.

Security

What scenario could be worse than arriving to present your program and discovering that the suitcase with the slides was lost by the airline? Or that you left the slides in a briefcase in a taxicab? Or that the slides were hidden, so they would be safe, in the closet of a hotel in another city? Such emergencies have motivated many companies to exercise security measures such as:

1. *Carry two sets of slides with you in two different places when you travel.* Keep one set in your suitcase and hand carry the other set.

2. *Make a backup set of slides and keep them in a safe place in the office.* Be sure someone else knows where they are and has immediate access to them. Should a set of slides disappear, the backup set can be forwarded to you instantly.

3. *Use a popular software package that is likely to be compatible with computers in most offices.* If you use a commercial slide service, be prepared to be able to send them data by modem—and if it's a networked service it may have offices in major cities. If your home office is in California and you're lecturing in Boston, your California office can send information by modem to the Boston office, which could reproduce the slides within a few hours—faster than they could be produced in California and shipped to you by express service.

If you use telecommunications, carry your software for accessing the system plus necessary telephone numbers for electronic mail where applicable.

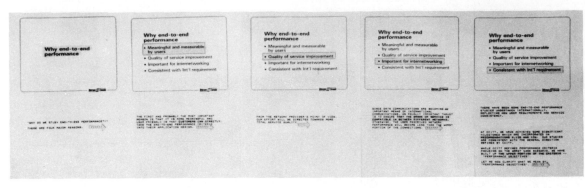

Courtesy, Mark Matsubara, Telecom, Canada

Lecture notes should contain copies of the slides and the comments to be made about each one. These notes indicate which line of a slide will be highlighted as the speaker makes the point.

4. *If you are planning an on-line slide presentation, carry two extra copies of the floppy disks with you, a copy of the program you need to run the presentation, and a copy of your disk operating system utilities to cover possible emergencies.* You can always rent or borrow a machine for showing the slides via computer if necessary. If you are traveling by car, a compact computer and the on-disk, on-line slide show can become your total sales presentation. It can be individualized with data changed instantly for each customer.

Finally, your lecture notes themselves should contain a hard copy replica of the slide as it will appear. It may help to reduce that copy and paste it in the text where you will be discussing it. Use glow-colored felt pens to underline the sentence you will be discussing. You can see it quickly both in a darkened room and when you must refer to notes in a bright room.

Each person develops a procedure that works best for him. Although many companies hire consultants to coach their executives to be effective presenters, few have helped them develop a personal approach that integrates the talk with the best types of graphics to use.

Do's and Don'ts for Professional Results

Established guidelines exist for presenting good visuals; these are discussed in depth and with examples in this chapter and those that follow. You will learn several common pitfalls to avoid, and a philosophy and psychology of visuals used in presentations. The following suggestions will help you begin on the right foot and avoid mistakes common to the uninitiated. Text slides, graphs and charts, and technical slides have standardized formats that are introduced in the appropriate chapter.

These guidelines are not carved in stone. Occasionally, a rule has to be broken, but you will know why and the best way to break it.

1. Don't mix 35 mm slides and overhead projections in the same lecture. They necessitate different lighting conditions and different interaction with the audience.

2. Always use a horizontal slide format. If you have a vertical image, push it to one side of the slide and add another picture, or add text at the side. If that's not practical, add a panel of black or a color at the side to achieve a horizontal format. A blank area of white is a "negative" poke in the side.

3. Do not crowd a slide with text. When bullets are used, the line should be short, with a maximum of four or five words per line. There should be no more than five or six lines per slide.

4. Don't use needless detail.

5. Don't use six slides when three or four will tell the same story.

6. Don't mix styles, type fonts, or colors indiscriminately. When in doubt, exercise restraint. You want the slide to call attention to the *content,* not the slide. The message is the medium; the medium is not the message. Too much razzle-dazzle in a slide presentation can make an audience suspicious and think it is being manipulated.

7. Select the right chart for analytical and report data. Use a chart to show trends rather than details that cannot be absorbed quickly as they flash on a screen.

8. Avoid red in business slides that deal with money and profit-and-loss figures.

9. Remember that the brightest colors jump forward. White is always safe for lettering; blue, for backgrounds. Or use a color that suggests the industry. Bankers and farmers like green backgrounds (suggestive of money and lush growth). Architects relate to blue backgrounds (blueprints). Black is always safe, especially if the room is not totally dark. If you're not sure how a slide will project in a large room, take your projector outside at night and project the image on the side of your house or a garage door to about the same size it will project on-screen. Is everything sharp? Readable?

10. To drive a point home, use the same message twice, but use a "glow" or other special effect the second time, and/or change its position on the slide.

A vertical format will be disconcerting among horizontal slides. If a vertical picture must be used, push it to one side and add text, a solid color, or a logo to convert it to a horizontal format.

Many aids on the market will help in the organization and evaluation of slides. Delete any slides that aren't absolutely essential.

A good text slide will have words that stand out against a dark background. The type style should be simple and easy to read.

Your Planning Checklist

Answer these questions before you begin to plan your next presentation. A strong identification of the who, what, how, when, and where in an organized manner is invaluable.

WHO is your audience?
    Number of people? _____

    Why are they coming to listen to you? _____

    _____

    What are they expecting to learn or gain? _____

    _____

WHAT do you have to tell them?
    How sophisticated are they about the subject?

    Level of understanding? Beginning _____ Advanced _____

    Peer group _____

    What are your objectives? _____

    What do you want to accomplish? _____

    What are the audience's beliefs and prejudices about the subject?

    _____

    How much time do you have? _____

    Is a question/answer period in order? _____

WHY are you telling them?
    What will they want to hear? _____

    How much will they be able to absorb? _____

HOW will you do it?
    Do you want to interact with the audience as you talk? _____

    Do you want to lecture, with questions afterward? _____

    Will you need hard copy handouts? _____

    What kinds of visuals will serve your needs best? _____

    Flip charts _____ Chalkboard _____

    Overhead projection with transparencies _____

    35 mm slides _____

    Computer presentation _____

    Videotapes _____

    Handouts _____

WHEN is it needed?

Date _____

How much time is there until the presentation? _____

In the time allowed, which medium is most practical? _____

What is the time frame for each step? _____

Planning _____

Organizing _____

Requesting visuals _____

Having the finished items in your hands _____

WHERE will it be given?

City _____

Building and room _____

Size of room _____

Arrangement of seating (see Chapter 3) _____

Facilities available _____

Products and Companies Mentioned in This Chapter

Aldus Corp.
Aldus Persuasion
411 First Ave. S.
Seattle, WA 98104
206 622-5500
800 333-2538. Dept. 24D
(information)

Cricket Software
Cricket Presents 2.0
Great Valley Corporate Center
40 Valley Stream Parkway
Malvern, PA 19335
215 251-9890

Charles Mayer Studios, Inc.
Converta-Wall Systems
168 E. Market St.
Akron, OH 44308
216 535-6121

Multiplex Display Fixture Co.
1555 Larkin Williams Rd.
Fenton, MO 63026
314 343-5700
800 325-3350 (except Missouri)

Reactive Systems, Inc.
222 Cedar Lane
Teaneck, NJ 07631
201 568-0446

Symantec Corp.
MORE II
10201 Torre Ave.
Cupertino, CA 95014
408 253-9600
408 441-7234
800 626-8847 (CA)

Symsoft, Inc.
HOTSHOT Presents
444 First St.
Los Altos, CA 94022
415 941-1552

Tymlabs Corp.
Terminal Emulator Software
811 Barton Springs Road
Austin, TX 78704
512 478-0611

Word Perfect Corp.
WordPerfect
1555 Technology Way
Orem, UT 84057
801 225-5000

3

Stage Set for Success

You've prepared your presentation material carefully. Your slides are dynamic and you've rehearsed your speech. Does that guarantee a super presentation, one talked about for weeks after and remembered months later?

Not at all. Consider all the presentations you've attended. Which have been dynamic and memorable, and which have been dull? Consider why.

Next time you listen to someone present a talk, take notes about what you liked and what you didn't like. You'll soon recognize what to do, and what not to do, when you are in the spotlight. The same general rules apply whether one is giving a talk with 35 mm slides or overhead transparencies. Room setups differ slightly; these are illustrated at the end of the chapter.

The medium you use is only one of three aspects of presentation. What are the others? (1) Your appearance, preparation, and content; and (2) the environment in which the presentation is given.

Assurance—Reassurance

The following points, carefully considered and followed, will help you clinch the presentation and come across as dynamically as the visuals you've prepared.

1. *Start on time.* A late start causes audience confidence to plummet; it requires extra time and effort to regain that confidence.

2. *Dress the role for a particular audience.* Casual attire in front of a formal group may cause the audience to have less regard for your ability. It may affect your own self-assurance. Being over-dressed can suggest snobbishness or the idea that someone thinks he is better than his audience.

3. *Know what you want to say.* For a slide show, use notes that clearly tell you which slide is coming up next and what you will say about it.

For overhead projections, place visuals in the proper order and right side up so you don't have to flip the boards or twist the film.

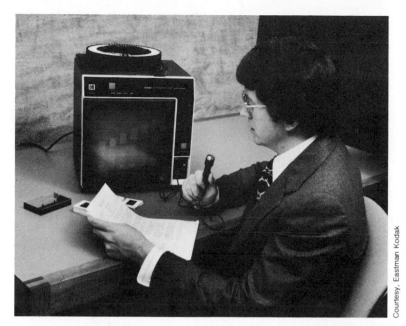

Courtesy, Eastman Kodak

Tape your talk with the slides and play it back. The Kodak Ektachrome 450 is one of several models that permit audio and visual input and output. After you tape the speech, play it back for yourself and someone else for a reaction. Listen for nonprofessional speech patterns.

4. *Rehearse with a tape recorder, or have someone videotape your presentation, or use an audioviewer projector/slide system.* Many seminars and companies provide videotaping and critiques as a business. Such a company may be hired to help coach potential presenters in the do's and don'ts of "presentmanship." Subconscious movements, such as jingling your money or your keys in your pocket, scratching your nose frequently, talking with your hand in front of your mouth, leaning on a podium, and not talking into a microphone are habits that some people are unaware of. They are like telegraph signals to an audience that you are nervous. They can be distracting if people focus on your habits and not on what you are saying. Remember:

> NEVER fill in pauses with ums, ahs, or ers.
> NEVER apologize for your discomfort in front of an audience.
> NEVER be modest about your accomplishments. If you don't think you're good enough to be up there, why should your audience?

5. *When you are at the lectern and ready to speak, is your audience ready to listen?* When you reach the podium, look out at the audience and wait until the room is absolutely quiet. It may seem an interminable amount of time to you, but it should only take a few seconds. You must command attention by your stance and by a look that says you "expect" them to be quiet and listen. Never begin a talk while others are talking. If they don't stop, continue to wait, or ask the offenders to carry on their conversation in another room.

6. *Pace your speech along with the visuals. Add enthusiasm!* Showing each slide for the same number of seconds and the same number of slides per minute can be subliminally boring. So can a monotonous voice and lack of rhythm when you speak. Speed up during different portions of the talk, and slow down during others. Inject excitement and enthusiasm into your voice and your actions. That enthusiasm will be imparted to the audience. For a fully illustrated slide show, plan an average of two to four slides per minute. This means that in some minutes four to six slides will appear to average the one or two in others (see Chapter 2).

7. *Adapt your writing style to the speaking situation.* Pose questions in your speech and answer them yourself. Use anecdotes or case histories to illustrate a point. Tell a joke only if it is appropriate and if you're good at telling jokes. Don't poke fun at people or at groups of people. Avoid puns and tongue-in-cheek comments; many people are too obtuse to understand them. Puns and idioms can vary in different regions, and those that are familiar to you may be so far out to your audience that no one knows what you're talking about.

Use words that suggest feelings for those in your audience who are aurally and kinesthetically conditioned.

8. *Keep attention focused on the screen by a smart use of visuals.* Smart use of graphics with reveals or build-ups (Chapter 4), highlights, and color for emphasis can eliminate the necessity for a pointer.

If you tend to be nervous, avoid using a light pointer or a stick pointer on a slide screen. A light pointer inevitably jiggles in the hand of a nervous speaker, darts over the screen, and confuses the audience. A light pointer may involve turning your head away from the microphone, and the sound of your voice may fade. If you must use a light pointer, practice turning it on and off as you move from one point to the next. If you see or feel the light shaking, brace your hand. Use a lapel or hand-held microphone if you pace or if you must leave the lectern to point to the screen.

Sometimes, a speaker plans to use a stick pointer, and when she sees the lecture room, she finds that the screen is out of reach. A stick pointer is acceptable with a small audience and when overhead transparencies or flip charts are used. With transparencies, the pointer is laid on the film rather than pointed at the screen.

9. *Look up at your audience frequently.* Don't constantly look at your notes. Make eye contact with three or four people as you talk.

10. *Smile.* If you observe someone nodding off or if your voice begins to sound monotonous to you, a smile will automatically change your attitude and pace.

11. *Stand up straight.* Don't put your hands in your pockets or cross your arms while you're speaking. Look alert.

12. *Don't let people ask questions that interrupt the flow of your topic.* Ask them to hold all questions until the lecture is over. Don't let anyone dominate the time period.

13. *Try to anticipate the questions that may be asked and have answers mentally formulated.*

14. *Close on a positive upbeat note.*

15. *Include handouts where possible.* It is preferable to do this after the presentation, unless you want your audience to refer to the paper as you speak. People like handouts and feel good to have something to take home and study. A handout recalls your presentation, and if an action is desired, the handout may clinch that action.

16. *Keep presentations down to 50-minute segments at the most, plus a 10-minute discussion period.* Any presentations that run over that time period should be broken into shorter time segments. People's attention spans are limited. Since the advent of television, those who study audience reaction have noted that people begin to squirm every 15 minutes (the usual commercial break time). Three 15-minute segments are tolerable; much beyond that is not.

17. *Finish on time.* Keep a watch handy, or have someone in the first row signal you. The formal portion of your talk should be timed so you know how long it will take. Allow for questions and discussion as part of the total time, not as additional time. Be considerate of your audience and the possibility that another speaker may follow you in the same room.

Survey Your Surroundings

1. *Is all equipment in proper working order?* Projectors should be pretested. Switches for dimming and turning lights on should be located. Are there ample extension cords and outlets? If you're using your own projector, carry one or two spare projection lamps and an extension cord. Know how to unjam a slide tray. If you're controlling the slide changes from the lectern, avoid fancy fingerwork on the remote controls, especially if you're using two projectors.

2. *Determine whether the image will be projected from the rear or the front of the screen.* Rear screen projection requires the slides to be placed in the tray differently from front screen projection.

3. *Place the projector for proper viewing.* Set the projector at the proper height and angle to the screen. Avoid tilting the projector; this results in a trapezoidal image on the screen—narrower at the bottom, wider at the top—which distorts the image. Place a logo slide or blank slide in the "O" slot of the projector tray so that the audience does not look at a bright, white light during the introduction.

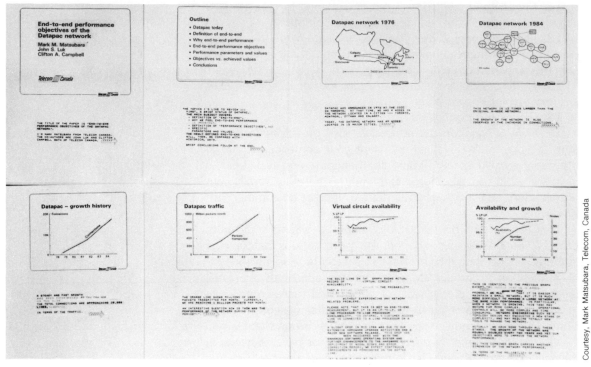

Each slide is reprinted on a sheet of paper with the spoken text that will accompany it. Points to be emphasized are highlighted. If certain phrases are to be spoken more slowly or more quickly, the speaker has notes to remind him.

4. *Run the slides through the projector quickly to be sure they are all right side up and forward.* (The emulsion portion of the slide should face the screen). An upside down, sideways, or backward slide is inexcusable for anyone who wishes to come across as a pro. If you have to apologize for a slide, don't use it.

5. *Can the slides or other visuals be seen and read clearly at the back of the room?* The setting for your presentation should be surveyed before the event, if possible, so you know how and where your audience is arranged.

6. *Check that no room lights will be shining on the projection screen.* Imagine spending hundreds of dollars preparing a slide show and then, in the lecture hall, floodlights remain on and pointed at the screen so that all the slides appear washed out and impossible to read.

7. *Have a lectern light for your notes.* Always carry a flashlight with you in case of an emergency. That same lectern light, or a poorly placed overhead light, can cast eerie shadows on your face. Often, there's not much you can do about such a setting, but if you have your own flashlight, it may be improved. Turn off lectern lights that may make you appear Mephistophelean.

8. *When you must interact with a computer, check all connections, cables, and power supplies.* Use a keyboard with which you're familiar, and have a flashlight handy so you can see the keyboard in a dark room.

9. *Remote control cords that you manipulate must be long enough so that you can stand a comfortable distance from the screen.* Remote control extensions are available for most projectors.

10. *If you must interact with a projectionist in a projection booth, arrange for a cue that will signal a slide change.*

Meeting Room Guidelines

Try to fit the size of the room to the audience. The size of the screen should be scaled to the size of the room and the audience. A small screen that is too low in a large room is worthless. Allow for ample room between you and the screen, and between the screen and the audience.

Do you want audience interaction? Keep room lights on and use overhead projection film, a chalkboard, or a flip board. This works best with small audiences not more than 20 to 30 feet from the screen. If you don't want audience interaction, a semi-darkened room and 35 mm slides work well in any size room.

If you have a sound track, it should be synchronized and amplified correctly.

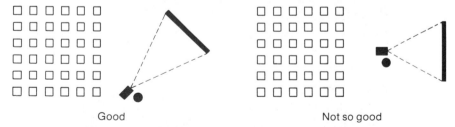

Good   Not so good

For any projection equipment, survey the seating and analyze the visual area from all parts of the room. In the seating plan at right, the people in the center would have their view blocked by the speaker, and those at the front corners may get a distorted screen image.

Overhead Transparency Projection Considerations

When using an overhead projector, try to place the projector about 8 feet from the screen. If the screen is high and the image appears wider at the top than the bottom, tilt the screen until the image is straight. The room may be light.

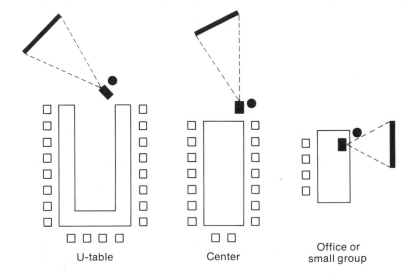

For overhead transparencies, use a u-table arrangement for 12 to 20 people. Use a center table arrangement for 6 to 12 people and for a small office group of 3 to 6 people. In each situation, the speaker is to the audience's left, out of the line of vision.

U-table   Center   Office or small group

For a small group of five or less, an acceptable arrangement consists of the overhead projector in the center with the viewers flanking it; the projector is at one side, with the speaker seated or standing.

Courtesy, 3M Meeting Graphics

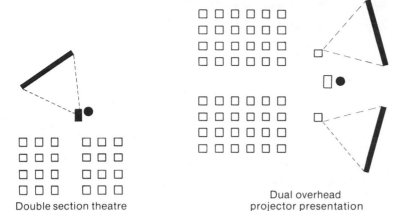

Double section theatre

Dual overhead
projector presentation

Use an auditorium arrangement for about 30 to 40 people. Seating should not be beyond four or five rows from the screen. If a larger audience must be accommodated, spread the seating widthwise and use two projectors simultaneously, one at each side of the room.

Dual overhead projector presentation is recommended for a larger audience. The speaker can be in the center with assistants handling the film and projectors.

Slide Projection Considerations

The number of people that can be accommodated for a 35 mm slide presentation is much larger than that for an overhead transparency presentation—literally hundreds. The room will be dark (there should always be a few lights on, but they should not affect the contrast of the slides), which discourages audience participation. Questions are usually held until the end of the presentation.

Generally, the screen is in the center front of the room and high enough for the audience to see it above the heads of those in front of them. Screen size is scaled to room size. Where possible, the speaker should stand to the left of the screen from the audience's viewpoint. People read from left to right, so it's logical that their eyes move from the speaker to the screen and back again.

Slide projection can accommodate larger audiences than can overhead transparencies. The speaker should be to the left of the audience, with a large screen high enough to be seen from the back of the room.

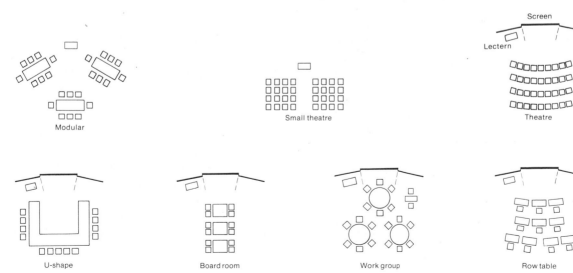

Modular

Small theatre

Screen
Lectern
Theatre

U-shape

Board room

Work group

Row table

Words Can Work
Visual Wonders

4

Estimates are that between 65 percent and 75 percent of the visuals used today are composed of words (text and titles). The remaining are business charts and miscellaneous graphics.

The reason? Text summarizes and emphasizes a speaker's main points in a direct manner immediately acceptable to an audience. "Word" visual aids are easier for a presenter to create and faster to prepare than drawings, photos, and charts. However, in today's presentation world, words have to be treated as art.

When they are done well, text and title visual aids can help a person communicate convincingly. When they are poorly planned and implemented, they can frustrate an audience, detract from the message, and present a negative image of the speaker.

Television has contributed, too, to the normal human condition of being more visually than listening oriented. Swirling words, logos, and slogans that spin and fade off into the distance splash across the TV screen every 15 minutes. How can a person using a typewritten or hand-scribbled visual compete? Only if he throws out the makeshift, slapdash sheets and uses either professional services or his own computer with professional techniques.

A computer is not a magic lamp. The keyboard is not a genie. Slides made on a computer can be bad—even worse than those made on a typewriter. Why? The user must still make choices. There are elements of good design—rules of the trade—to be followed. The examples in this chapter have been designed to show you how these rules are applied.[1] They are aimed at helping you understand the differences between slides that are dynamic and those that are only so-so, or worse. The chapter provides you with guidelines so you can critique slides. You can emulate the examples.

Are you aware of problems common to slide presentations? Think of presentations you've attended. Use the list below to analyze other people's slides and your own. How often have you seen:

---

[1] Because of the number of people and companies who contributed slide examples, it was impossible to document, in the credit line with each slide, the specific software, hardware, and image recorder systems used. Note the company credit line, then locate the company name in the appendixes. Most have host equipment or software. Contact the company for information.

Visuals that can't be read at the back of a room?
Too much to read while the speaker is talking?
One slide on the screen too long?
Letters too small to read?
Poor color contrast between text and background, making the text illegible?
Too many colors?
Slides so busy you don't know what to focus on?
Disconcerting layouts?
No apparent continuity in the presentation?
Charts and diagrams with so many symbols on them you don't know where they lead, or which element the speaker is discussing?

Types of Text Slides

There are four major types of text slides:

Title slide.
Title with text as outline points. Bullets, numbers, or a,b,c's may precede each line.
Those that build up or reveal each point in a topic line-by-line.
Titles or text with images.

Word messages used for slides, transparencies, or hard copy require several decisions in the planning stage: How much to put on one slide? Which type style or font to use? What about color, layout, emphasis, and any special effects? Can you select these features using your own hardware and software? Will you order

IN-HOUSE Business Graphics

- Computer Generated Slides
- Large format paper pen plots
- Overhead transparencies
- Laser generated hard copies
- Deluxe Slides

Courtesy, Caramate Visual Master Systems and In-House Graphics

IN-HOUSE Business Graphics

- Computer Generated Slides
- Large format paper pen plots
- Overhead transparencies
- Laser generated hard copies
- Deluxe Slides

Courtesy, Caramate Visual Master Systems and In-House Graphics

Capital and lowercase letters: A yellow title and white bullets with green capital and lowercase text on a black background.

Same as at left, but with a white frame around a background of dark blue with light blue letters. Black around the outside of the frame.

Courtesy, Genigraphics Corp.

Elements to observe in a slide: Five lines of copy in addition to the title, two type styles—all capital letters, yellow drop-shadowed title with white text; the lightest color carries the most important part of the message, special effects background.

Avoid overcrowding a slide. It results in letters that are too small to be read at a distance.

slides from a service? Can you exercise good artistic judgment based on rules and not by "feeling it looks right"? Can you exercise restraint when faced with literally hundreds of options from which to choose?

Many people think they can successfully make all these decisions. If they could, there wouldn't be so many ineffective, poorly conceived visuals. There wouldn't be a need for people to teach these skills or to write articles and books about them.

How Much to Put on One Slide?

Probably 75 percent of the text slides used are crammed with too much information.

The rules for text slides are:

1. Each line is a basic thought.
2. Don't have the visual tell everything.
3. Use a maximum of five or six lines per slide.
4. Use no more than six words per line.
5. Keep titles short.

What is the purpose of a visual? To "aid" or support what you have to say. When the slide appears, don't read it aloud; the audience can read. Use the same words, but phrase them in complete sentences spoken in a conversational tone. If you want your audience to read your speech, give them a printed copy to take home. Don't put it on the screen while you're talking.

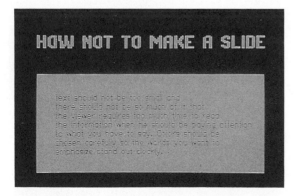

Avoid using complete sentences. Edit each thought to no more than six words.

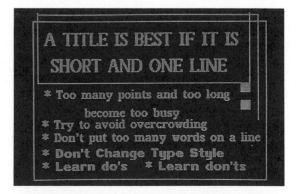

Avoid overuse of underlines and borders. Use color to emphasize.

Type Styles

Computer software packages provide a choice of more type styles than most people would know what to do with in a lifetime. That choice can be a trap for the novice designer. The tendency is to try this style and that, and toss them all into one slide like a vegetable stew.

Four rules govern type style decisions:

1. Select simple type styles.
2. Use only one or two type styles per slide.
3. Retain those styles throughout.
4. Style should enhance, not overpower, the message.

It's safest to use one typeface per slide in different weights and designs. If you use Helvetica, it is better to mix sizes of type, regular with bold, a drop shadow, or an outlined letter. A slanted or italic version can be mixed.

Safest typefaces are Helvetica or one of its look-alikes. Roman style type faces generally have a serif, or extra line, at the ends of each letter. The type style should not overpower the message; it is the medium for the message.

A specialized, or fancy, type style is legitimate if it suggests an image for a product. If you're selling women's perfumes, select a light-looking, gracefully designed typeface with a slight slant. If you're selling tractors, select a boldface type style to project a sturdy, reliable, rough appearance.

A flourishing type style is apropos when it suggests an idea, a mood, or a feeling for a product.

Artist: Raymond J. Lasky. Courtesy, The Hartford Insurance Group

Two type styles are used here— one for solidity and one for emphasis.

Artist: Raymond J. Lasky. Courtesy, The Hartford Insurance Group

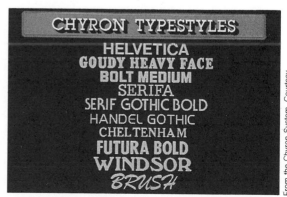

The same style can be varied by using special effects as drop shadows, outlining, sweeps, and others (see Chapter 8).

From the Chyron System. Courtesy, Raymond J. Lasky

Software offers a variety of type styles. For slides and transparencies, select a simple, direct typeface. Shown are 10 of 20 available typefaces in the Chyron System; the user can generate additional styles.

From the Chyron System. Courtesy, Raymond J. Lasky

Courtesy, Hewlett-Packard Co.

PAINTBRUSH applies its own program to its own sell slide using two simple type faces in all capital letters. Variety is added by placing the entire text on an angle within a frame.

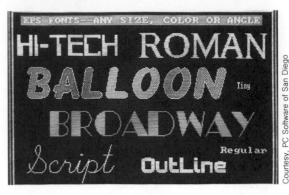

Courtesy, PC Software of San Diego

Executive Picture Show software offers a variety of fonts that can be sized and slanted at different angles.

Generally, type styles have standardized names, but companies vary a typeface design or develop a new one, and then name and trademark it. Type styles are available in different weights: bold, extra bold, heavy, italic, and so on. Gently italicized letters can add emphasis to a visual, but those that are too fancy can be difficult to read and should be avoided.

Opinions vary about the use of capital and lowercase letters versus all capital letters. Some experts adamantly avoid all capital letters as being too difficult to read; other experts use all capitals throughout the slide, as you will observe in the examples. Consistency

FONTRIX can exploit all the capabilities of a dot matrix printer in its incredible font styles and foreign language characters.

Proclamations in Ye Olde Engli

Several point sizes of Easy Readi

Several point sizes of Easy

Several point sizes of

INNOVATIVE NEW

FONTS for making HEA

Fonts A Calligrapher Would Write

FUTURISTIC FONTS   NO

Textual fonts for letters and correspondence THREE IN ONE

Courtesy, Data Transforms

is the key, regardless of which you use. The same type style should be used for titles and text throughout a presentation, unless there's a good reason for varying it.

Color

Color can be as enticing an aspect of slides as a wide selection of type styles. New graphics hardware and software are capable of producing hundreds of colors and shades of each color. This capability can be a pitfall when color relationships are not understood. Even when you know what you're doing, use color sparingly and with restraint.

Observe how colors are combined and contrasted in television newscasts, advertising, and in the slide libraries of the catalogs and books available with software and commercial slide services. Make a conscious effort to look at colors used for backgrounds and for lettering. TV stations hire top artists and use expensive equipment. Their colors, layouts, and methods are well worth copying.

Two rules for color dominate:

1. Limit the color palette to two or three colors on a contrasting background.
2. Lighter colors highlight and emphasize.

There are other concepts to be aware of. Avoid colors that have a negative effect in an industry. For example, don't use red in slides for business executives; the connotation is sagging profits. Avoid

Courtesy, Professional Presentations

A text slide can become an image when it both says and shows the message. FEAR is red outlined in white; smaller letters are purple outlined in white on a black background.

If a vertical photo or drawing must be used and it occupies only one third or one half the space, don't center it with white space on both sides.

Move the illustration to one side; add a title or text and color on the other side.

using red and green together. People with red-green color blindness view the slide as being one shade of muddy brown.

Blues and blacks are safe background colors. They dominate in slides created by professional services. Yellow and white are safe for lettering, bullets, and numerals. They stand out and can be easily read in almost any lighting situation.

Avoid changing background colors frequently during any one slide presentation. Consistency in typeface, color combination, and layout give a feeling of unity. If your presentation is designed to upset or unnerve or change the direction of an audience's thinking, then change the backgrounds and images. If you want to instill fear, use harsh, bold colors such as reds and purples.

Layout

Balance, as a design element, creates a feeling of equilibrium in a space. When all text is centered, the balance is "formal." An off-centered title, with text arranged to balance it, is "informal." If something is off-centered and nothing is used to equalize it, the viewer's equilibrium is disturbed.

Within a balanced composition, variety can be achieved by angling or tilting the text, or by using a special effect as shown in several examples.

Rules for composition are:

1. Keep all slides in a horizontal format.
2. Balance the text within the space.

Layouts can be varied, but usually *not* within one presentation. Establish formats and adhere to them. Will the title be flush left,

Formal balance: Everything is centered.

Informal balance: Title is flush left and text is off-centered to balance the title.

No balance: The result is chaotic.

Artist: Raymond Laskey, Courtesy, The Hartford Insurance Group.

C *A simple build series with formal balance, using the Hartford Insurance logo. The title "NEW CREATIVE ELEMENTS" is carried on each slide in light blue against a dark blue background. Each new topic is introduced and highlighted in yellow. Once* *highlighted, they drop back to the light blue color. It's a good way to carry the audience with you.*

(Throughout this book, the symbol C indicates that the slide is reproduced in color elsewhere in the book.)

centered, or flush right? Will the title be underlined? What width and color will the line be? Observe layouts of titles in relation to underlines, color, text, and logos in the examples. Choose a style and use it consistently.

Emphasis Using Reveal or Build-up Slides

Among the most popular text slides used by lecturers and seminar leaders today are those that present only one idea at a time. They are referred to as "reveals" or "build-up" series.

The principle is simple and the reasons for using such slides are practical. Consider a subject with five topics. The usual approach is to show all five topics in one slide, then talk about each topic in order. The audience must read the entire slide. Its members may have difficulty concentrating on the particular point you are making because they are mentally jumping ahead to the next. When each slide adds one more point, they can't jump ahead until you are ready for them to do so.

With the reveal concept, five or six slides may be required. Each slide will introduce one new topic that is highlighted as it is presented. The previous topic, or line, drops back to another color. The final summary slide may show all five topics with none highlighted.

This approach pulls the audience along with you. It justifies more frequent slide changes on screen and avoids exposing your whole subject at the beginning. The impact as each point is made is greater.

As you observe presentations, become aware of slide techniques. Sit at the back of the room, and observe that, in a large lecture hall, people may leave more frequently when a projected slide shows all topics at once than during a presentation that reveals each topic individually.

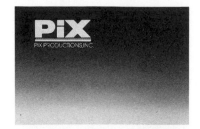

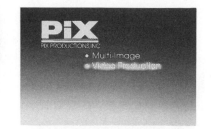

Pix Productions Inc. selects a light blue for its own logo on a background shaded from almost black at the top to a dark blue at bottom. The balance is informal with the title off-centered and balanced by the off-centered revealed text. Each new topic is introduced with a bullet and white letters with a glow effect. The previous line becomes the same blue color as the logo. The final slide is the logo centered in large red letters against the same background.

(Some of these slides are reproduced in color elsewhere in this book.)

Another successful format is to build the discussion with each topic highlighted in a large type size, then drop each topic to a less bright and smaller type size when the next topic appears. In this series, the logo remains in corporate colors on a blue background. The framed inner background is dark green with white highlighted text dropping back to a light green and smaller typesize.

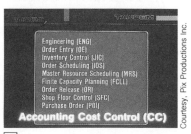

Interpreting Text into Drawings

Text can be developed so it becomes pictorial. It carries the same message as if it were solely words, but it carries greater impact. Not all text slides lend themselves to pictorial representation, but when you can think of a way to do so, it can add variety and interest to a presentation.

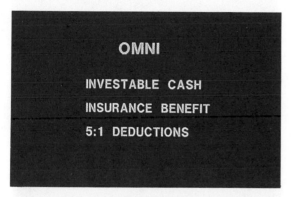

A text slide outlines advantages of the OMNI plan using high-contrast white letters on a dark blue background.

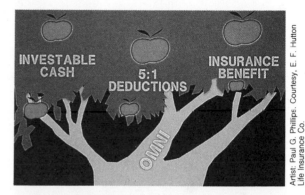

The same message is developed visually as though the benefits were apples ready to be plucked from a green tree. The tree trunk is pink, the background, a dark blue, with white letters.

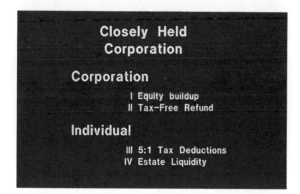

The Closely Held Corporation in words alone.

The same message is visually presented using stored images brought together to compose the needed concept.

Artist: Paul G. Phillips. Courtesy, E. F. Hutton Life Insurance Co.

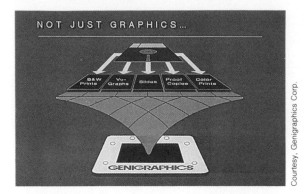

Courtesy, Genigraphics Corp.

NOT JUST GRAPHICS is one of a build-up series in which the speaker discusses each medium possible from data on a disk to final output. This one emphasizes the slide-making procedure.

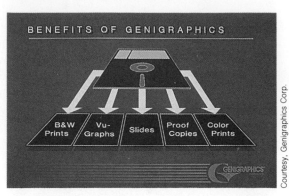

Courtesy, Genigraphics Corp.

BENEFITS OF GENIGRAPHICS is the summary slide containing the major points. Imagine it as only a text slide with a title and bullets and the difference is apparent.

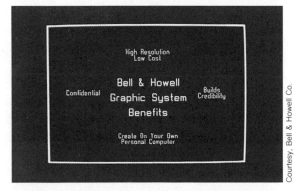

Courtesy, Bell & Howell Co.

Bell & Howell Graphics System Benefits could have been a title with numbered or bulleted text lines. Converting it into an illustration adds impact; it performs a "show and tell" role describing the company's software capability.

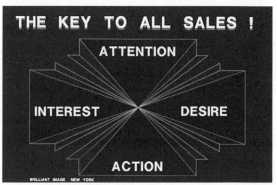

Artist: David Lapidus. Courtesy, Brilliant Image, Inc.

The yellow title, KEY TO ALL SALES, might have been only a title with each point listed in white lettering on a plain background. This is certainly a more impressive approach.

The Text Becomes the Image

A word or a concept can often be presented dynamically with an illustration alone or with a combination of the word and the illustration. Text can be designed to represent the meaning of the word and create a double impact. Imaginatively and artistically created slides pack punch into a theme. They can be combined with text, business graphics, and other visual aids within a totally integrated presentation. The same lettering can be used for a printed brochure and for an advertising campaign.

"Creative" and "Budget" represent stock slides available from commercial slide services; or you can create your own. They can reduce overall costs and extend a slide budget (see Chapter 13).

Assorted slides with a universal message can be purchased from commercial slide companies. These slides must be added to a presentation judiciously, especially if colors, graphics, text style, and general tone are not consistent with other slides in the series.

Companies sell stock slides with images that can add to your message; the slide is semi-customized. A fully customized series, or new slides compatible with existing ones, can be created (see Chapter 13).

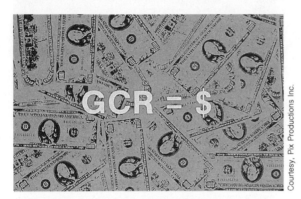

Replace a word only in a stored slide to suggest savings, spending, budget, or any reference to "dollars" by placing the words against a background of dollar bills.

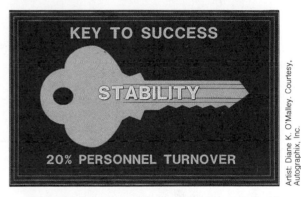

Stored illustrations can be quickly customized with new data. How many ways can you think of to use the picture of a key?

When you want to make the point that your service opens doors, do it with words and a picture, using a stock slide that can be popped into any presentation where applicable.

Artist: Jack Curtis for Pencept. Courtesy, Celtic Technology, Inc.

A cartoon character expresses joy at the sales upturn.

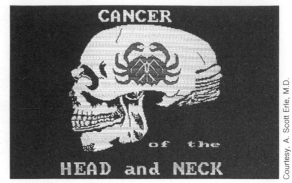

Courtesy, A. Scott Erle, M.D.

Cancer of the head and neck is a dramatic introduction to a medical lecture: yellow skull, red cancer, green lettering on a black background.

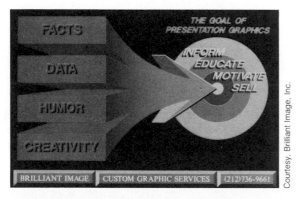

Courtesy, Brilliant Image, Inc.

An oversized arrow with four boxes for its tail carries the message that targets the circle. The blocks and major portion of the arrow are blue, gradating to a green tip outlined in yellow. Text is yellow, the title is green, and the target is grey.

Artist: Marilyn Abers. Courtesy, Jones Photocolor, Inc.

An arrow can serve to suggest a trend and simultaneously list the points to be made. Imagine this image as only a text slide and you can grasp the difference in impact.

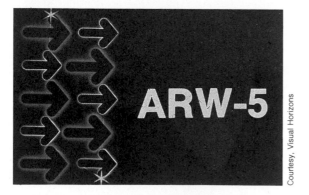

Courtesy, Visual Horizons

Stock arrow slides from a commercial slide service can be customized with your message.

Courtesy, Visual Horizons

Or perhaps a slide with question marks would help keep an audience on its toes, trying to answer the question you ask.

Artist: Raymond J. Lasky, Courtesy,
The Hartford Insurance Group

The title is a take-off on a movie, and the concept is visualized with a rocket aiming for the money target.

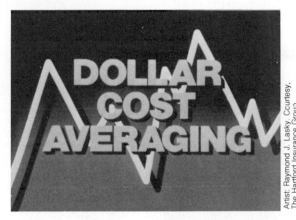

Artist: Raymond J. Lasky, Courtesy,
The Hartford Insurance Group

Here, a charted line suggesting trends illustrates the words.

Pictures give the words greater impact; you can visualize money, taxes, and rainy days when the images are there.

Artist: Raymond J. Lasky, Courtesy,
The Hartford Insurance Group

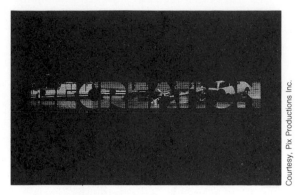

Courtesy, Pix Productions Inc.

Courtesy, Pix Productions Inc.

CRIME shows photographs of police and street scenes dramatically and advantageously when the slide is projected on a large scale. Computer-generated outline letters are filled with a photographic image of the subject assembled in a photo lab.

RECREATION is treated the same, with a beach scene photograph within the open lettering.

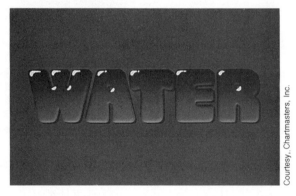

Courtesy, Pix Productions Inc.

Courtesy, Chartmasters, Inc.

FRANCHISING has a fragmented photo that suggests money and business news.

A blue-green background with soft-edged letters filled with shaded tones of green suggest the visual image of the word.

An astronaut landing on a stylized version of the moon suggests the future. The shadow behind the lettering and the astronaut create a third dimension.

A word repeated and placed on an angle within a frame is balanced by the logo at the bottom right.

Artist: Marilyn Abers. Courtesy, Jones Photocolor, Inc.

Courtesy, Genigraphics Corp.

Courtesy, Visual Horizons

Repeat figures scaled in different sizes are yellow with a metallic glow against a partial background effect called luminescent. The white lettering is on black.

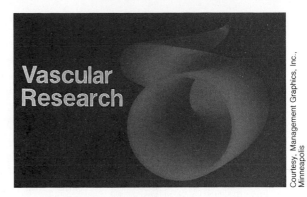

Courtesy, Management Graphics, Inc., Minneapolis

Vascular Research: white letters on black with a red tubular image suggesting a blood vessel.

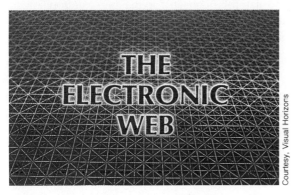

Courtesy, Visual Horizons

Black letters are given a white glow effect to suggest electronics against a weblike design that fades from blue-green in the bottom half to red in the top half.

Courtesy, Visual Horizons

Yellow outlined lettering with shades of orange within are simple, yet dramatic, against a black background. A punchy finale to a sales pitch will leave the audience on an upbeat note.

Artist: Diane K. O'Malley. Courtesy, Autographix, Inc.

Thank you; a rose is a pleasant touch that could be carried over to any applicable topic and presentation using your own message.

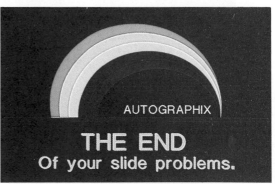

Courtesy, Autographix, Inc.

Chromatic rays can be produced with sophisticated software; similar effects can be improvised with other equipment. This is nice for an ending slide with your own message, or only "The End."

Courtesy, Genigraphics Corp.

How many ways are there to communicate a message? There is no one answer, but there are many dynamic answers when the basic rules for selecting fonts, colors, layout, and special effects are followed and imagination added.

Printed proceedings from conferences and seminars are packed with a wealth of information. Those that repeat illustrations which accompanied the talk will simplify reader recall, especially when read months after the presentation.

Printed and Plotted Text Handouts

A presentation followed with hard-copy supportive material stands a better chance of creating a lasting impression and motivating further action than a presentation alone. The easiest course is a typewritten sheet summarizing the outline, highlights, or a further explanation of a product or service.

But avoid those typewritten handouts at any cost if you want to stand out from the crowd. Carry through a total visual package in the hard copy. It is not difficult with so many software packages on the market for use with today's printers and plotters, copy machines, and printing services.

Text can be attractively formatted and can become a logical extension of your talk. Text and graphics can be integrated. Your logo can appear on the page, with different type sizes in bold or italic, along with other effects. If a color printer is used, the copy can mirror the colors so carefully chosen for the presentation, much of it coordinated with the colors of the slides or overhead transparencies. Corporate colors can be repeated on hard copy.

Charts used in a presentation ideally show only trends; a hard-copy supplement could repeat the trend chart, then expand it with detailed data. This integrated total image concept is becoming more visible. Proceedings from a conference are often compiled in a printed book containing each presenter's lecture. Those that repeat the slide presentation images will stand out and will stimulate almost instant recall weeks, or even months, later when someone refers to the information.

For board meeting presentations, copies of charts, statements, concepts, and directives can be studied, discussed, and acted on when the data can be easily referred to by everyone present.

Dull, unattractive, lengthy lines of typewritten copy, unrelieved by illustrations, are difficult to follow. Main points are buried. Those that are succinctly developed will help to propel the presenter to a prominent position. They are a reflection and an extension of the presentation.

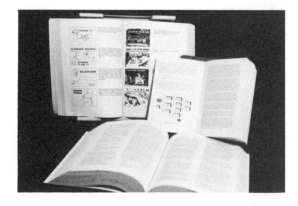

People who work with sophisticated reproduction equipment in an industrial and corporate environment can request what they need from an art department. Every available facility should be explored for its application to a total presentation package. Art directors who may think only of 35 mm slides or overhead transparencies should help their clients evolve a total package.

Those who do not have such facilities at their fingertips can take advantage of computer systems that are able to integrate text and image, such as the Macintosh, and programs such as GEM, by Digital Research, Inc., for the MS DOS market. There are many routes to investigate and select. Graphics programs can dump the images to a printer or plotter. Printer support packages, such as Fontrix and Magic Font, can make your printer perform as a typesetter.

Such systems can reduce time and expense. A salesperson demonstrating with an on-line slide show for a client could leave that client with a printout of the demo taken almost as is from the screen. There is no need for typesetting and printing, especially when short runs of a handout are required, or when handouts must be customized for different occasions.

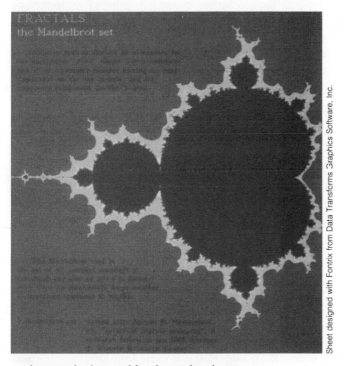

Sheet designed with Fontrix from Data Transforms Graphics Software, Inc.

Attractively designed hard-copy handouts developed with software to take advantage of a printer's or plotter's capabilities are almost as easy to create as plain typewritten output.

Getting a Grasp on Business Graphs

Graphs and charts that portray performance pictorially are the backbone of business graphics. Columns, bars, pies, maps, and wiggly lines are the elements used to represent analytical data, compare numbers, show where things happen and how they are organized, and indicate how different systems relate.

This need—this expanding practice to impart information visually and quickly—has evolved into standardized styles for specific graph and chart formats.

Why are business graphics popular? They illustrate, at a glance, trends that would require longer study if presented as numerical data. And therein lies the key to effective business graphics. Their purpose and their ultimate effectiveness result from their proper use as a support tool in a presentation environment. They should show trends, movement, and comparisons that can be evaluated readily, not finite details or figures.

If an inordinate number of legends or much descriptive material is required to interpret the chart, suspect that the chart has not been properly prepared and that the impact of the message may be lost.

A business visual image must:

Be accurate.
Be easy to interpret.
Have impact.

As more people begin to create visuals, one or more of these essential factors may be missing—but not lost to the perception of an audience.

A question was posed recently to columnist Alan Paller, president of AUI Data Graphics and a consultant on the subject of business graphics, in the magazine *Computer Graphics Today:* "Why are conference speakers so bad at using computer graphics?" Paller offered four reasons:

Speakers do not prepare their presentations in advance and do not allow ample preparation time.

Secondly, they may have time but not the in-house resources nor the budget needed to make effective visuals.

Third, they do not know how to design good visuals.

Fourth, they are unaware that speakers who do not use visuals are perceived to be less professional and less interesting than other speakers.

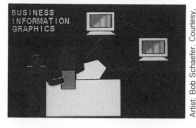

To help remedy the situation, the National Computer Graphics Association presents awards to the 50 speakers rated highest by audience evaluation sheets. Those speakers, without exception, used visuals effectively. Those who receive poor ratings are not invited to subsequent conferences.

Business charts and graphs can be treated with creativity in addition to accuracy and clarity.

Effective business graphics have to be more than well-placed titles and text that use readable type styles and good color combinations. They must be accurate. The proper chart or graph must be selected to explain the information. A dynamic chart may not be required when you call up data for your own analysis, but it should be accurate. When you display that information for an audience, it should be clear and dynamic and accurate.

Why Some Charts Miss the Mark

Computers are incredibly docile. They do exactly what you tell them to do. Yet, sometimes they misinterpret what you mean—an aberration especially applicable to charts and numbers. A poorly designed chart can be misleading. There are people who purposely "misdesign" charts so that numbers will *appear* to be different from

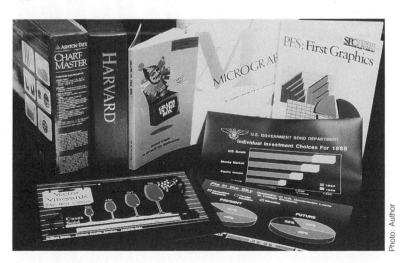

Several programs emphasize chartmaking. Most are able to interface with a film recorder for 35 mm slides. All have good output to printers for overhead transparencies and hard copy. Some programs have only 8 or 10 basic chart formats; others may have 20 to 25 formats with analysis capabilities.

Progression of a chart design

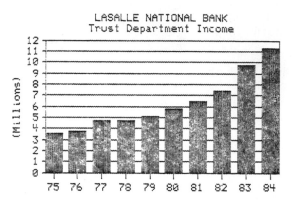

A. *A basic chart is generated by Lotus 1–2–3 data, then edited with The Grafix Partner.*

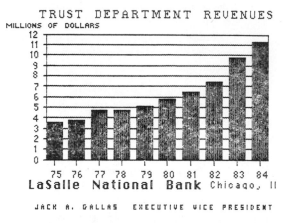

B. *Titles are enhanced and "millions of dollars" moved to a horizontal position.*

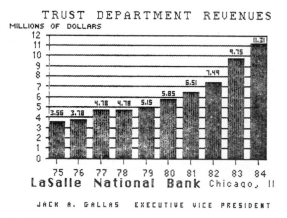

C. *Values are placed at the tops of the bars.*

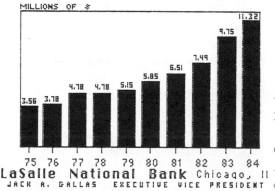

Courtesy, Raymond Jacobson, LaSalle National Bank, Chicago

D. *Finally, horizontal grid lines and vertical numbers on the axis are deleted, and "Millions of $" is shortened to fit within the chart rectangle. The result is a clean appearance that focuses attention on the succinctly illustrated data. The eye isn't floundering and being distracted by unnecessary lines. The chart is tight and well designed.*

what they really are. Just a little "optical illusion," may be their explanation. Officially, it's more like check forgery and counterfeiting.

Given the ability of some people to falsify charts with malice intended, the same effect, accidentally achieved, can inadvertently produce glitches in pitches. Designing charts is not a hit-or-miss venture. It is like anything else worth doing: it helps if you know the ground rules before you begin to play, so you can minimize the mistakes. It's like knowing the proper etiquette and the correct form to use before you have dinner with your chief executive officer.

Many more problems will be covered, but for emphasis, and forewarning, here's what you should begin to observe and avoid assiduously.

1. Incorrectly placed scales on the horizontal or vertical axis can cause a curve to appear exaggerated.
2. Changing grid divisions halfway in a chart can cause one portion to appear as gradual and another as a fast drop or rise, even though the rates are the same.
3. Broken lines and segmented bars, compared with those that are not broken, can change the appearance of the data and the final readout.
4. Design elements can visually alter the effect of correctly presented data; certain colors, such as red and black, when assigned to some bars or lines, make them appear more important than those in yellow or light blue. Solid bars appear weightier and more important than those that are outlined.
5. Hatch marks and textures can be used to visually distort; vertical lines filling a horizontal plane make the surface appear higher.

What other errors are likely to make charts miss the mark? For one, businesspeople, in their zeal to convince a viewer, tend to cram too much information onto a chart. It's going to get worse before it gets better. With a microcomputer and spreadsheet or

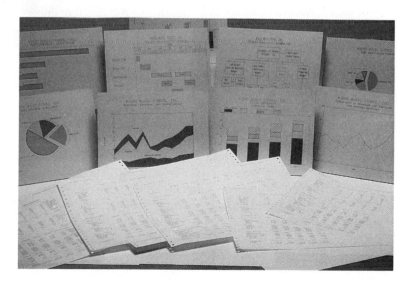

Spreadsheet data can easily be transformed into charts for easy analysis using chartmaking software. Many spreadsheet programs generate charts, but they may not be as versatile and well designed as those in a chartmaking program. Most chart and presentation programs can import spreadsheet files so that it is never necessary to rekey the data.

chart-generating software, almost anyone can produce a graphic representation of data in seconds. Many charts will look like they were produced in seconds. Some may look worse, as people begin to add extra titles, logos, and fancy printing.

The excitement of working with the computer and its ease at spurting out beautifully colored, well-titled, and tagged charts are making people complacent. They think any chart the computer can produce is faultless. One salesman boasted that he had made the longest bar chart ever seen in his company—40 bars wide! No one ever told him there are suggested limits to the number of bars included on a chart.

Corporate officials, top-ranking sales managers, everyone who uses graphics can unwittingly produce and present poorly designed material. Why? They know what they want to say. They are driven to succeed, but they refuse the input of people who are in the business of creating dynamic presentations. They don't hesitate to hire consultants for other phases of their business, but they fail to see that the same expert advice applies to graphics.

There is another reason why many charts are poorly designed and presented. Because of limitations in computer memory and capability, much software available for the microcomputer is not yet capable of producing output that conforms 100 percent to recommended standards. Some charts can be enhanced, but the time required to do it would be prohibitive, especially in a bank, brokerage firm, or company where 50 to 100 charts must be produced daily. It's a case of living with what you have and doing the best you can with it. It's still faster and more efficient than hand drawing.

Charts generated by many of the microcomputer programs are perfect for peer group presentations. They can be used to generate film or slides. When a program does not produce charts that adhere to accepted design rules, there are ways to compensate for the software shortcomings or to break the rules judiciously. When the software cannot produce the quality needed for the purpose, the data can be sent to a professional service.

For example, many chart programs cannot produce charts where line thicknesses can differ for the plot, axes, and grid lines. But those lines could be changed with a draw program. If the chart will be plotted, a thicker pen tip could be used for the different lines. Color can suggest line thickness when the lines are the same weight. Black appears heavier, red is medium, and yellow may appear thinner. Often, you can eliminate grid lines. The result? A more professional appearing chart that creatively compensates for the program's limitations.

A TYPICAL CALL
ORIGINATING IN SAN DIEGO
BASED ON 2½ MINUTES

SALT LAKE CITY	$ .75
DENVER	1.05
CHICAGO	.96
PHOENIX	.60
NEW YORK	1.20
SEATTLE	.85

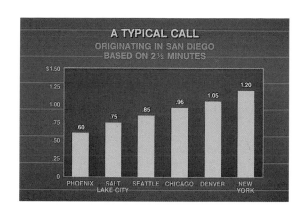

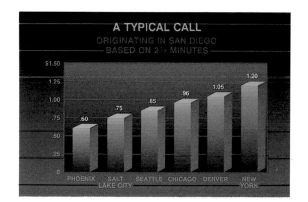

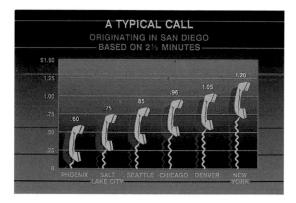

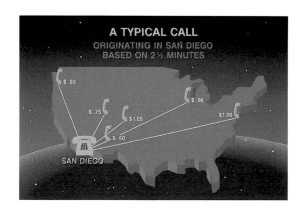

1984 ADVERTISING
NEW CREATIVE ELEMENTS
NEW MEDIA STRATEGIES

1984 ADVERTISING
NEW CREATIVE ELEMENTS
NEW MEDIA STRATEGIES
EXPANDED PROGRAMS

1984 ADVERTISING
NEW CREATIVE ELEMENTS
NEW MEDIA STRATEGIES
EXPANDED PROGRAMS
MARKET TESTING OF
CONCEPTS

PiX
- PIX PRODUCTIONS, INC.
- Multi Image
- Video Production
- Filmstrips
- Photographics
- Photography
- Audio

PIX PRODUCTIONS, INC.

Engineering (ENG)
Order Entry (OE)
Inventory Control (JIC)
Order Scheduling (IOS)
Master Resource Scheduling (MRS)
Finite Capacity Planning (FCLL)
Order Release (OR)
Shop Floor Control (SFC)
Purchase Order (POI)
Accounting Cost Control (CC)

Service opportunities

Services	Business	Industry group	Residential
Circuit switch			
Packet switch			
Leased line			
Network management			
Value added services			

Service opportunities

Services	Business	Industry group	Residential
Circuit switch	Centrex		
Packet switch	Private line substitution		
Leased line	Bandwidth pipe		
Network management	By customer		
Value added services	Many		

Service opportunities

Services	Business	Industry group	Residential
Circuit switch	Centrex	Standard interfaces & application protocols	
Packet switch	Private line substitution		
Leased line	Bandwidth pipe	--	
Network management	By customer	By carrier	
Value added services	Many	Many	

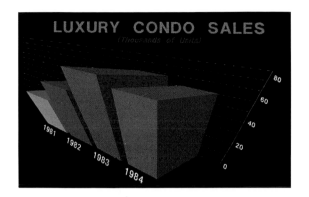

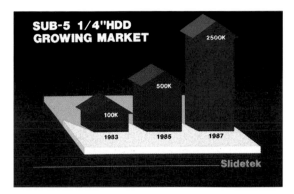

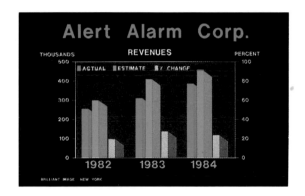

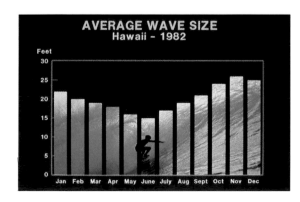

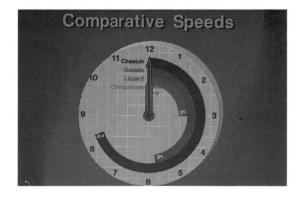

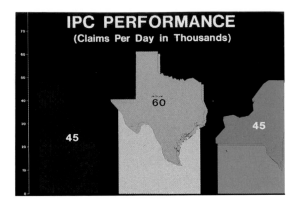

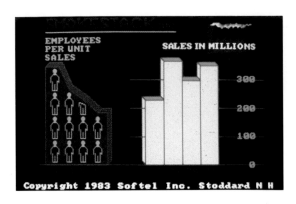

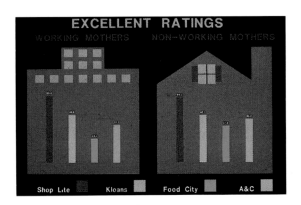

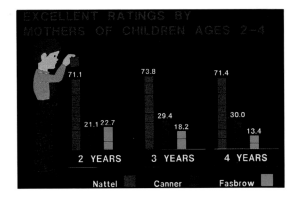

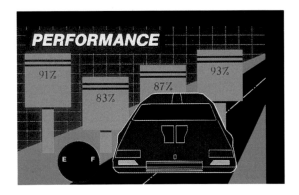

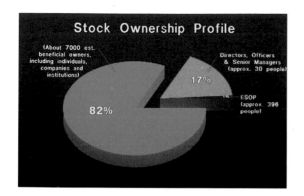

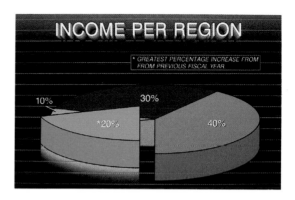

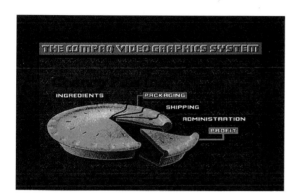

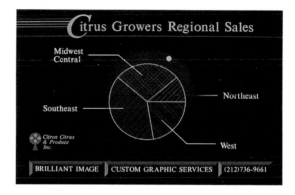

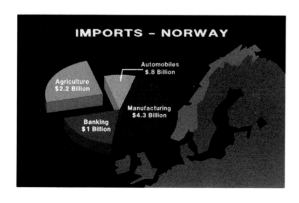

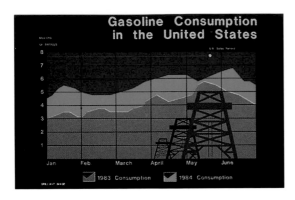

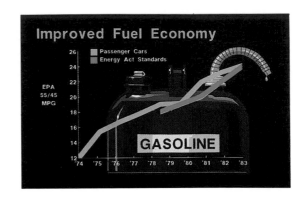

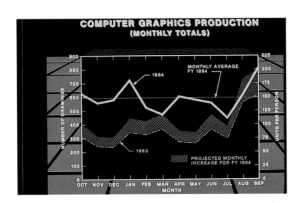

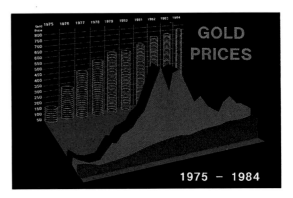

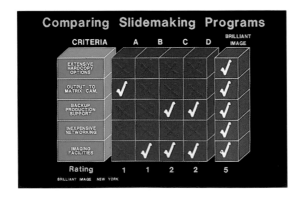

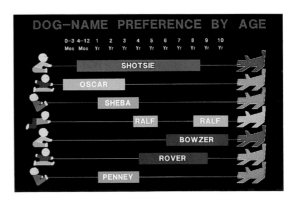

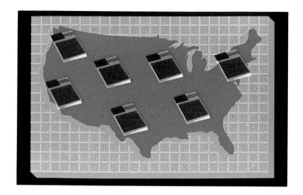

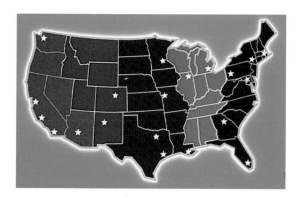

The Organizational Concept
Endemic to This Strategy

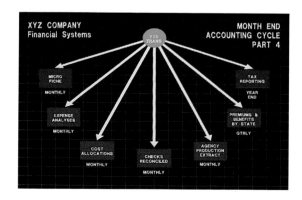

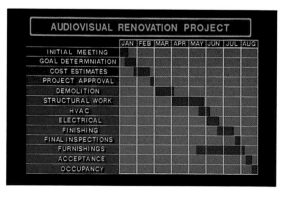

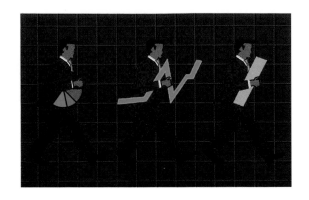

LIBRARY SYMBOL

BRILLIANT IMAGE NEW YORK

Legal and Technical Trends

TECHNICAL EQUITIES CORPORATION, INC.

Poorly Designed Software Compounds the Presentation Problem

Don't be fooled by the "cookbook" type of graphics packages on the market "guaranteed" to make you a perfect presenter. Some packages reviewed for this book generated slide formats that would make an audience cringe.

People who create software are programmers or engineers who rarely have a graphic arts background. The charts generated are poorly designed. Title and text sizes are too small to be read from the back of a large lecture hall. There may be inflexible positioning for legends and labels. The picture library is static and dull. In some programs, the chart you see on-screen is not what you get when it is printed.

Some software appears to have been written by a committee. One isn't quite certain what the program is supposed to accomplish, and it does nothing well. Still other programs appear to have been thrown into the expanding graphics software market just to get something out there; the software serves minimal needs and is impractical. For the learning curve involved, it offers too little in return.

Graphics is no different from other software research. It requires asking people how they like the packages they bought, reading reviews, purchasing programs until, by trial and error, you find what you want. One, two, or more packages may be needed to satisfy your requirements (see Chapter 12).

There Are Excellent Software Packages

On a positive note, be assured that there are excellent packages that quickly and accurately produce exactly the graph and chart you want and provide options for enhancing it. The Grafix Partner and IBM PC Storyboard, for example, are programs that can enhance charts generated by other programs. Many packages are extremely versatile and clever. With imagination, you can make them perform tasks and output beyond their original intent. If you lack that expertise, send your information to a service that will redesign basic charts and produce the final visual you need (see Chapter 14).

As you delve into the capabilities of current software, you'll discover that there may be more chart formats than you've heard of. Selecting the correct chart that will interpret and display your data to best advantage is a prime consideration. The programs provide input forms; you pull the data from a spreadsheet program or type it in. With the given data, you can often test your preference for data appearance in a horizontal or column bar format or in a line chart.

Each program provides a skeletal input form for your data. If it's to be a pie chart, you request that format. Fill in the blanks. Select the color or textures you want, and then display the chart on screen, completely drawn with the data you provided. (All programs do not have the display capability.)

Twelve Rules for Creating Analytical Graphs

The overriding consideration when developing charts is to select the correct format for the information to be displayed. However, you might suspect, by now, that there are many ways a chart design can evolve. You've probably seen pie charts with so many segments, labels, and legends that any attempt to analyze them is formidable. The figure resembles a maze rather than a chart.

It's easy to study chart styles in the proliferating number of business publications, not so much for the data, but for the way the data is shown. Watch magazines such as *Business Week* and *Fortune,* and newspapers such as *USA TODAY* and the *New York Times.* These publications hire the best designers in the field. Clip examples of various graph styles and begin a reference notebook of ideas. These media employ top graphics designers whose work is well worth studying and emulating.

When you must show data to an audience, you will command greater attention and be perceived as a sharper presenter if you use well-prepared visuals. Learn how the data you show can be clear, yet dynamic; correct, yet attractive; easy to read, yet tell the story.

Generally, the "right and wrong" suggestions apply to slides, overhead transparencies, and printed handout material. Use the following 12 rules as a checklist each time you must prepare visuals.

1. Simplicity.
2. Emphasis.
3. Unity.
4. Balance.
5. Spacing.
6. Scale.
7. Shade and color.
8. Texture and pattern.
9. Grid line use.
10. Line thickness.
11. Data and tic mark placement.
12. Placement of numbers and labels.

1. Simplicity

Limit the number of elements used. Try to show trends rather than detailed data in a chart. Supplement a trend chart with handout hard-copy material if detailed data must be presented. That allows the audience time to study the detailed material at leisure. When complex data must be presented, instead of one single complex chart, design a sequence of simple charts.

Rule 1: Simplicity

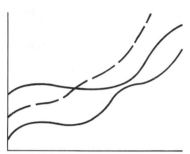

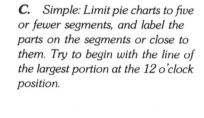

A. *Simple: Arrange lines in layers and in different widths and textures or colors. Use no more than three or four lines.*

B. *Too busy: When too many lines cross and go in conflicting directions, data are almost impossible to sort out and understand.*

C. *Simple: Limit pie charts to five or fewer segments, and label the parts on the segments or close to them. Try to begin with the line of the largest portion at the 12 o'clock position.*

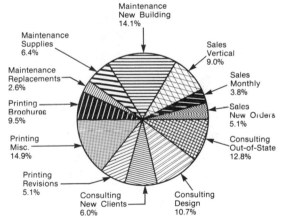

D. *Too busy: Use straight lines or arrows. Avoid using too many textures, too many segments, or too many tags.*

2. Emphasis

Give one element special treatment if you want it to stand out from the others. A brighter color, a filled-in area contrasted with outlined areas, and an "exploded" section (one shape moved out of the geometry of the other shapes) are techniques that create emphasis.

Rule 2: Emphasis

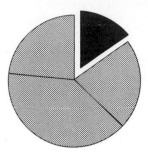

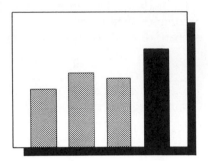

A. *All segments are of equal importance.*

B. *One segment is exploded for emphasis.*

C. *One bar is of a darker or heavier value.*

---

3. Unity

Unity is the relationship among elements that make them function as a whole rather than as separate parts.

Rule 3: Unity

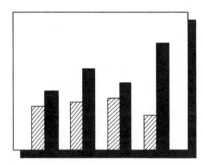

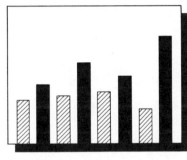

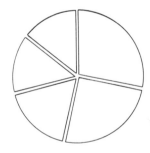

A. *Unified elements: Combine dissimilar elements to unify them when they are to be compared with the same groups.*

B. *Separate elements: Using too much space between the elements to be compared leave a few wondering what elements are being compared to which. Each element can appear to be more important individually than in combination.*

C. *Unified divisions: Show separate parts of one item in relation to a whole as one color or shade.*

---

4. Balance

Placement of different elements in relation to each other can create a formal or informal balance. A formal balance is most frequently used in charts, but an informal balance can be a practical design solution when chart elements create an imbalance.

Rule 4: Balance

A.
B.

A. *Formal balance: Elements are arranged symmetrically.*

B. *Informal balance: Elements are placed asymmetrically, but the total area is balanced.*

5. Spacing

Space the same elements so they relate as positive shapes to the negative space. (Positive is the element itself; negative is the space that surrounds the element.) Bars and columns should be wider than the space between them. The elements should fill the space and balance within the dimensions of the chart.

Rule 5: Spacing

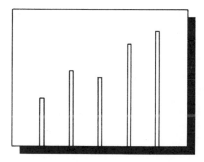
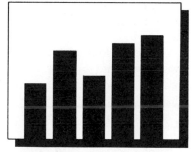
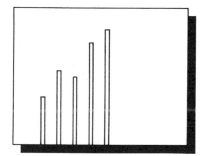

A. *Bad: Bars that are too narrow with too much space between them appear awkward.*

B. *Good: Bars and columns should be wider than the space between them.*

C. *Bad: Bars should not be squeezed into one side of the chart.*

6. Scale

Develop the data so it will not appear disproportionate to the image to be conveyed. Use the same grid increments in the horizontal and the vertical axes. On a curve chart, for example, poorly selected proportions on the x-axis (horizontal) can alter dramatically how the data is read. A dip in sales would look worse on a chart where the x-axis is broken into shorter increments than it would on a chart with longer increments.

Rule 6: Scale

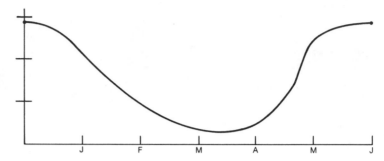

A. *Bad: Contracted or uneven scale marks alter the appearance of the curve, and sales figures can appear as having a severe dip in a six-month period.*

B. *Good: Evenly placed scale marks present a more realistic, and smoother, picture.*

7. Shade and Color

Place shades or textured patterns so they move from darkest to lightest. Work from darkest colors in the foreground to lighter colors as you progress backward. Lighter colors tend to jump forward; by ordering colors from dark to light, the elements will appear to be next to one another.

Avoid red to represent data shown to businesspeople; it connotes business failure. For the 4 percent of the male population that is red-green color blind, the two colors next to each other cannot be distinguished; they appear as one muddy brown shape. Blues and greens are good background choices for charts and slides.

Rule 7: Shade and color

A. *Bad: Unorganized mixture of colors and patterns.*

B. *Good: Order colors or shade patterns from darkest to lightest.*

A.

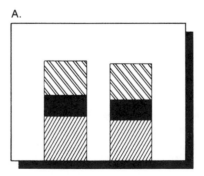

B.

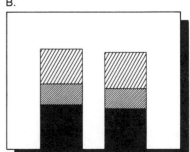

8. Texture and Pattern

Avoid placing garish patterns next to one another. Avoid juxtaposing any two patterns that cause distortion. Vertical lines make a vertical bar appear taller; if used next to other bars with horizontal patterns, the vertical will appear even taller than it is. Placing bolder patterns in selective bars can distort the way information is perceived. Bolder colored and patterned bars will jump out and suggest greater importance, although they are equal. Use bold patterns and bright colors for emphasis only in individual elements.

Rule 8: Texture and pattern

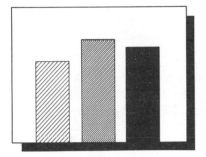 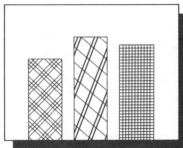 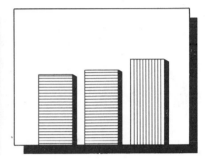

A.   *Good: Values and directions of textures should be similar.*

B.   *Bad: Garish, dissimilar texture or colors next to each other on the same chart are an eyesore.*

C.   *Bad: Don't use dissimilar fill lines next to one another if they optically distort the size of an element.*

9. Grid Line Use

When charts are used to illustrate trends or comparisons, it often is practical to omit grid lines; they may not add to chart readability. Use only enough grid lines to help the eye follow and interpret the data. Major and minor tic marks may be adequate. Do not allow grid lines to pass through bars, columns, lines, or surface areas that represent data. Keep grid lines in the background unless they contribute to the facts or design of the chart.

Rule 9: Grid line use

A.   *Grid lines should stop at solid areas; if data can be placed at the intersecting numbers, they may appear there, and the grid lines may be removed completely.*

B.   *Lines through solid areas representing data serve no function.*

A.

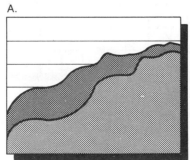

B.

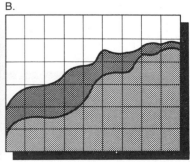

C.

D.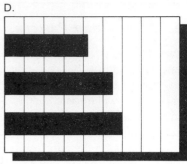

C. *Grid lines are not necessary with most bar charts and column charts.*

D. *Do not let lines intersect bars. Tic marks will serve as dividers.*

10. Line Thickness

Chart lines should not be all of the same weight or thickness. The plot line should be the heaviest, the horizontal (X) and vertical (Y) outer lines of a medium width. Grid lines should be the lightest weight. When two or more plot lines are used, use different shades, weights, textures, or colors in relation to the importance of the data assigned to each line. When color is used, the plot line can be the brightest or darkest; for X and Y lines use a medium color; for grid lines use a darker color (light colors come forward, darker colors recede).

Use solid lines for primary data that refer to real trends. Use dashes or dotted lines for secondary data, projections, or extensions. Use dots for missing data on a line.

Rule 10: Order of line thickness

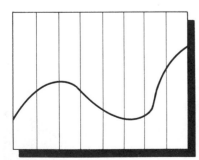

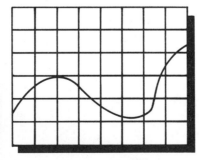

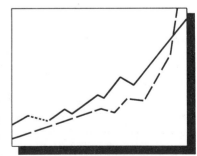

A. *Good: Three line weights: lightest for grid, middle for horizontal and vertical axis, heaviest for plot line.*

B. *Bad: Lines are the same weight and blend together.*

C. *Missing data are represented by a dotted line the same weight as the data line. Projected data can be dots, dotted lines, or dashes.*

11. Data and Tic Mark Placement

Usually, scale figures should be on the left side of the vertical axis and at the grid or tic marks. They may appear on the right side if the chart is wide or if the upward progress is to the right. Use only one set of scales on an axis, even when two sets of data are being shown.

Rule 11: Data and tic mark placement

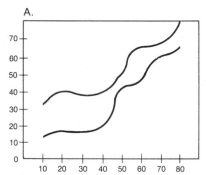
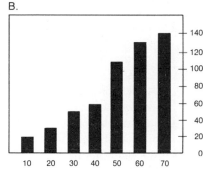

A. Labels are usually placed on the left side and bottom of the chart.

B. Values can appear on the right side if that makes the information more readable.

12. Placement of Numbers and Labels

Numbers and letters should be large enough to be read easily. Labels should be placed horizontally rather than vertically so they can be read without tilting the head. Place labels on the chart where practical. Start the beginning of the data with 0 (zero) at the base. If you don't, be sure that the numbering is large and clear and there is a reference shown to suggest 0 so the chart is not misread.

Rule 12: Placement of numbers and labels

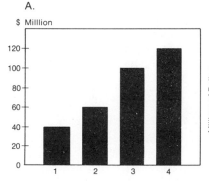
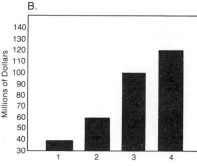

A. Plan so that numbers are large enough to read easily. Begin with 0 (zero) where the horizontal and vertical axes meet. Write labels horizontally.

B. Numbers are too small on this chart. Data begins at 30 instead of 0. "Millions of dollars" is placed sideways unnecessarily.

A Note about Titles and Legends

Generally, titles can be capitals and lowercase letters or all capitals; in any series of charts, this lettering order should be consistent. A type style without serifs (the tiny tails on some letter styles) is preferred to busy, fancy fonts (refer to the rules for text slides in Chapter 4). Charts should especially use simple type styles that do not add clutter and confusion. Use no more than three letter sizes in one chart. Use the same styles and reference colors on legends as in the chart. Select lettering large enough to be read at the distance required for specific audience setups and distances.

Here are some general guidelines to follow:

> For report graphics, select a size that will not be smaller than $\frac{1}{16}$ inch when reduced.
>
> For overhead transparency, make the letter size at least $1\frac{1}{4}$ inches for titles, subtitles, and charts that contain only text. Use lettering at least $\frac{1}{8}$ inch high to label X and Y lines and for plot curves and lines.
>
> On 35 mm slides, letter size will depend on chart proportion and the distance from which the slides will be viewed.
>
> Use a single family of type on one chart and within a total presentation for consistency. Keep the size of type for titles the same. Changing the size of one title will alter its importance in the group.

Chart Style Is the First Consideration

The primary consideration in analytical presentations is to know which chart style should be used for the data to be presented and, within that style, which format is best.

Table 5–1 organizes types of data and appropriate charts. Define the data you have and see which style chart may be selected. Following the table, each chart style is discussed with a drawing of the basic styles. Entire books have been written defining each family of charts; some consist of a hundred or more possible design formats. Refer to the appendixes for titles.

A variety of examples that build from simple to complex is offered in each category; they are meant as a stimulus for producing dynamic graphics. When chart and text slides are to be mixed, follow overall rules for presentations so that colors, titles, and type style are consistent throughout.

Which Chart to Use When?

The majority of charts are designed to show the following: quantities related to a fixed scale, comparison of items with one another, parts of a whole, and trends. Diagram charts are used to present items in a structure or show how parts of an object or process perform in relation to other parts or processes (see Chapter 6).

TABLE 5–1

When Data Is:	Chart to Use
Quantities—trends	
One item with another	Column chart: all types
	Bar chart: grouped bar, stacked bar, deviation bar, sliding bar
Divisions	
Parts of a whole	Pie chart
	100 percent bar chart
Quantities—trends	
One item over another	Line: curved surface
	Type of column: grouped column, stacked column, deviation column, histogram
Correlation	Scattergram
	Paired bar chart
Percentage of change	Semilog chart
	Index chart
Precise data	
Tabular	Table
Where things are	
Distribution	Map
Organization	
Items in a structure	Diagram: organization, relationship, Gantt, PERT, flowchart
How things work	Specialty charts
How much—volume	Specialty charts

Bar Charts: Vertical and Horizontal

Bar charts are either vertical or horizontal. Vertical bar charts are often called "column charts." They probably are used more than any type of chart when data must be compared in simple and compound relationships and within a fixed scale. There are literally over 100 column chart variations. The following are examples of those most often seen:

Single column–shows a comparative quantity; the amount of a subject in direct visual relation to other subjects of the same character.

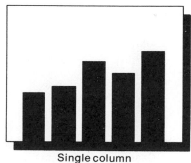

Single column

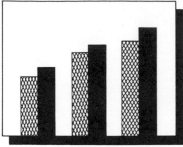

Two columns

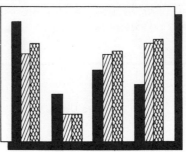

Three columns

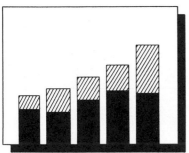

Stacked or divided columns

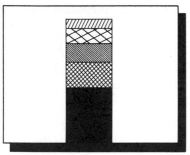

100 percent column

Two columns–a compound quantity showing two or more subjects and their amounts concurrently. Each bar represents two (or more) distinct quantities compared to one another, then both compared to others.

Three columns–a triple compound quantity, in which each successive subject is measured in terms of three standard situations. These are sometimes called "clustered charts."

Stacked, or divided, columns–show a subject amount, with the bar split into segments that indicate fractional amounts of the whole. Each segment is divided visually by shading, color, or texture. The number of stacks should be limited to four.

100 percent column–the parts total a 100 percent quantity. Similar to a pie chart for dividing a whole amount into portions.

Characterized column–the bars differ to show unlike characteristics. They may be shaded, colored, patterned, or shaped to represent the object.

Split columns (deviation charts)–show an amount in relation to a dividing line that separates the whole amount into two areas with a quantity on each side. It may indicate positive and negative values, with the dividing line being 0 (zero).

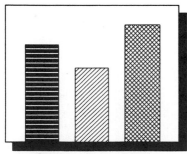

Characterized column

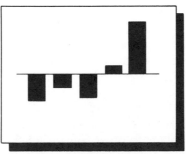

Split or deviation column

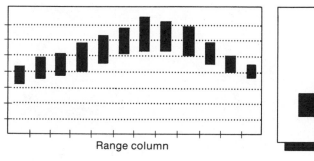

Range column

Histogram

Range column –shows a periodic quantity, or frequency distribution, of a subject related to a measured value, such as time.
Histogram –similar to a frequency distribution or range chart.

Horizontal Bar Charts

Bar charts (horizontal) serve the same functions as their vertical counterparts. Sometimes, data and titles lend themselves more conveniently and naturally to the horizontal format, especially when titles or tags must be placed in the same horizontal line as the bars. Sometimes they can be placed on the bar itself.

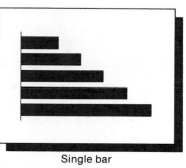

Single bar

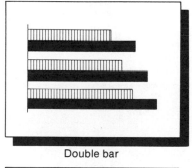

Double bar

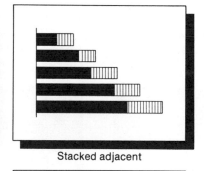

Stacked adjacent

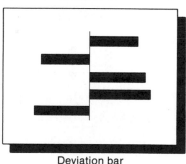

Deviation bar

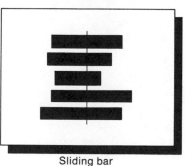

Sliding bar

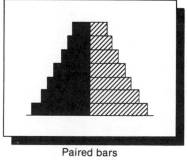

Paired bars

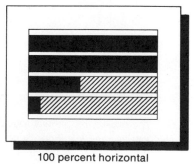

100 percent horizontal

C. There's more than one way to present a given set of data, as illustrated in this series by artist Sondra Berryman of Genigraphics Corp., San Diego, California. Tabular data could be shown as a table, but it may be adaptable to a variety of formats that will be more exciting and add impact to the information. (These slides are reproduced in color elsewhere in this book).

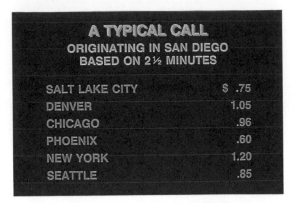

A. The information in a text slide is perfectly acceptable: white data, yellow title, orange subtitle on a blue background.

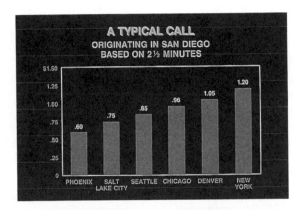

B. It can be shown on a single bar chart. The same title and subtitle are used in each example.

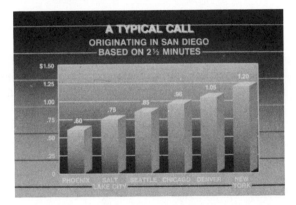

C. A drop shadow placed behind the bars creates a three-dimensional effect that makes the bars appear to jump out of the frame.

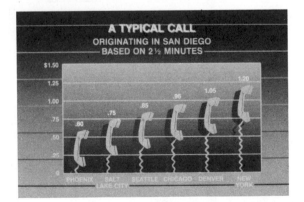

D. The artistic imaginative touch has been added: The bars become telephone hand sets.

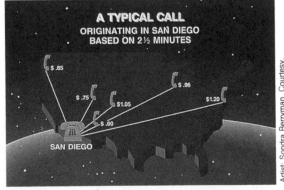

E. Now the data is placed on a map showing distances and costs; the map is superimposed on a portion of the globe with stars suggested on the shaded blue sky background.

Artist: Sondra Berryman. Courtesy, Genigraphics Corp.

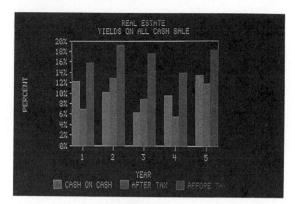

A chart generated by personal computer software isn't bad, but it's not good either. Titles are too small, framing is weak, colors are pale, and the percent tag is too far to the left.

The same data enhanced using *The Grafix Partner*. Titles now have weight, bars are given dimension and color contrast. The frame is red, with larger numbers set in a panel. The word percent is changed, but is redundant.

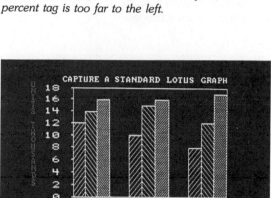

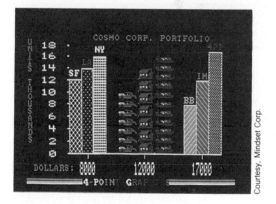

A standard four-column vertical stacked chart generated by Lotus 1–2–3 using three different textures—

—is enhanced using the program *4 Point Graphics*. The bars have been colored and the center group has been converted to products. The purpose of the chart was to show how the graphics program could change the basic chart so the busyness is not a factor.

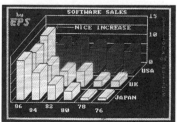

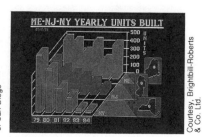

Left: A three-dimensional bar chart created by *PC Software Executive Picture Show* illustrates the potential of the program. The program has the draw capabilities to enhance it.

Right: A similar chart (slightly different data) enhanced using *The Grafix Partner*.

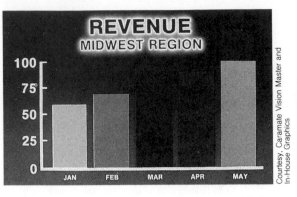

Courtesy, Caramate Vision Master and In-House Graphics

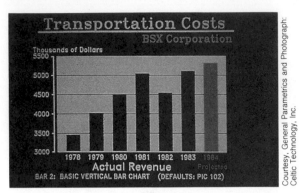

Courtesy, General Parametrics and Photograph: Celtic Technology, Inc.

Colored bars are more dramatic than black and white bar charts. The title has been enhanced with a glow effect. When color is not possible, different textures, or solids and textures, can be used.

VideoShow 150 in the default mode offers format title and structure elements shown in this bar chart. The final column, in green, is brighter and represents a different characteristic—projected change compared to known change.

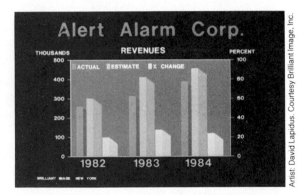

Artist: David Lapidus. Courtesy Brilliant Image, Inc.

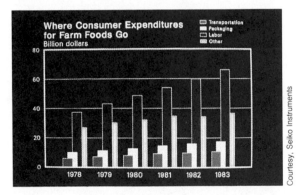

Courtesy, Seiko Instruments

C   *A three-column chart. Each group contains a column in green, blue, and orange. An extra set of marks showing percent is on the right axis. Normally, different sets of measures are not used on each side, but when the data require it, rules can be bent.*

Four-column chart that reads well; colors are consistent, and horizontal grid lines carry the eye across to the bars. The words Billion dollars *are properly written horizontally at the top of the column rather than as a vertical string of letters at the side.*

Left: An informal balance of elements. The data in chart form can be compared more quickly by simultaneous use of bars.

Right: Text and bar chart work well; when only a few bars are shown, the trend is emphasized.

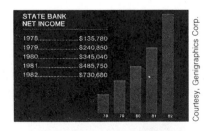

Courtesy, Genigraphics Corp.

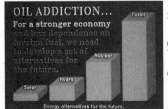

Courtesy, General Parametrics and Celtic Technology, Inc.

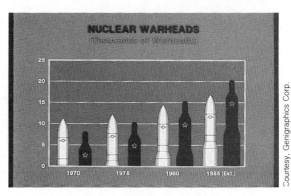

Sales profits; the bars are blocks in perspective with drop shadows that make them appear to float. The fencelike background represents the industry, producers of wooden fencing material.

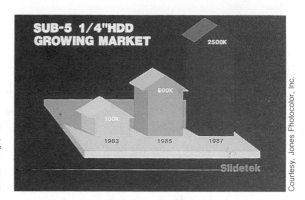

Nuclear warhead production is represented with images of the warheads replacing the standard bar columns.

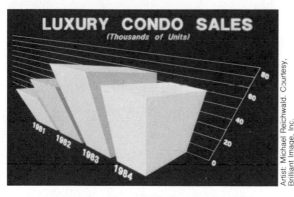

[c]   Luxury condos sales are represented by building shapes against a tilted grid.

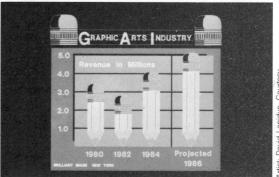

[c]   When only three columns are involved, it's a challenge to have the columns fill the space. The bars have been made into dimensional arrows, but the same shape could be interpreted for sales of houses, garages, and so on.

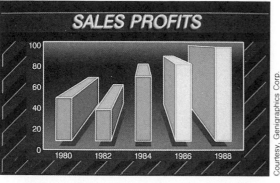

Business charts should be easy to read, be accurate, and have impact. The slide artwork is related to the industry and data represented, but the style format is retained in this single-column chart.

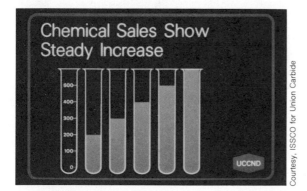

It's appropriate to show revenues in the graphic arts industry as brilliantly colored pencils. Pencil caps, repeated at top, appear as cupolas of an art museum.

GRAPHWRITER

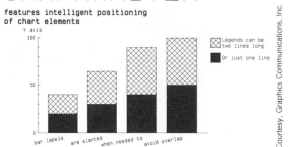

features intelligent positioning
of chart elements

A basic stacked column chart format can be easily generated with Graphwriter; it combines a solid base with a textured top.

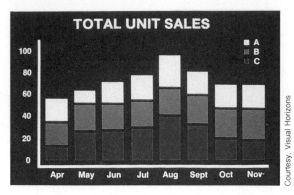

Colors progress from blue to green to yellow (darkest on bottom, lightest on top) in an example of a stacked column chart.

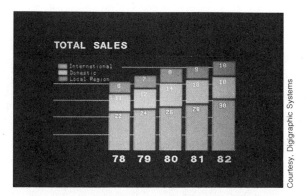

An informal balance in a stacked column chart. The designer pushed the four columns to the right of the space and balanced them with the title and legend at left.

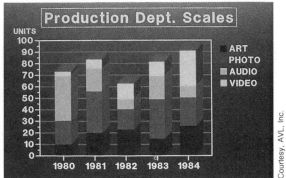

A three-dimensional stacked column chart. Colors progress from red on the bottom, to blue, to yellow, to green. Bars are framed and the legend is on the outside.

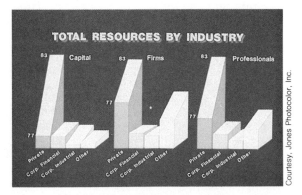

Another idea for illustrating grouped columns when data must be shown for four elements in three different groups. The frame has been dropped.

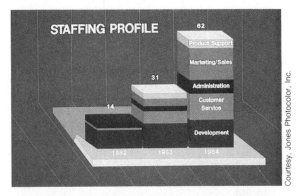

Three stacked columns with the same color sequence. The labeled final column suggests that the same labels apply for the shorter stacks so additional labeling is not required.

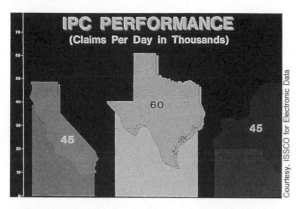

C *Performance in three states is indicated by the shape of the state at the end of the column. The speaker, or the accompanying copy, would tag the state names for those who don't recognize the shape of each.*

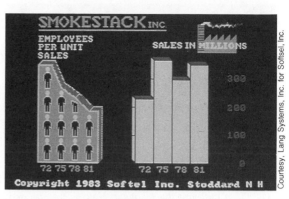

C *The subject of the comparisons is instantly evident where drawings symbolizing employees are used in one element. (These slides are reproduced in color elsewhere in this book.)*

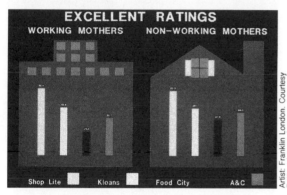

C *MOTHERS: Columns indicating statistics for working mothers versus nonworking mothers are placed in an appropriate "environment" of factory and home.*

C *BUILDING BLOCKS is composed of children's blocks with an image of a child adding to the data.*

C *A stored drawing of an airplane is easily added to an appropriate company's data, and the chart will become customized.*

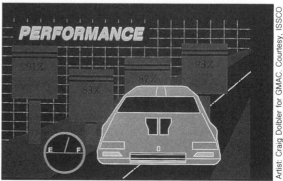

C *Clever use of a highway, car, and road signs to show automobile performance.*

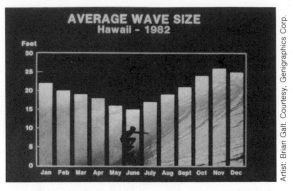

Artist: Brian Galt. Courtesy, Genigraphics Corp.

C How high are the waves in Hawaii during each month? A surfer and water within the bars leave no doubt regarding the subject of the data.

Artist: Franklin London. Courtesy, Brilliant Image, Inc.

A chart combined with a map suggests a wide world sales network.

Courtesy, Genigraphics Corp.

Although column chart data is generally associated with a rectangular format, it can be placed in a circular design that suggests the product, such as a beer keg, top background, for bars topped with dripping beer foam.

Courtesy, Dicomed Corp.

C Data that might normally be given a column chart format is placed on a time-clock background to show the comparative speeds of four animals.

A horizontal single bar chart is given impact by using a different color for each bar set against a black background. Bars are usually arranged in a descending order, with the larger value at either the top or bottom.

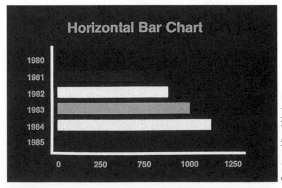

Courtesy, Visual Horizons

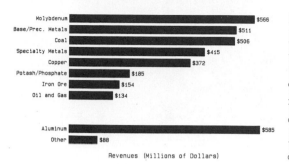

Courtesy, Graphics Communications, Inc.

Long word labels and long bars lend themselves to interpretation in the horizontal format. This one was generated with Graphwriter.

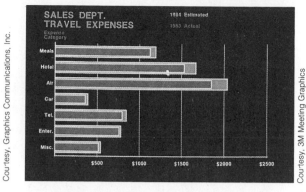

Courtesy, 3M Meeting Graphics

A typical horizontal bar chart may be preferred to a column (vertical) chart when the labels are words that are easier to read in the horizontal format. By using one color bar within another, the data shows estimated and actual expense in each horizontal.

Generated with VideoShow. Courtesy, General Parametrics Corp.

A drop shadow is placed behind each bar, which makes it appear to stand away from the light green background. The chart itself is also shadowed, so the image appears as an entity against the background rather than a flat sheet.

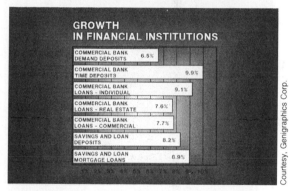

Courtesy, Genigraphics Corp.

Labels are placed on the bar itself so no external tags are required. The scaling is not in descending order, but in the order in which the presenter will discuss the topics.

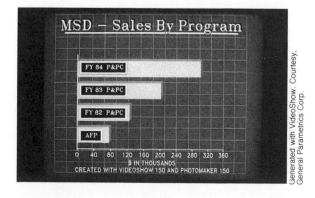

Generated with VideoShow. Courtesy, General Parametrics Corp.

Tags appear on shadowed bars against a grid with data on the base line.

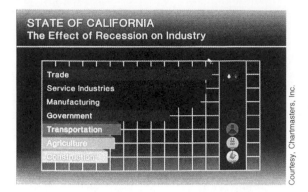

Courtesy, Chartmasters, Inc.

General trends can be reported without using actual numerical data. Shadowed bars have no space between them; the shadow separates one from another.

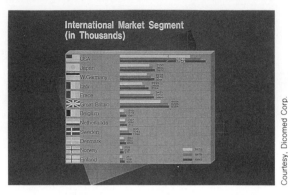

Courtesy, Dicomed Corp.

A grouped bar chart, with each group representing a specific country, compares items at different points in time. Three colors are used consistently in each group, a legend is at the bottom. Flags are a clever addition of color.

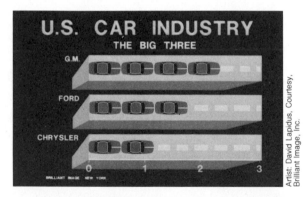

Artist: David Lapidus, Courtesy, Brilliant Image, Inc.

When comparing factors in the automobile industry, use automobiles on the bar.

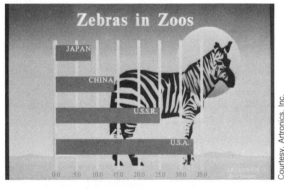

Courtesy, Artronics, Inc.

No question here what animal resides in which country's zoos and the general relationship of quantities.

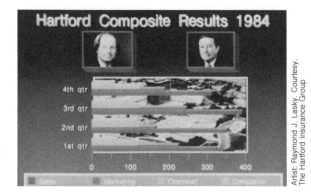

Artist: Raymond J. Lasky, Courtesy, The Hartford Insurance Group

Digitally stored images of corporate officers were recalled from disk storage and placed in boxes for the top of the picture. The graph pictures the company building complex. The basic graph was generated on an IBM PC, but the combination was made with a Chyron System.

Pie Charts

A pie chart illustrates relations of parts to the whole. The circle represents the whole amount. The segments represent proportional quantities or percentages of the whole. All segments may be visually related to give a feeling of a unified total; or, a segment can be differentiated in character to distinguish it. An important segment, or segments, can be emphasized by pulling them away from the whole (exploding), changing color, or shading.

The basic pie chart formats are:

Simple pie chart—one shade or color shows a whole amount of one character.

Differentiated divisions—each segment of the whole has an independent character that is shown by shading or coloring each segment differently.

Exploded segment—emphasizes one segment. A characterized segment is shown, but it could be an emphasized part of a whole pie with a single character. It could be a group of segments.

Two pies of characterized segments and different sizes—may be used to compare parts and their relationships at different times, and to show growth.

Pie chart drawings

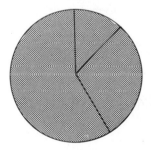
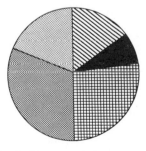
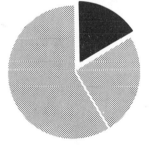

A. *Whole amount of one character.*

B. *Differentiated divisions; each segment illustrates a different character.*

C. *Exploded for emphasis.*

D. *Two pies of different sizes and with different characters for comparisons at different times. The smaller pie could represent another division of the largest segment of the big pie.*

Pie chart drawings (concluded)

E.   *Two pies of same size for similar comparisons under different conditions.*

F.   *Three pies compare the same subject at different times.*

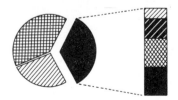

G.   *Combination pie and bar; bar becomes a 100 percent quantity of a single pie segment.*

Two pies the same size—compare the same object under different conditions; the relationship of the segments differs.

Three pies—compare value changes of the same object at different times.

Combination pie and bar—one segment of the pie becomes the 100 percent quantity for the stacked bar chart illustrating the value of its parts.

Design Considerations

Pie charts would run a close second to bar charts in a popularity poll. They would probably run neck and neck in a race for general abuse of design fundamentals. The major offenses: too much information, poorly labeled parts, lack of understanding about how the pie should be cut up, and type too small to read.

Pie charts become confusing when too much information is squeezed onto them. If necessary, they can be broken into two or three separate slides, with each portion of the pie described individually.

The general rules to follow regarding pie charts are:

Use as few slices as necessary, preferably not more than four, five, or six unless more are absolutely necessary.

Keep labels short and place them next to, or within, the segment.

Remember that visuals are used to show trends. If the pie has too much information, use handouts for detailed data.

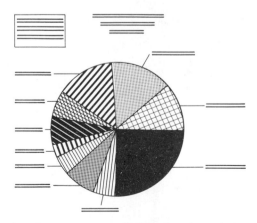

Avoid entering so much data that the pie's format is overcrowded. This example suggests too many segments, more textures than the program is capable of outputting, two and three line tags per segment, double or triple headings, an extra legend, and an annotation.

Use a different shade, color, or texture for each segment, to help visual clarity. Segments can share a slice line, or they can be a complete slice with a space between each. Labels may carry the same color as the referenced segment.

Avoid using textures that confuse or colors that are incompatible next to one another. Place pies on a background of a dark or neutral shade.

Emphasize one segment (or series of segments) by exploding it away from the circle and highlighting it with color or a special texture.

Show comparisons by using two or more charts, or combining a pie and a bar chart.

Arrange pie data so it reads in a clockwise direction. Consider a vertical line drawn from the 6 o'clock to the 12 o'clock position as the base line. Position the most important segment beginning at the 12 o'clock position. If no single segment is more important, arrange the slices from the largest to the smallest or vice versa. If two or more pies are used in the same chart, have them all begin at the same point, use the same colors, and follow the information segments in the same order.

Acknowledge a source by placing the information in the lower left-hand corner in the smallest legible lettering size available.

The slices themselves, the tilt of the chart and the placement of legends and titles have infinite design potential—and pitfalls. Titles, text, and special effects used in other examples throughout the book can be applied to and combined with pie charts. The examples offer variations on a pie adaptable to any type of content.

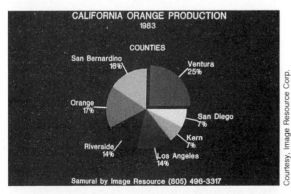

A basic pie chart with the largest segment "exploded" or pulled away from the circle for emphasis. Each segment is large enough to hold the percent value, which would have simplified the design.

A similar basic exploded chart design with labels inside the slices. The exploded segment is a bright pink compared to the muted colors in the other segments.

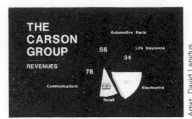

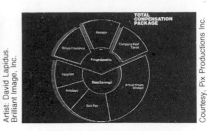

The pie has a drop shadow behind it for depth. Labels repeat the segment colors.

Courtesy, Lang Systems, Inc.

Shadowed pie segments: numbers are inside; labels are outside. The pie is off-centered with the company logo at top. Observe placement of the words so they follow the circle design.

Artist: David Lapidus. Brilliant Image, Inc.

Outlined pie segments with a circle remaining in the center. Only two colors are used: yellow lines and text on a blue background.

Courtesy, Pix Productions Inc.

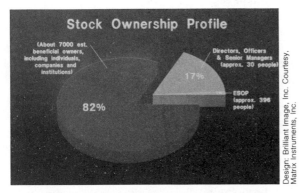

Design: Brilliant Image, Inc. Courtesy, Matrix Instruments, Inc.

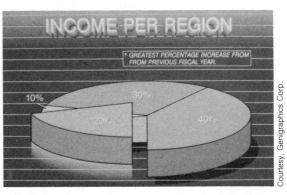

Courtesy, Genigraphics Corp.

C *Tilting a pie shape alters the position and the audience's attention because it represents a changed image, yet it is not so shocking that it detracts from the message.*

C *Four different colored segments; the highlighted piece is placed in the front position and reflected on the background.*

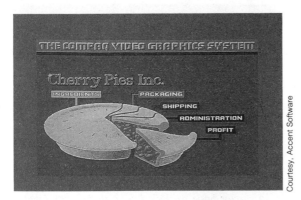

Courtesy, Accent Software

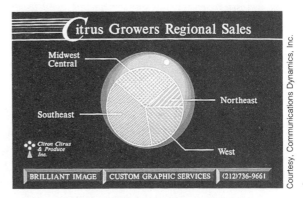

Courtesy, Communications Dynamics, Inc.

C *A literal pie is the pie chart. This is one screen from a demonstration disk developed for Compaq Computer Corp.*

C *Instead of a pie, a phonograph record representing the industry under discussion becomes the "pie." Created with CDI ImageBuilder Software.*

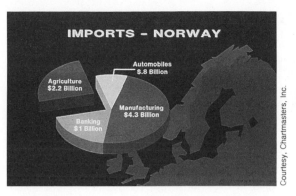

C *Both the pie and the title are tilted; the image is combined with a map of the Scandinavian countries with Norway highlighted.*

C *An orange is the circular pie image for the Citrus Growers chart. Observe that the title design and the logo placement are used throughout the presentation.*

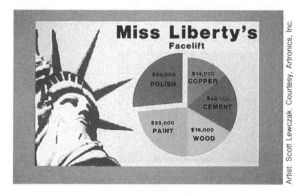

The pie chart can be simple yet dramatic by associating it with an image of the subject.

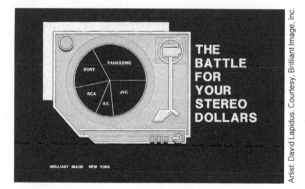

The pie is placed on top of a drawing of a stereo set; the title is at the right; words are at left, justified.

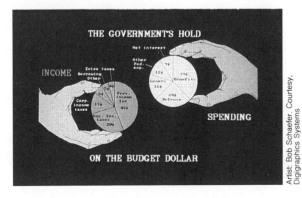

Two or more charts can be compared in a single panel. They are not quite so bland if they are given a theme—a little pizzazz. The word hold *suggested the use of hands holding the pies.*

Line and Surface Charts

Line and surface charts

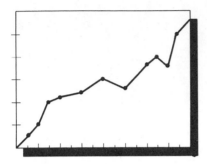

A. *Plotted dots connected with straight lines.*

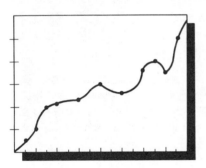

B. *Same dots with gentle curve lines.*

A line chart, also referred to as a curve chart, shows trends and emphasizes movement and direction of change over a period of time. Graphically, it is based on a succession of coordinate points. The trend may be shown by connecting each of a series of coordinated points on a grid with a sharp line or a generalized curve.

A line chart can depict many more points than can comfortably be illustrated with a bar chart. It can reflect more subtle differences in data. By using two or more lines or curves, comparative directions can be observed instantly. Consider a chart showing the rate of inventory in and out of a warehouse per month in one year compared to another. A 12-point flow (1 point each month) is easier to follow on a line chart than on a bar chart. By assigning each product to a different line, three or more product movements can be illustrated simultaneously and in relation to each other.

Emphasis can be shown by changing the character of a line: making it heavier than comparative lines on a multiline chart, or making parts of one line heavier. On an upward trend line, the line character might change from thin at the bottom to heavy at the top.

A surface chart results when the area between the lines or curves is shaded or filled in. This approach emphasizes total amounts rather than changes in amounts, as in a single curve chart. However, filled-in surfaces are often used to add a more solid, impressive look to a single or double-curve chart.

Comparisons may be clarified with two or more charts on one panel.

The primary caution, already noted, bears repeating. The scale of the line and the grid divisions must be chosen to accurately reflect the information without distorting it. Try not to show too

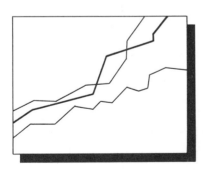

C. *Emphasis on a multiline chart.*

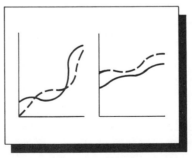

D. *Two charts on one panel, same data at different times.*

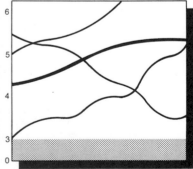

E. *When 0 is not the logical starting point, add a texture or another base line to clarify that the starting point is different than 0.*

many elements (and lines) in one chart. Four or five data lines should be the maximum and then only if they don't cause confusion as they overlap.

Grid lines should not look like a checkerboard or a venetian blind on the chart. If grid lines must be extended for clarity, keep them lightweight. Have them stop or change at the data line, or integrate them as a design element. If your software does not support different line thicknesses, use a dotted line, try to eliminate the line, or use a draw program to change the chart appearance.

Always begin the vertical axis number at zero. If the axis must begin at a higher point, make that change very clear! Keep legends to a minimum. Place tags within an area where possible, but use lettering and colors that will show. Arrange labels to read horizontally as the eye would read. Vertically strung words require extra time for the reader to assimilate.

Never use the *y* axis line as a data line. The *y* axis acts as a border and carries the information for clarifying the data.

When textured lines rather than colored surface areas are used to differentiate sections, line directions should be compatible with one another. Avoid using textures that distort the appearance of a section. Horizontal lines can appear to soften the sharp vertical of a downtrend.

On a surface chart, arrange data so that the data forming the flattest, or smoothest, band is on the bottom. If all bands are relatively smooth, put the most important band data, or the widest band, at the bottom.

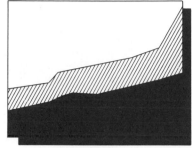

Surface

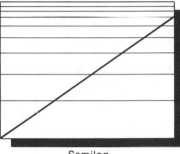

Semilog

Other Types of Comparison Charts

Other charts that fall into a "line" category and are used to show a comparison of data are:

> *Semilog charts*–show a relative change. They are useful when comparing large quantities with small quantities and when comparing relative change of data expressed in different-units. The grid used is uneven, as shown.
>
> *Index chart*–also shows relative change by converting data into percentages of a base period. It compares two or more series of data measured in different units or different-sized units.
>
> *Scattergram or scatter chart*–shows how two sets of data correlate. When both sets of data increase at the same rate, correlation is positive. When both sets decrease at the same rate, the correlation is negative. A line may be drawn between dots to plot the relationships. When there is no relationship between the sets of data, the correlation is zero.

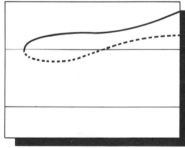

Index

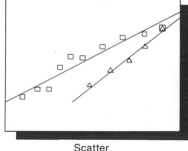

Scatter

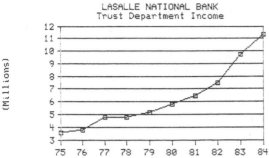

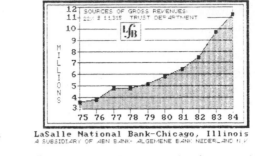

A. *Plot of a screen from Lotus 1–2–3. Notice data starts at 3.*

B. *Titles added in new styles, frame, and legends; logo added. Many design elements are still placed incorrectly.*

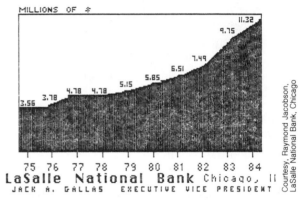

C. *Simplification begins. Number begins at 0, Millions of $ moved to top. Grid lines do not go into surface area. Titles changed.*

D. *Complete revamp. All changes accomplished with The Grafix Partner.*

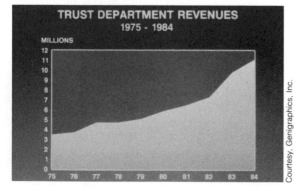

The same data as above, interpreted in a simplified surface chart. The surface area is a gradated red-orange color, and the background is gradated dark to lighter blue.

Another interpretation of the same data. The surface area is a solid light blue three-dimensional shape; the background is a gradated dark to lighter blue. The titles are yellow.

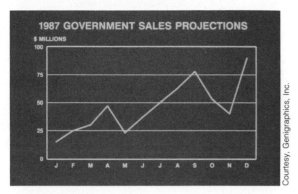

Courtesy, Genigraphics, Inc.

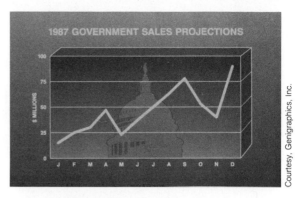

Courtesy, Genigraphics, Inc.

When possible, keep line charts simple for easy readability. Ideally, the line should show a trend rather than infinite detail.

The additional dimensional box for the chart and the subtle image of the White House add visual interest, but the data is still the major emphasis.

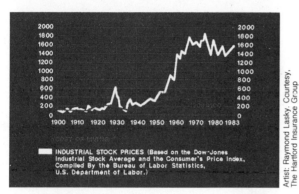

Artist: Raymond Lasky. Courtesy, The Hartford Insurance Group

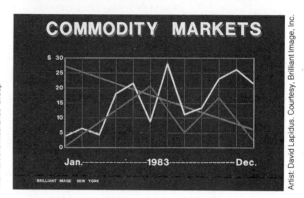

Artist: David Lapidus. Courtesy, Brilliant Image, Inc.

Numbers may be placed on both vertical lines of a very wide chart.

When data lines are extremely erratic, grid lines help make the points easier to read and to compare within an area. The blue grid appears to fall behind the red and orange data lines.

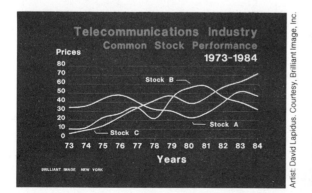

Artist: David Lapidus. Courtesy, Brilliant Image, Inc.

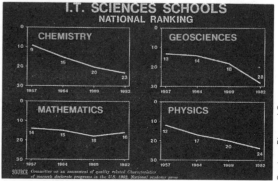

Courtesy, Dicomed Corp.

Crisscross curved trend lines show comparisons. Each line must be a different color; or, if printed in black and white, it should be a different thickness, texture, or shade.

When data cannot be compared clearly on a single line chart, four "like" charts may perform the analysis effectively.

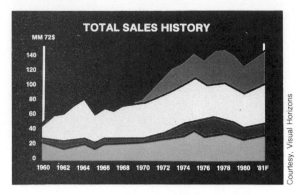

Courtesy, Visual Horizons

Sales history in millions of dollars is simply presented in a surface chart. The surface fill is separated by the lines that become part of the background. The darkest color and smoothest data is on the bottom.

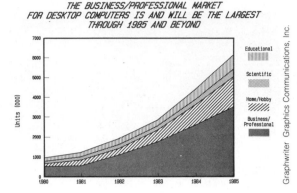

Graphwriter Graphics Communications, Inc.

When areas are not wide enough for tagging, a legend can be placed at the side of the chart with references that match each surface. Solid and textured areas separate data visually.

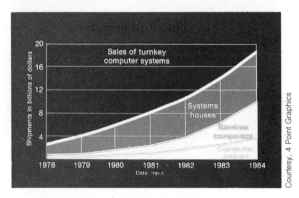

Courtesy, 4 Point Graphics

Observe the different widths of data lines and the use of thin grid lines; labels appear on the section.

Courtesy, Lang Systems, Inc.

Unequal grid divisions do not distort the data shown. Grid lines do not enter the solid surface areas.

Here is a surface chart that has been developed dimensionally. Because the highest points appear at the right of the chart, the scale marks are placed at the right.

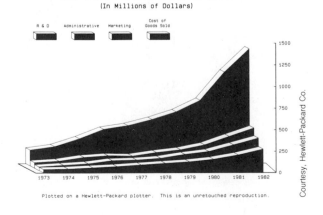

TEN-YEAR CONSOLIDATED SUMMARY
(In Millions of Dollars)

Courtesy, Hewlett-Packard Co.

Plotted on a Hewlett-Packard plotter. This is an unretouched reproduction.

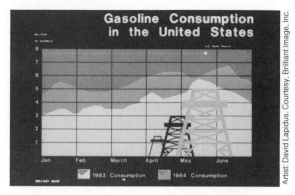

Artist: David Lapidus. Courtesy, Brilliant Image, Inc.

C Drawings of a product or an industry symbol added to a surface chart customize it without overpowering.

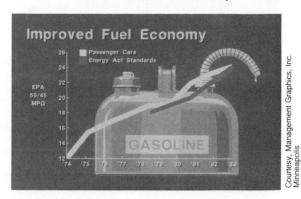

Courtesy, Management Graphics, Inc. Minneapolis

C An oil can is an attractive and logical fill image for a line chart showing a trend. It is novel and dynamic.

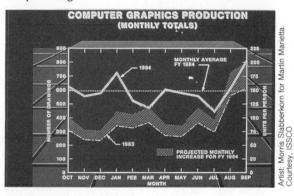

Artist: Morris Slabberkorn for Martin Marietta. Courtesy, ISSCO

C Example of an index chart. Tags and labels on each side of the chart differ. Reading and analysis have to be done carefully to understand the various factors.

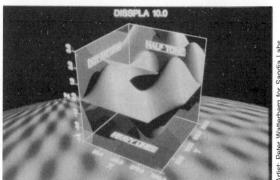

Artist: Peter Watterberg for Sandia Labs. Courtesy, ISSCO

A three-dimensional surface chart.

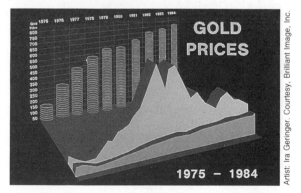

Artist: Ira Geringer. Courtesy, Brilliant Image, Inc.

C Data can be shown on one chart using two formats when cleverly accomplished. A shadowed surface chart seems to appear in front of the column chart. It's more dramatic and readable than it would be if the surface chart were on the same plane or superimposed on the column chart.

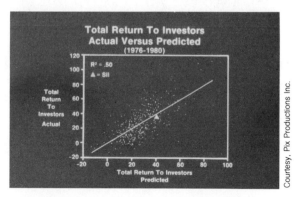

Courtesy, Pix Productions Inc.

A plotted scatter chart compares data increasing at the same rate.

Table, Or Tabular, Charts

Charts that show rows of tables with words and numbers usually contain precise information that the viewer is expected to comprehend in a short time. Presenting that data interestingly is a challenge. Many programs offer picture libraries and draw capabilities for enhancing a chart, but applying these requires time and imagination.

When straight data are presented in tabular format and the table is constructed clearly, logically, with color and carefully chosen spacing and lines, the data can appear dynamic. Reveals can be applied to tables as they can to text and picture slides. An example is shown. Your objective is to arrange data so it is as easy as possible for the viewer to analyze and compare, and thereby reach valid conclusions. There are practical rules and resulting formats that can accomplish that objective. They are:

1. Captions at the head of each column should be short and specific. Include an overall measurement such as dollars, thousands of people, years, and so on, at the top of the chart or in the appropriate column.
2. Columns that contain words should be aligned with the words at the left. Numbers should be centered in a column and aligned by decimal points or commas.
3. Use underlines for headings and major column divisions; avoid crossing lines for all horizontal and vertical columns. Let spacing suggest column divisions. Use short underlines to show totals. In the examples, lines exist for different purposes, but they are used discriminately so the charts don't appear as checkerboards.

Tabular charts

Connecticut OSHA
Incident Rates by Major Industry

	Total	Lost Workday Cases	Non-Lost Workday Cases	Avg. Days Lost
Private	8.1	3.8	4.3	15.0
Construction	15.8	6.4	9.4	18.0
Local Gov't.	16.8	7.5	9.3	18.0

Artist: Raymond Lasky, Courtesy, The Hartford Insurance Group

Statement of Consolidated Financial Position
(Dollars in millions, except per share)

Investments and Other Assets		
Investments in affiliates	175.1	158.2
Other	160.7	152.1
Property, Plant and Equipment at Cost		
Land	57.7	57.0
Buildings	665.4	670.3
Machinery and equipment	4,600.1	4,628.4
Mineral rights and oil and gas properties	475.4	352.0
Construction-in-progress	418.9	365.9
	6,217.5	6,073.6
Less accumulated depreciation and depletion	3,033.6	2,964.5
Total Assets	$6,069.2	$5,796.4

Color is used in the title and subtitle. The final line showing the highest incidence rate is colored to call audience attention to the data to be stressed. Observe the use of column headings, lines, spacing, and how words and numbers are lined up.

This example is not nearly as effective. Because so much information must be placed on the slide, the letters are small. The title does not stand out and the number column does not have a heading over it. The result is a less readable chart with information that is hard to assimilate readily.

Only a few graph-making programs include automatic generation of tabular chart formats. A text chart may be used if the data will fit within the limits of the input file. A spreadsheet program or word processing program can do the job efficiently and retain rows and columns as you work. The data can then be transferred to another program for enhancing with more attractive type styles, titles, and colors.

Artist: Diane K. O'Malley. Courtesy, Autographix, Inc.

LIFE INSURANCE BY AGE GROUP. Columns and headings are boxed.

BUDGET. Underlines appear only where data totals will be shown.

Artist: Paul Phillips. Courtesy, E. F. Hutton Life Insurance Co.

Courtesy, Genigraphics Corp.

FINANCIAL HIGHLIGHTS. Separating lines are used between entries.

Service opportunities

Services	Business	Industry group	Residential
Circuit switch			
Packet switch			
Leased line			
Network management			
Value added services			

Service opportunities

Services	Business	Industry group	Residential
Circuit switch	Centrex	Standard interfaces & application protocols	—
Packet switch	Private line substitution		
Leased line	Bandwidth pipe	—	
Network management	By customer	By carrier	
Value added services	Many	Many	

Service opportunities

Services	Business	Industry group	Residential
Circuit switch	Centrex		
Packet switch	Private line substitution		
Leased line	Bandwidth pipe		
Network management	By customer		
Value added services	Many		

Courtesy, W. S. Wong for Bell-Northern Research, Canada

|C| *A table chart can be treated with a reveal or build effect in which each slide reveals the next column of information. As the new column appears in a red color, the previous column falls back to a dimmer blue. Section headings and dividing lines are white. The first slide shows only the headings.*

|C| *The second slide reveals the first column of information in red text. Adding a column at a time offers the data gradually and is not a formidable display of information at one time.*

(Five of these slides are reproduced in color.)

|C| *The third slide reveals the next column of text in red; the first column fades to a blue, and so forth until all three columns have been shown and explained. This is a more effective way to present tabular data and keep the audience along with you than putting all data on the chart at once while you vie for audience attention.*

Comparing Slidemaking Programs

CRITERIA	A	B	C	D	BRILLIANT IMAGE
EXTENSIVE HARDCOPY OPTIONS	✗	✗	✗	✗	✓
OUTPUT TO MATRIX CAM.	✓	✗	✗	✗	✓
BACKUP PRODUCTION SUPPORT	✗	✗	✓	✓	✓
INEXPENSIVE NETWORKING	✗	✗	✗	✗	✓
IMAGING FACILITIES	✗	✓	✓	✓	✓
Rating	1	1	2	2	5

BRILLIANT IMAGE NEW YORK

Artist: David Lapidus. Courtesy, Brilliant Image, Inc.

|C| *A table chart becomes a drawing with symbols where yes's and no's might be. The columns representing different companies are separated and colored differently. The one meant to stand out is bright pink for greatest emphasis.*

EXCELLENT RATINGS BY MOTHERS BY CHILD SEX

	INFANT	MALE	FEMALE
Health-tex	73.3	65.2	65.4
Carters	56.0	39.8	50.0
Oshkosh	38.9	33.0	32.2
Izod	32.9	43.6	44.8

Artist: Ellen Rosenthal. Courtesy, Brilliant Image, Inc.

MOTHERS WITH SIGNS interpret ratings of children's clothing.

DOG-NAME PREFERENCE BY AGE

0-3 4-12 1 2 3 4 5 6 7 8 9 10
Mos Mos Yr Yr Yr Yr Yr Yr Yr Yr Yr Yr

SHOTSIE
SHEBA
RALF   RALF
BOWZER
ROVER
PENNEY

Artist: Ellen Rosenthal. Courtesy, Brilliant Image, Inc.

|C| *DOG NAMES are shown on a colorful illustrated bar chart.*

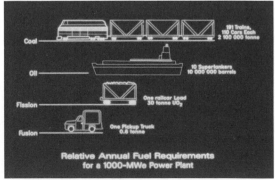

Coal	191 Trains, 110 Cars Each 2 100 000 tonne
Oil	10 Supertankers 10 000 000 barrels
Fission	One railcar load 30 tonne UO₂
Fusion	One Pickup Truck 0.6 tonne

Relative Annual Fuel Requirements
for a 1000-MWe Power Plant

Mary Jo Koelbl for Argonne Labs. Courtesy, ISSCO

A chart that probably began as a tabular entry with headings such as "fuel," "vehicles," and "tonnage" is reinterpreted with visuals. The data might be tried in horizontal bar chart format, too.

Maps as Charts

A map of the world or of a country, or a detailed map of an area, can show general trends and comparisons for sales saturation, routing, strategy in targeted areas, and so forth. When maps must be specific for locations of travel routes, historical sites, or geological conditions, the zoom feature of most programs will enable the user to create detail, pixel by pixel, if necessary.

Generally, one thinks of a map with pushpins indicating locations. But charts, slightly customized with the aid of a computer and an artistic approach, drive home the points to be made clearly and pictorially. Areas can be readily emphasized with color by exploding or breaking up the map and showing the important parts separately.

The simplicity rule applies to maps as it does to other charts. Avoid unnecessary detail. Use color or textures to divide areas. Company logos or symbols of the product may be substituted for pins. Think of using slides that reveal only one portion of the map at a time if that technique fits the presentation.

The majority of chart and draw programs contain library images of maps of different countries. Some have individual states predrawn. Following are several ideas for map design:

A map may show all locations of all objects with the same character. If a large mass occurs in one area, the symbols may become a larger group.

Elements that are not alike can be shown by different symbols and properly placed in relation to one another. Any of these areas can be enlarged to show a more detailed distribution.

The elements described may have a definite physical shape

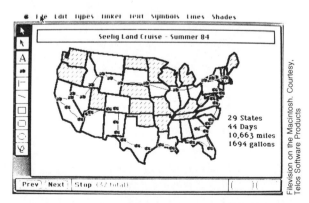

Filevision on the Macintosh. Courtesy, Telos Software Products

The same map may be stored in a picture library, then called up and filled in as necessary. This map of the United States shows routes of a land cruiser. States that are all white are those where the bus traveled; the vehicle is drawn as a bus.

Sales activity nationwide as analyzed by the Chicago office (outlined). Two other symbols represent different amounts of money as stated by the legend, right. Observe the different file patterns possible with the program.

in relation to the surrounding environment. A specific area and a specific location can be illustrated.

Routes of vehicles, communications networks, and so on are logical elements for portrayal on a map chart. A lapse in a route, or a projected route, could be displayed by a dotted line. If the connecting points are important, they can be designated with a symbol such as a circle, triangle, square, tent, oil well, skyscraper, and so on.

Drawings—maps

A.

B.

C.

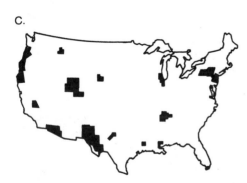

D.

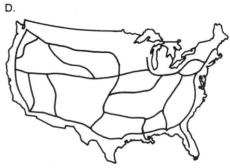

A. All locations of objects have the same characteristics.

B. All locations of all objects have different characters.

C. The elements have a definite physical shape in relation to the surrounding environment.

D. Routes can be shown by lines with varying characteristics; those characteristics should be explained with a legend.

E.

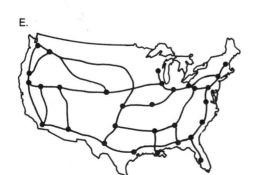

E. A network map would have the points connected by a symbol.

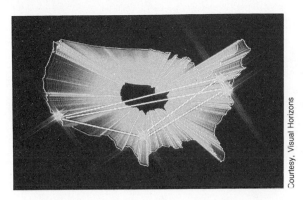

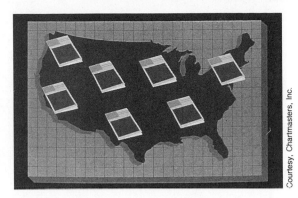

A generalized map becomes an abstract drawing. There are no details, yet the points to be made are obvious by the highlighted route lines.

[C] *An accurately drawn, but not detailed, map of the United States with a product symbol. The product appears to have nationwide distribution because no areas are pinpointed.*

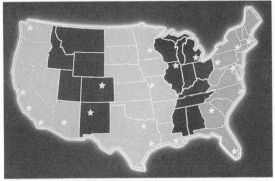

[C] *You know instantly how the country is divided into five sales divisions because each division is its own color. Stars indicate sales offices. The entire map is "eclipsed," a special effect that gives the appearance of light behind the subject.*

Three applications for the use of predrawn maps from the program ExecuVision.

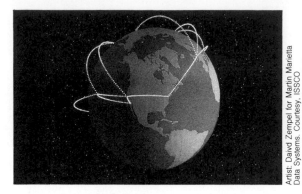

Artist: Daivd Zempel for Martin Marietta Data Systems. Courtesy, ISSCO

Routing in three dimensions has been created with the program DISSPLA.

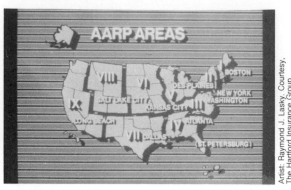

Artist: Raymond J. Lasky. Courtesy, The Hartford Insurance Group

Geographic sections of the map are exploded, and drop shadows are placed behind each section and the lettering. The map appears to float away from its striped background.

The Eastern United States in two separate panels compares the affected portions of the areas at different times.

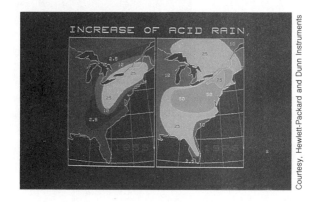

Courtesy, Hewlett-Packard and Dunn Instruments

A detail of a location showing the route and specific places along the way.

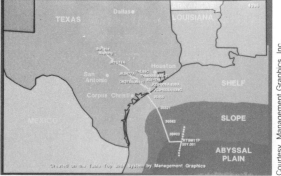

Courtesy, Management Graphics, Inc., Minneapolis

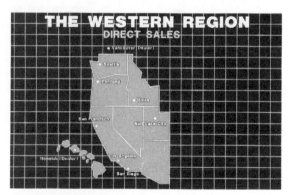

A.

A. A build-up series that illustrates growth of the western sales regions begins with a title slide for an introduction.

B. This focuses on the southern section. All city names are white against a red map on a lighter red grid with a black background. The orange title is carried through in the orange "sky" around the globe on the final slide. Different colored dots next to the city may indicate the range of sales figures for that particular color or number of dealers, depending on the presentation.

C. The northern coastal area is added.

D. And the expanded northern territory is filled in.

E. The final slide is an overview of the map area from another viewpoint.

B.

C.

D.

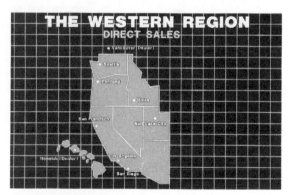

E.

Artist: Diane K. O'Malley. Courtesy, Autographix, Inc.

Diagram Charts

Diagram charts are pictorial representations of a subject with the elements arranged in terms of the whole. The elements are generally abstract and appear as symbolic shapes: squares, rectangles, circles, triangles, or volumes. Charts may show spatial organization of a subject: the hierarchy in an office command, the structural organization of a physical object, a time frame for a job, or steps required to complete a project. Relationships can be portrayed simply or in complex and layered arrangements. Subject elements can be illustrated as grouped, divided, subdivided, declining, and ascending in importance.

Current software excels at producing these charts in any and every possible interrelationship. Programs provide geometric shapes; you have only to assemble them and add text. These programs also offer a library of pictures that may be used to replace the traditional geometric shapes for greater visual interest.

The programs are so good that one needs only to select typeface, color for shapes, and overall design. The finished chart can be ready in a few minutes and can be readily revised. Once you learn how to generate certain diagram charts by computer, constructing them by hand drawing them will be as ancient a practice as traveling by horse and buggy.

Basic shapes provided by programs are only the first step in creating good diagram charts. You have to add the dynamic design elements and plan carefully how you wish to add each element as you discuss it. The examples that follow will provide a wealth of ideas.

Squares and rectangles can be shadow-boxes; certain levels can be colored or shaped differently. Arrows can be made more forceful for each new point to be made by changing thickness and color.

Emphasis can be created with endless variety. Build-up and reveal techniques are effective. Each slide may emphasize or add a new element, with the previous element dropping back onto the chart in a subdued color. The final slide puts the whole chart together. Changing the color of a box, its outline, and the lettering within can emphasize a point. Changing line thickness, or having the lettering overlay the box, can also provide emphasis. The line or lettering can drop to match the other previously shown boxes as the next slide with a new box emphasized appears on the screen. A dotted line can surround a temporary box as it is discussed and become a solid line, perhaps in another color, when added to the chart.

Moving too far away from a traditionally recognized form may create problems for the viewer, so exercise restraint. Content is the most important ingredient; it becomes gourmet fare when presented tastefully and eloquently.

The chart forms used most frequently are:

Diagram charts

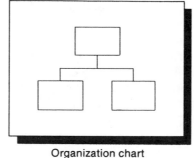

Organization chart

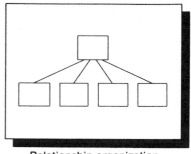

Relationship organization

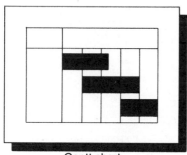

Gantt chart

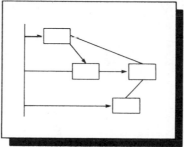

PERT chart

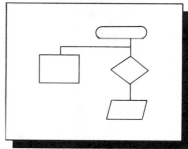

Flowchart

Organization–a chain of command in a company or a family. An elementary organization is like a tree with branches; each element leads to others which, in turn, lead to yet others.

Relationship–an arrangement where there is a central deciding element from which all others extend (not branching as tree-like).

Gantt–used for product management purposes. Gantts show the amount of time required for an individual task, and the order in which each will be performed in relation to the total job.

PERT (Program Evaluation and Review Technique)–depicts tasks and their dependencies.

Flowchart–a schematic representation of the actual path, showing the sequence of a set of functions or steps.

Within the format of each of these charts, elements can be simple or complex. The design must reflect the relationships, and can depict a set of three or four squares with connecting lines up to complex dynamic representations that are a challenge to develop.

In minutes, computers can produce scores of choices for arranging the elements and coloring, and emphasizing them.

The diagrams shown may not appear to fall within familiar forms, but generally they are variations on the usual themes. Observe the subject covered, how the elements are depicted in these variations, the lettering and its placement, and how elements are emphasized, characterized, and colored. The examples may provide exactly the idea you need to interpret and illustrate an abstract organization concept in a meaningful and dynamic manner.

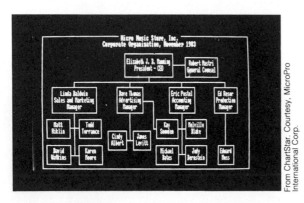

A basic organization chart format can represent complex relationships.

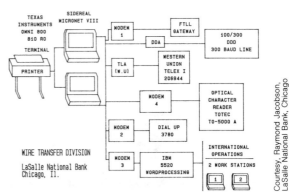

Predrawn objects are used instead of boxes (created with PC-DRAW).

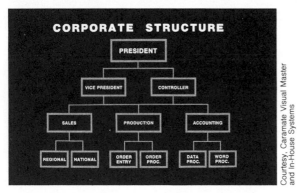

Specific boxes that are being discussed by the presenter can be highlighted with different colored lettering. Different color lettering within groups of boxes tends to separate and define relationships.

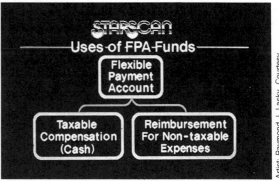

Only three boxes, but they tell the story with greater impact than a text slide alone might, and they organize the concept visually. Connecting lines are curved instead of straight.

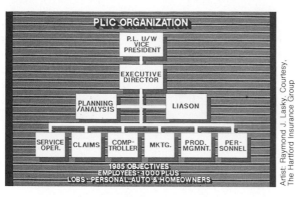

A relational organization chart using drop shadowed grey boxes with yellow lines on a striped background. Chyron System.

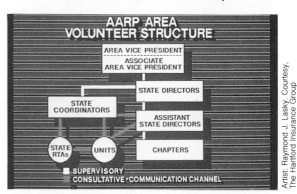

Circles are used to symbolize elements that are different but associated with the main elements. The circles are the same color but the lines to and from them are red; others are yellow.

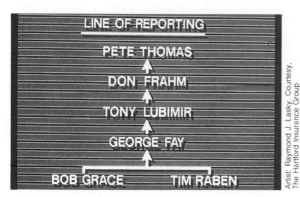

The line of reporting is a variation on a chart that might be interpreted in traditional squares. Chyron System.

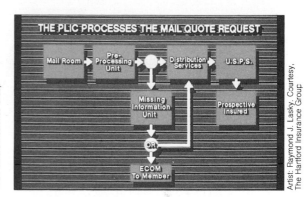

Work flow is depicted graphically. Chyron System.

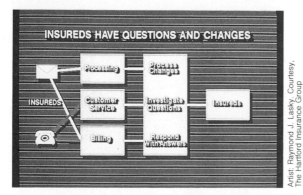

A telephone and an envelope symbolize the input from customers more dramatically than would a box with the words telephone and mail on them. Chyron System.

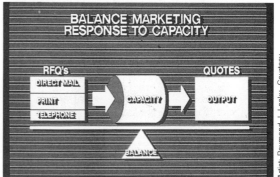

An organizational concept is interpreted as a system of symbols balanced as a scale. The scale is the basic element; the other shapes would correspond to symbols on a flowchart.

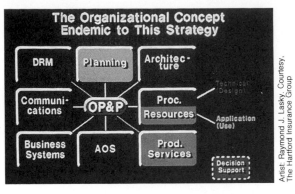

Artist: Raymond J. Lasky. Courtesy, The Hartford Insurance Group

C *All elements revolve around the central element. Chyron System.*

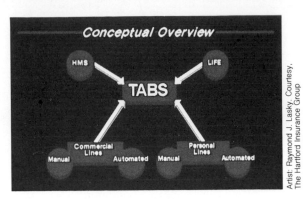

Artist: Raymond J. Lasky. Courtesy, The Hartford Insurance Group

A conceptual overview where all elements report to a central element. Chyron System.

C *When everything flows from a single point, it can be illustrated with a circle and squares using a hublike design rather than one square with a row of squares beneath.*

(Three of these slides are reproduced elsewhere in this book.)

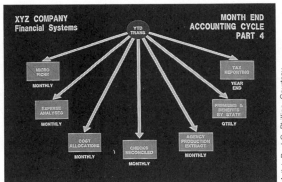

Artist: Paul G. Phillips. Courtesy, E. F. Hutton Life Insurance Co.

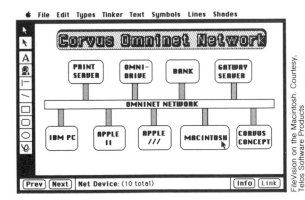

FileVision on the Macintosh. Courtesy, Telos Software Products

A network is a relationship organization with all dependent elements emanating from the central element.

Artist: Raymond J. Lasky. Courtesy, The Hartford Insurance Group

C *A Gantt chart for job tracking is attractively designed and more dynamic than the basic Gantt or PERT chart generated by most software programs. Most are so dull they scream for customizing.*

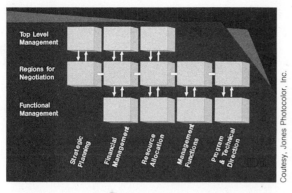

A relational diagram uses arrows to show back and forth channels, and straight lines to show a single level.

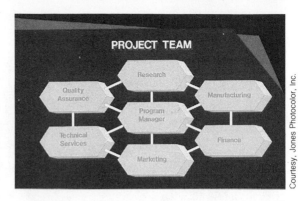

The same background can be used for a chart with a different set of communication lines.

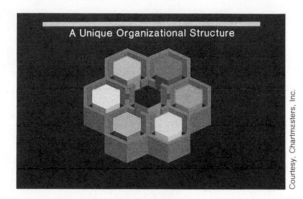

An opportunity to make an unusual organization structure unique.

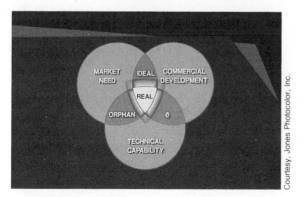

All levels of management are involved in negotiations in some way.

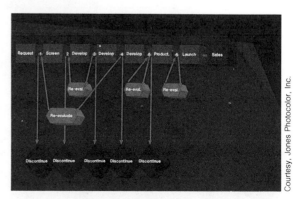

A PERT chart illustrates a series of procedures.

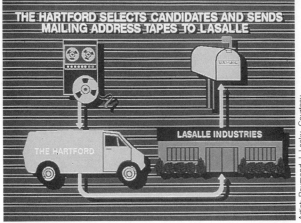

Every "square" becomes a recognizable element.

A pyramid is a variation of the simple organization chart.

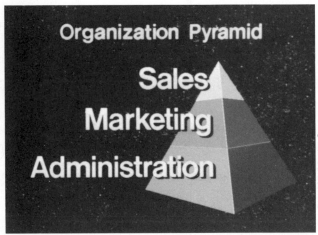

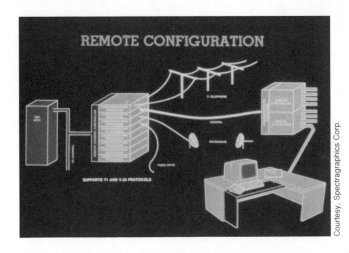

All objects are picture images so the slide no longer appears as a "symbolic" chart, yet it illustrates flow from one area to another.

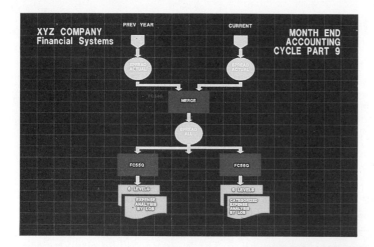

Part of a total flowchart series uses symbols from the picture library planned to cover:

A. The presentation design with the whole flowchart. Tasks that generated report 1 were highlighted.

B. Tasks that generated report 2 were highlighted.

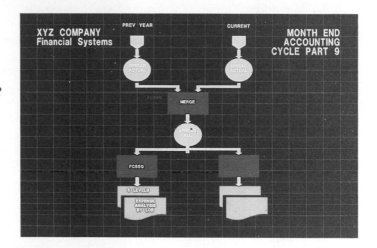

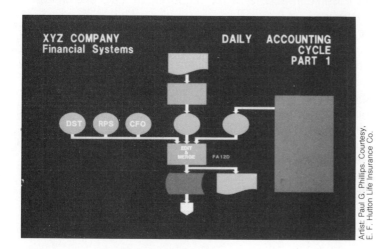

C. Then individual discussions of each part were supported with an expanded portion of the subsection. Highlighting was accomplished by using white text for the section being discussed. Finally, the entire flow was shown again.

Artist: Paul G. Phillips. Courtesy, E. F. Hutton Life Insurance Co.

Showing How Things Work

6

How do objects work? What systems are involved? How can the volume and size of an object be illustrated?

To answer these questions visually requires converting the idea into a pictorial representation. That's the role of technical drawings and specialty charts that may show physical movement, materials, and an object in relation to its surrounding space.

The application of computers to these tasks has produced innovative changes in industries that require mechanical drawings, drafting, technical directives, architecture, renderings, and so on. Computer graphics have considerably reduced the number of man-hours spent in labor over drawing boards. Computer Aided Design/Computer Aided Manufacturing (CAD/CAM) and Computer Aided Engineering (CAE) applications permit you to generate a rough set of plans, store them, and revise them as often as required.

But there's more to computer use than storage and recall for later manipulation and revision. Once a drawing is in the computer, it can be developed to limitless visual advantage, given the proper software for the purpose. It can be rotated, can be translated into different views, or have its sizes changed or textures altered. Software with powerful two-dimensional and three-dimensional capabilities makes possible in minutes what might require days and weeks of hand drawing.

Blueprint drawings, traditionally confined to blue-tinted paper, can now be brought to life with color, with zoom details taken from the original drawing, and with different views exposed instantly. One can make selections in seconds from choices that weren't previously available, all at the push of a few keys or the movement of a mouse. Details need not be redrawn by hand or blown up via time-consuming photographic processes. They can be generated almost as fast as the operator and the computer can implement the change, then quickly duplicated in hard copy, slides, or prints.

When changes are required, data for the revised area are entered and the computer recalculates, redraws the area, and reintegrates it into the original. A data change that affects other areas of the system is also recalculated automatically.

Computers simplify the creation of drawings that describe how a system works. They easily and efficiently produce labeled mechanical drawings, floor plans, renderings of complex architectural projects in two and three dimensions, in wire cage, or solid modeling depiction. Similar concepts for medical illustration benefit from this wondrous technology.

All the above may be required for in-office use, client presentation, showing a project publicly, sales promotion, training, fund raising, and publications. They can be a dynamic image or series of images that will sway potential users toward a desired decision. They can also be dreadfully dull and poorly composed.

The various principles for composing presentation visuals described in the preceding chapters are equally, perhaps more, applicable to technical presentations. Attention to accuracy, simplification, color selection, line quality, type style, and succinct statement are elemental. If the visual is clear, with easy-to-follow points, the workings of a mechanical shaft in a diesel engine could hold the interest of the most nontechnical person in the audience.

Therein lies a major problem. Engineers think in minute detail, which often results in visuals that are overly complex and crowded with text and image. Trained in a "design discipline," engineers believe they know what a visual should look like. They may disapprove of a graphics designer who encroaches on their territory and purports to have skills applicable to the creation of a mechanical device. Without exception, design services that deal with engineers and technical people report that such persons are frequently difficult to work with and are the hardest to convince that design has several meanings and applications.

Many graphics packages today enable images to be developed in levels; a series of steps can evolve, one over another, as in, for example, the steps required for a manufacturing process. Then the steps can be peeled back and regenerated for the audience, so the object is literally "made" before the audience's eyes.

Until recently, CAD/CAM software required mini machines; now sophisticated software, such as AutoCAD by Autodesk and Polycad 10 by Cubicomp, are available for microcomputers.

The examples shown illustrate paths computers are paving for those involved in illustrating technical concepts. Note that for clarity and simplicity, 95 percent of the technical and diagram slides use black or dark blue backgrounds. Directions are emphasized by color, width of an arrow, and size and shape of an object.

How Arrows Depict Movement

Movement is usually expressed diagramatically with an arrow. A subject element can show *direct* movement, *fixed* movement, or *circular* movement. It can indicate the *entrance* or *exit* of an element, and several elements can be joined to form a *compound* or grouped movement. Multiple motions that indicate the movement of a group of elements can also be expressed.

If the movement of an object is *obstructed,* the direction of the arrow changes course and becomes *modified.* The movement may also be *reactive* when the object is obstructed. Reactive and obstructed movement occurs if a continuous route is shown, as in a *circuit* that moves between two points.

Movement

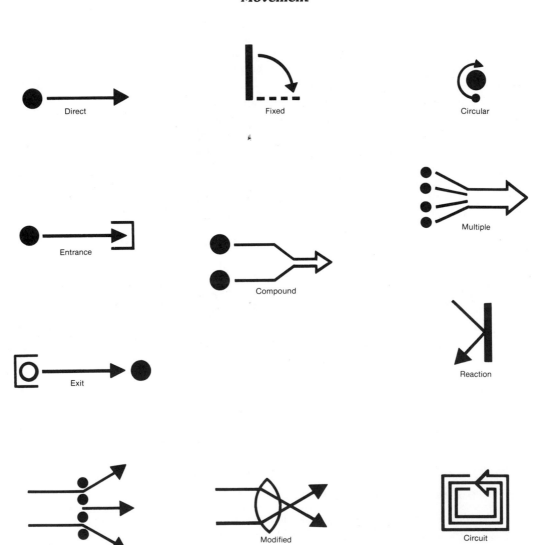

Illustrating Size in Physical Space

Size refers to the physical space an object occupies. Graphically, the object must be shown within a defined space such as the frame of the slide or edge of the paper, or in relation to another object. Measurements, actual or suggested, are introduced. The object may be shown as having *volume.* Its size may be based on showing its *plane* or suggested by showing space between objects in a *distance* relationship. When absolute size is required, numerical measurements must be shown.

Physical size

Volumetric

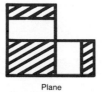

Plane

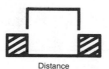

Distance

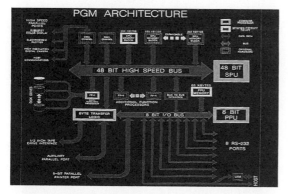

Diagrams of PGM architecture are presented in two ways. Above: All parts are labeled and identified to show specifics. Note the various categories of movement represented by the arrows: direct, obstructed, entrance, multiple.

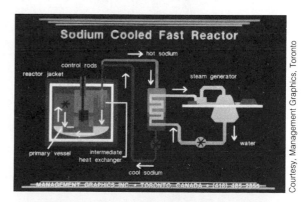

Shapes of objects, arrows, and different colors all help differentiate the flow of the sodium to and from the primary vessel. Labels are carefully placed.

Courtesy, Management Graphics, Toronto

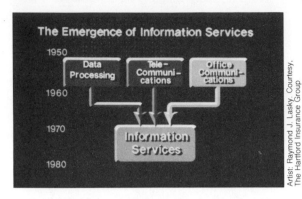

Artist: Raymond J. Lasky. Courtesy, The Hartford Insurance Group

Directional arrows can be used to diagram how a service has worked over the number of years.

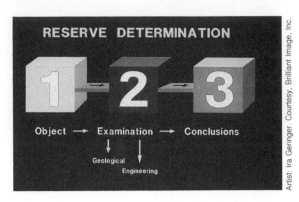

Artist: Ira Geringer. Courtesy, Brilliant Image, Inc.

A subtle use of direct arrows establishes the equation.

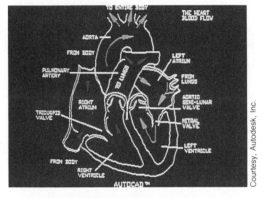

Courtesy, Autodesk, Inc.

A diagram of the heart has been drawn in a free hand mode. Direct, obstructed, and curved, entry and exit arrows illustrate how the system works (AutoCAD on an IBM PC System).

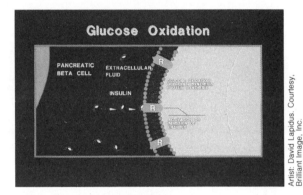

Artist: David Lapidus. Courtesy, Brilliant Image, Inc.

A diagramatic representation of oxidation. Chemical functions that can't be seen are perfect subjects for understanding systems with drawings.

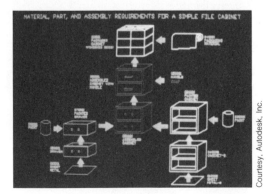

Courtesy, Autodesk, Inc.

The parts of a file cabinet exploded with directional arrows indicate parts to be assembled (AutoCAD on an IBM PC).

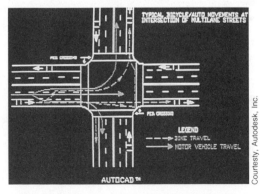

Courtesy, Autodesk, Inc.

Highway traffic management application in a civil engineering application (AutoCAD on an IBM PC).

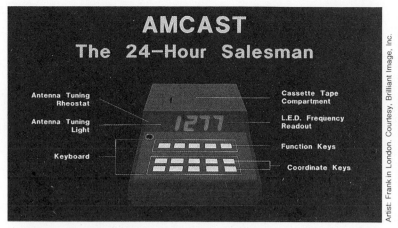

Artist: Frank in London. Courtesy, Brilliant Image, Inc.

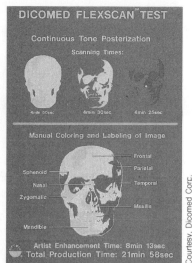

Courtesy, Dicomed Corp.

AMCAST sales presentation showing the parts of the system is simple, direct, uncluttered. Labels and lines are consistently and carefully placed. Those on the left are right justified. Those on the right are left justified, so the lettering creates a visual line. The volume of the object is captured (Executive Presentation System).

A diagram shows the time taken to scan and enter a drawing, then develop it to finished slide. The skull appears dimensional in space.

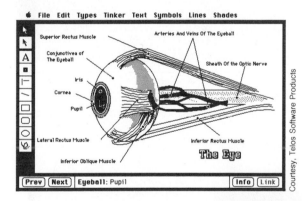

Courtesy, Telos Software Products

The parts of an eye show as a two-dimensional subject labeled as though it were a one-dimensional plane. It is developed with a data base and graphics program (Filevision, by Telos Software Products, on the Macintosh).

Artist: Anne Marie Rossi, Jones Photocolor, Inc.

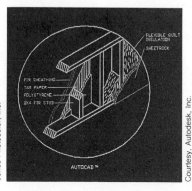

Courtesy, Autodesk, Inc.

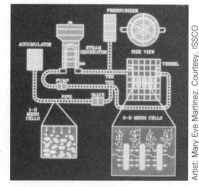

Artist: Mary Eve Martinez. Courtesy, ISSCO

An internal layout; the color of the label text is the same as the component it references.

Diagram of a detail wall cutaway (AutoCAD).

Parts of a steam generator have been created with DISPLA software.

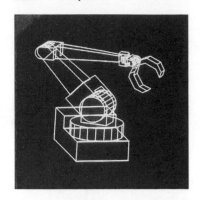

Left: A robot arm in a wire frame drawing. Right: Solidly filled (Prism software).

Courtesy, Spectragraphics Corp

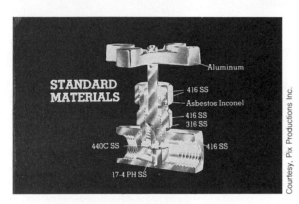

Courtesy, Pix Productions Inc.

A cutaway shaded planal drawing of a faucet is shown with parts labeled.

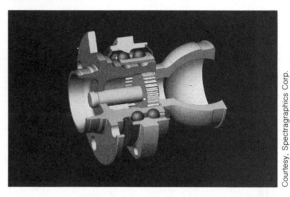

Courtesy, Spectragraphics Corp.

A solid modeled object, once in the computer, may be rotated and tilted for different viewpoints (Prism software).

Courtesy, GE CAE INT.

The under-structure of an automobile is exploded—   *—then put in place.*

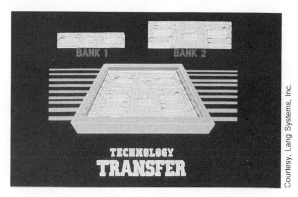

A circuit board with two parts lifted out and detailed at the top of the slide.

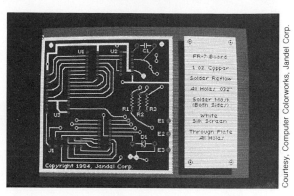

On a single-level drawing of a circuit board, the different elements can be separated by color (The Digital Paintbrush System used on an Apple II+, IIc, or IIe).

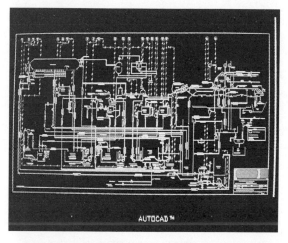

A diagram of the entire circuit board shows layers using dotted and solid lines and different colors (AutoCAD on an IBM PC system).

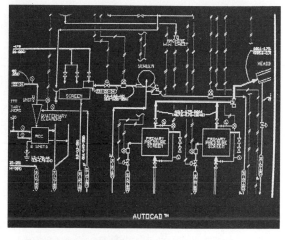

Zoom detail of a circuit board.

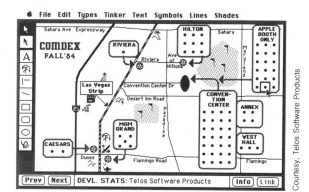

A map of Las Vegas and the Comdex Convention Center, developed on the Macintosh computer with Filevision.

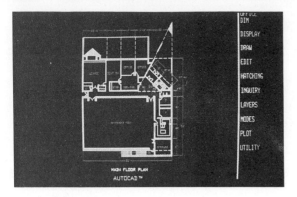

Floor plan of a church—

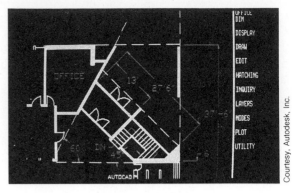

—and zoom detail (AutoCAD).

Courtesy, Autodesk, Inc.

Courtesy, Cubicomp Corp.

A form can be modeled in minutes by beginning with the simplest basic geometric shape and adding circles, rectangles, and other geometric shapes. The model can be viewed in any orientation by using rotate and translate commands. It can be shaded, and jagged lines can be removed (Cubicomp Polycad 10 solid modeling system on an IBM PC).

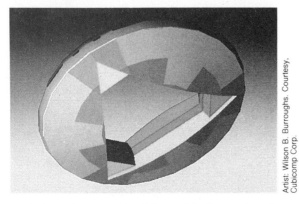

Artist: Wilson B. Burroughs. Courtesy, Cubicomp Corp.

A three-dimensional solids model of a machined part (Cubicomp Polycad 10 solid modeling system on an IBM PC).

Artist: Wilson B. Burroughs. Courtesy, Cubicomp Corp.

The rendering of a house (Cubicomp Polycad 10 solid modeling system on an IBM PC).

An office designed by using Cubicomp Polycad 10 solid modeling system on an IBM PC.

A representation of a software structure called system tables; the blocks represent interchangeable tabletops.

The aircraft was created by merging together parts which were created using the Surface Revolver of a 3-D package. Background was created with the e FGS-4000 paint program. The scene took the artist about two minutes to render.

Chess set was rendered using different software for 3-D to create the volumetric shapes, then colors and special properties were edited with another package called ShEd (Shading Editor). The board is the product of a text compiler known as ROb (Read Object). The system was the Robert Bosch FGS-4000.

7

Picture Libraries Speed Presentation Preparation

Every picture is composed of one or more elements: each bar on a chart, a company logo, a product that appears often, words or phrases frequently used, titles, or a symbol. Each of these elements can become an image in your personal picture library. Each can be combined with others or used with new picture elements for a particular slide.

You will save time and money when images are composed ready for use, each in a separate file. (It's the same idea behind a boilerplate paragraph in a word processing program.) An image, like a paragraph, may be captured and pulled into a new slide. If it isn't exactly what you want, you may retain desired parts, delete those you don't need, and redraw new areas.

The images you process will depend on both your needs and the software and hardware you have. As software companies have discovered the need to compete, more have added comprehensive picture libraries to their offerings. Executive Picture Show, ExecuVision, Grafix Partner, PC Slide, PC-Draw, Softslide, and so on all offer assorted images of varying subjects and complexities.

Draw and paint programs include a library of geometric shapes: circles, boxes, parallelograms, ellipses, triangles, arrows, and so on can be called into a file, stretched, and reduced (a process called rubberbanding). Programs may contain elements for a mechanical drawing, flowchart, or floor plan, so you need only grab, edit, and use them. After you have completed a drawing, store it for future use. Next time, the same slide may require only minor editing and cosmetic changes.

CAD/CAM packages, such as AutoCAD2, include templates of objects applicable to architecture and interior design, plus fonts. Predrawn patterns for standard materials used in the industry, such as bricks in different layouts, clay, grates, insulation, honeycomb, cork, and more are available. The scaling and precision drawing capability of AutoCAD2 is based on X-Y coordinate input (it also has a freehand draw mode).

Create Your Own Library of Images

Consider creating your own library of customized picture elements. The resulting slides will be consistent with the general appearance of the other slides. Strive to use the same colors and type style throughout.

How would you approach the task? Consider the individual elements you use most often: a logo, a title slide, a diagram or illustration of your product, your name in an appropriate type style. You may generate images symbolic of your industry: a computer, file drawers, mainframe storage units, airplanes, a street setting, a street map showing your location.

Assume you're in the lumber-producing business. If your software can't generate a logo as complex as the one your company had designed, simplify it and suggest either the basic shape or an interplay of its initials.

Rather than use a vertical column for a chart, design an abstract tree. For a horizontal bar, design an ax or a handsaw. A pie chart might attract more attention if it is composed of a series of circles that suggest the age rings of the tree trunk rather than a plain circle.

But you're not an artist, you argue. You can't draw a straight line. You don't have to be an artist to produce dynamic images. You can use the predrawn images and enhance or customize them. You may wish to hire a designer to create images with your software that you can use for a long time. Often, the simpler the better. Almost every object can be distilled to its component shapes: circles, squares, rectangles, ovals, or triangles.

How can you begin to think of the shapes and elements of an object? Observe drawings in children's books, comic books, greeting cards, posters, catalogs, encyclopedias, advertisements, and in the pages of trade magazines. If you have an input tablet, such as the Koala or PenPad; a digitizing tablet; and a mouse, you can outline the image from a drawing on paper and it will be in your computer in minutes.

You can tape a sketch to your CRT screen and draw around it as closely as you can, using the keyboard or other input devices. Untape the paper, and refine or embellish the drawing as necessary. You may draw on the screen with a wipe-off pen and repeat and simplify the shapes as necessary. As you analyze shapes that make up a drawing, you'll observe that shadows, for example, are another shape, dropped slightly behind the first shape and filled in.

Start a notebook or file folder with ideas for images. Clip appropriate pictures of charts from newspapers and magazines that suggest ideas. Watch carefully for examples in trade publications that deal with your industry.

Refer to the hints in each chapter of this book regarding the graphics design of a slide, and use the examples as a reference for good placement of titles, pictures, text, and so on.

Drawings can also be captured by new devices on the market, such as image scanners and optical character recognition devices, discussed in Chapter 15.

Stock Slides

There are 35 mm stock slides (those already prepared and sold by commercial slide services—Chapter 14) that apply to many situations. You can pop them into a slide tray (they may be available for overhead transparencies, too), and you have instant professional graphics. If you're presenting directly on-line from a CRT, you won't be able to use these, but you could emulate the effect of the drawing and incorporate it into your slide show.

Stock slides available with artistically drawn messages—"Intermission," "End," "ACT NOW!"—are usually inexpensive, colorful, and well designed. Sometimes, they may be so well designed that they call attention to the cleverness of the slide and shift the audience's attention from the topic, especially if the slides you've produced are not as professional looking. So be careful.

Left: One drawing of a telephone and its stand has been replicated and reduced to illustrate a progression.

Right: Drawings from the slide library in ExecuVision were captured and manipulated to create a customized slide.

Artist: David Lapidus. Courtesy, Brilliant Image, Inc.

Courtesy, Raymond Jacobson, LaSalle National Bank, Chicago

A forest of trees was created by drawing one tree and "rubberstamping" it to create a larger clump. Then the clumps were repeated to result in the forest. Program: Flying Colors on an Apple IIe.

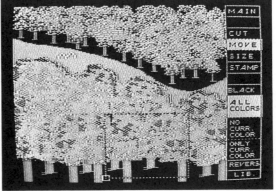

Courtesy, Computer Colorworks

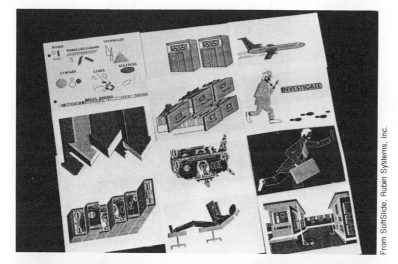

From SoftSlide, Rubin Systems, Inc.

Graphics libraries included in many draw programs offer pictures that can be reused, reduced, enlarged, edited.

Photo, Author

Drawings from the program PC Slide (Management Graphics Inc. of Toronto, Canada) can be printed for reference. A user can design a picture, then order 35 mm slides selecting from a color chart included with the software. The disk can be mailed to the company or the data can be transfered by modem. ExecuVision (Visual Communications Network) includes a picture library with the main program; additional disks, each with a library of picture categories, can be ordered. Also shown: a page from the border library and the library included with the program.

Courtesy, Data Transforms Graphics Software, Inc.

The software program, Fontrix, has an incredible assortment of predrawn fonts and images available in its different Fontpaks.

People can be drawn in their infinite variety.

The image of a manager.

C *Three men preparing to create a chart are placed against a grid background.*

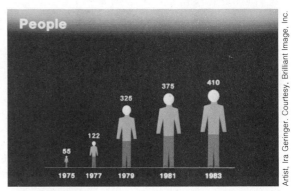

A people slide using the same "people" drawing scaled in place of columns.

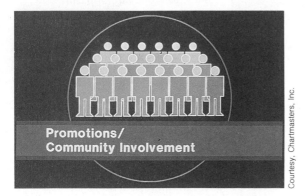

People are repeated, scaled, overlayed, and enclosed in a circle with a title placed in a rectangle. The entire picture is composed of circles and rectangles.

An artist and a monitor are individually stored images that can be used separately or together.

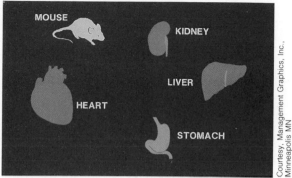

Courtesy, Management Graphics, Inc., Minneapolis MN

For the person who deals with subjects about health, perhaps a library of human organs, the heart, stomach, kidney, liver, and a mouse, if it applies.

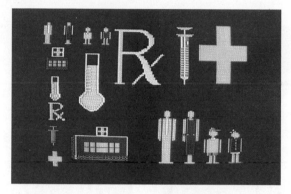

Library images in the program Flying Colors could be used for newsletters, labels, flyers, and slides by those in related health professions.

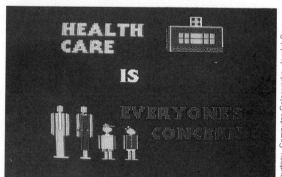

Courtesy, Computer Colorworks, Jandel Corp.

An application uses several of the images. (Produced on an Apple IIe.)

Courtesy, Management Graphics, Inc. Minneapolis MN

A generic cityscape or skyline. Each time you're presenting a seminar in a new city, announce, "It's a pleasure to visit in . . ." 35 mm or on-line slides could be made in advance, naming each city in which you normally make presentations.

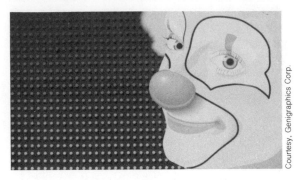

Courtesy, Genigraphics, Corp.

A clown face drawn to the right of the slide leaves room for text at the left. This is a stock image that can be customized.

Courtesy, E. F. Hutton Life Insurance Co.

Frontal view of a telephone. Observe the use of simple geometric elements with some planes shaded for depth. Avoid getting too detailed, too complex.

Courtesy, Hewlett-Packard Co.

A top view of a telephone is also simply drawn. The image can suggest the object. If it must be reduced, it will still be a clear picture.

Courtesy, E. F. Hutton Life Insurance Co.

Money tree.

Courtesy, E. F. Hutton Life Insurance Co.

Hand and dollar sign.

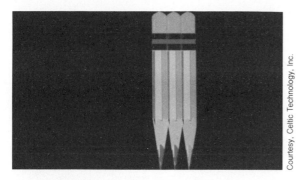

Pencils created on DEC PRO 350.

Courtesy, Celtic Technology, Inc.

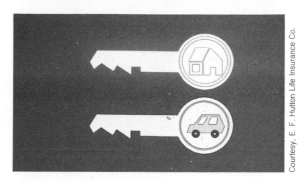

Keys, one in pink with a house inside, the other yellow with a car inside.

Courtesy, E. F. Hutton Life Insurance Co.

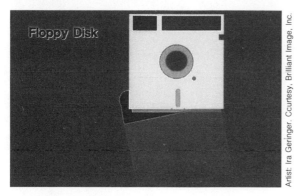

Floppy disk.

Artist: Ira Geringer. Ccurtesy, Brilliant Image, Inc.

C | *Computer.*

Artist: David Lapidus. Courtesy, Erilliant Image, Inc.

A cheeseburger has been drawn abstractly with lettuce, etc., as designed shapes.

Artist: Tony Meador, Courtesy, Jones Photocolor, Inc.

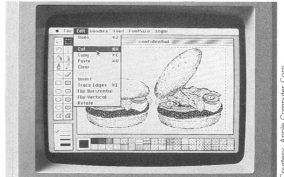

A more realistic version of a hamburger is being created with MacDraw for the Macintosh Computer.

Courtesy, Apple Computer Corp.

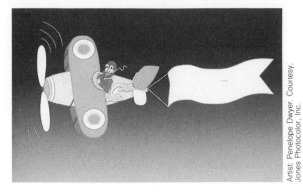

Artist: Penelope Dwyer. Courtesy, Jones Photocolor, Inc.

Airplane pulling a banner.

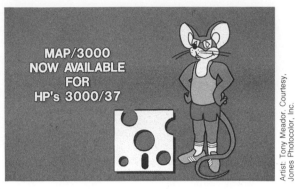

Artist: Tony Meador. Courtesy, Jones Photocolor, Inc.

Mouse and cheese.

Courtesy, Genigraphics Corp.

Library symbols in the Genigraphics Corp. selection book.

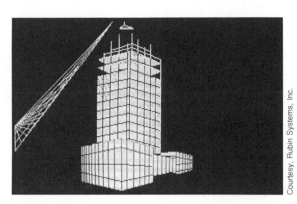

Courtesy, Rubin Systems, Inc.

Skyscraper (Softslide).

Courtesy, Rubin Systems, Inc.

Pile of dollars (Softslide).

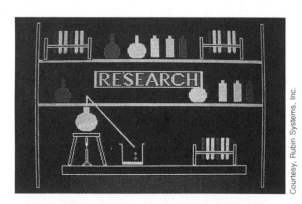

Courtesy, Rubin Systems, Inc.

Research. Each set of elements can be stored individually (Softslide).

A medallion and a stag, logos of The Hartford Insurance Group, are used so frequently that each picture is stored in hard disk memory and can be recalled with a single keystroke. The medallion was captured with a black and white TV camera, then electronically shaded and enhanced. The stag was scanned; there are 12 versions of the stag available for recall.

Another application of the Hartford Stag logo. Here it is combined with a predrawn frame and background, then lettering is added. Each image is stored individually and assigned a key on the keyboard, which performs as a macro.

The stag is placed on a blue field with the company name in the corporate typeface. Each picture and each line is assigned one key. This version is used at the end of all slide shows and some videotapes.

8

Special Effects—Electronically

Artists who create slides have developed a large electronic paint box of special effects designed to make ordinary pictures and words extraordinary.

Hardware and software used by corporate art departments and by commercial slide services have state-of-the-art, high-cost computer tools for creating spectacular images.

Software available for personal computers cannot yet match the ability of their big brothers' systems, but the small computers can tap into their siblings' muscle and memory. Services such as AVL, Genigraphics Corp., Autographix, Dicomed Corp., Management Graphics Canada, Pix Productions Inc., 3M Company, Visual Horizons, and others offer equipment and telecommunication tie-in with personal computers. Contact these companies (listed at the end of Chapter 13), and explore the potential of generating the information you want for a presentation and sending it to them. They in turn can transform that information into slides with special effects, if and where appropriate. Their systems are capable of outputting thousands of colors compared to the 8 or 16 available from a personal computer.

But don't be intimidated into thinking you can only get what you need with megabuck equipment. Personal computer software packages are constantly offering more capabilities. Perhaps you can't capture exactly the same effects as those shown here, but you can emulate and simulate many of them by using a program creatively or combining the outputs of two or more programs. New software packages are able to perform amazing feats, and more appear in every update.

You can apply tricks of the photographer, too, by dipping into methods for cropping slides, sandwiching two or more pictures, or a picture and a mask. Many more methods can be found in photo publications, in catalogs from Gepe, Visual Horizons, Wess Plastic, and at the specialty counter in your local photography shop. Zooms, mirror images, eclipses, wipes, pinwheels, step-ups, and stepdowns are among the methods used often. Color effects for backgrounds on title slides are a blend of shaded tones, chromatic rays, rainbows, perspective, shiny and shaded grids, frosted blends, and more.

Presentation graphics are not confined to business reports, technical drawings, charts, or text to accompany a talk before an audience. They may be used for an infinite variety of applications in every business. Architects, systems designers, or planners can use them for board artwork, audiovisual applications, technical illustrations, and more. You'll note these applications and others in television logos and commercials and in the minigallery in Chapter 10.

There is a good reason for including special effects in this discussion: When you understand what can be created, you can:

1. Observe how special effects are used in various media.
2. Think of how to apply them to your specific applications.
3. Learn to recreate the effect or something close to it.
4. Know what to visualize in your own presentation, and what to look for and ask for from an artist or commercial slide service.
5. Judge software on the basis of what it can and cannot accomplish.

As you observe the special effects shown here and see how they are used in TV, film, training programs, and other videos, you may never again be satisfied with plain vanilla slides. You may hunger for presentations with extra topping, an artistic flourish, and flavors blended to make an unforgettable entrée.

Wild and wide describes the mask shapes that Visual Horizons supplies on a long roll of film. Cut them apart, lay one over a slide for a special effect, and remount them in the slide holder.

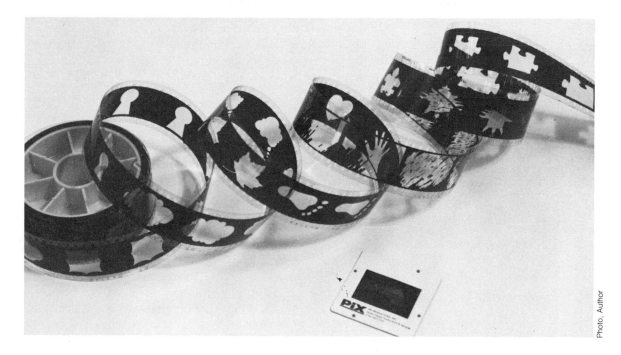

Photo, Author

Photo, Author

Courtesy, Wess Plastic

Slide masks in a variety of shapes will allow only certain portions of the film to display. Try highlighting and cropping with mounts. You slip your film into the Gepe slide mount so that only the portion you want emphasized is displayed.

Soft edge slide mounts perform the same crop function but yield a soft edge.

But caution is advised. The effects are so delectable that they can be like desserts on a buffet table; you want one of everything. Remember that the message is the medium; the medium is not the message.

Combining the Effects

Several special effects can appear in a single slide and are dynamic when not overdone. Each must be designed specifically for a purpose; the effect can suggest the topic.

BAIN-O'REILLY ADVERTISING, INC.

Neon style lettering is used for this attractive logo; a starburst is used at the end.

Courtesy, Visual Horizons

Artist: Raymond J. Lasky. Courtesy, The Hartford Insurance Group

A large outlined letter or numeral can be filled in with as many effects as the software can produce. Metallic appearances that simulate gold, silver, bronze, and Mylar are among the possibilities.

A glow effect, rounded letters, and colors fading within the letters are combined special effects.

Glow or Eclipse

The color and treatment of a word can carry the message. A glow surrounds individual letters or an entire word; this is called an eclipse effect because the letters eclipse the light. Use this treatment on stark, dark backgrounds.

Courtesy, Pix Productions Inc.

The logo is surrounded by a glow effect, and a starburst is used that appears to come from behind the word. Black background.

Courtesy, Pix Productions Inc.

A build-up treatment with a special effect. Words and a logo are outlined, but both the logo and background are black; the glow only suggests the logo.

Courtesy, Pix Productions Inc.

In the next slide the logo is dropped into the blank space; the glow treatment is dropped. The logo is blue; the other words are yellow.

Zoom

Zooming in on a detail from an overview slide is effective. An overview in an illustration is like a summary in a text slide. Details are like individual topics. In a mechanical drawing or a layout, the ability to zoom into one section and explode it helps to clarify areas. Software that supports the zoom ability lets you blow up any portion of the screen and edit the details in several size increments, beginning with the pixel.

A portion of a drawing of the TransAmerica Building can be blown up using the zoom feature in the program AutoCAD2.

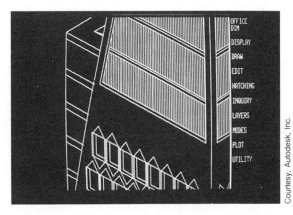

Here is a closer detail of the building. Additional zooming could blow up one portion of a window. A detail of a section.

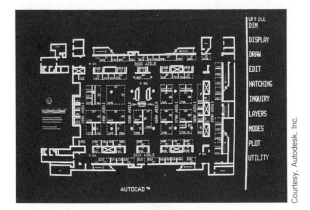

The floor plan of the Comdex Convention, 1983, notated in red, white, and blue on a black background is dynamic, but measurements and scale would not be legible from a viewing distance of only a few feet.

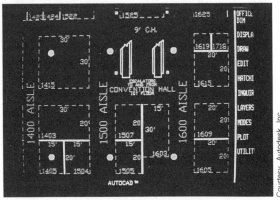

Zooming in to the detail clarifies all the markings. A better space relationship of booth to aisles is shown (AutoCAD2 software).

Mirrors—Vibrations—Neon Lighting

A reflection of your company name, a logo, or a welcome slide can add impact to a presentation when used once or twice in a talk. This technique lends itself well to businesses that deal in travel, fashion, or high-design service. A company that manufactures a reflective product could apply reflection so the image suggests the product.

Words repeated in the same size with some overlapping will appear to vibrate. It is possible to simulate different "light" effects such as in the "neon" example.

A true mirror image is shown in the same color.

A computer can alter a "mirror" image. Top letters are mirrored in another color, yellow.

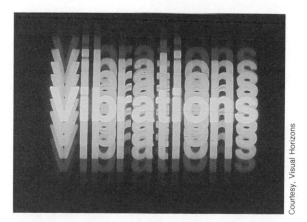

Send an electronic, scintillating feeling to the viewer by showing an image or a word that seems to vibrate.

A word surrounded by light-emitting rounded corner bars imparts the look and soft glow of neon.

Courtesy, Visual Horizons

Courtesy, Visual Horizons

Courtesy, Visual Horizons

Courtesy, AVL, Inc.

Starburst, Starbeam, and Laser Highlights

Highlighted background effects suggested by bursting light images can add colorful special effects to a title slide.

Starburst.

Starbeam.

C *Laser.*

Swirl, Spin, or Pinwheel

No matter what it's called, the effect of spinning letters and words that take the shape of the letter or another shape is dynamic.

A square spinning around and around behind a word can emphasize the meaning of the word.

Thank you.

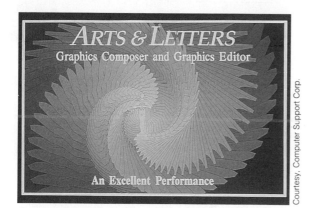

A spin effect can also be created in the paint program Arts & Letters. Directions can be freeform and flowing compared to the distributed effect between two objects in presentation graphics programs.

Distributed lettering can produce a spin or pinwheel effect when used in a circular design. The same distributed technique can be used with horizontal or vertical letters or shapes. Draw APPLAUSE software was used.

The Effect of Movement in Lettering

You can make a message appear to move up, down, or sideways, or to zoom out from the viewer by repeating it in progressively different sizes, using shades of one or more colors. Letter styles may be solid or outlined. They are effective when only one or two words are used on a black or dark background. The impression is three dimensional on a two-dimensional surface. The effects are called wipes, zooms, zips, step-up and step-down, step and repeat, and so on. Names may vary by software and by the commercial services that create them.

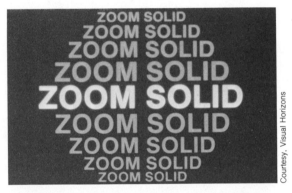

Solid white letters; red letters in diminishing sizes above; blue below.

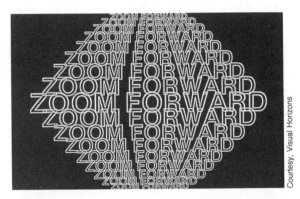

Outlined white letters are shown with purple above and below for the diminishing letters.

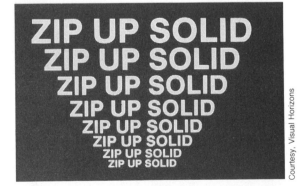

Small yellow letters increase in size and zip up to a white top line. A program that has different type fonts that can be centered can accomplish this effect.

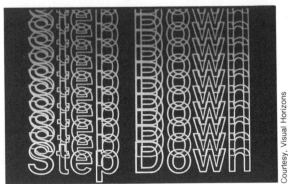

Wipe and zoom are shown using outlined letters with blue wipe on a black background. The wipe can be pulled down. The letters appear to jump forward on a frontal plane.

Courtesy, Visual Horizons

Another example of wipe and zoom features different placement of the words and the wipes toward the center.

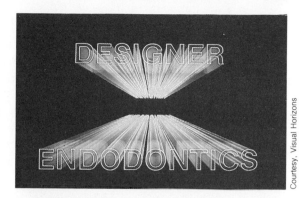

Courtesy, Visual Horizons

The effect can be changed infinitely with the type style or design, the colors, and the directions of the wipes.

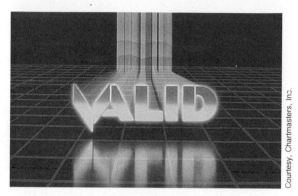

Courtesy, Chartmasters, Inc.

Mirror and wipe effect shown on a grid base and blue mountain background.

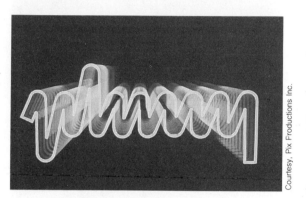

Courtesy, Pix Productions Inc.

The words can be stepped down in the same plane. White outlined letters appear to jump in front of the yellow to orange shades behind.

Courtesy, Raymond Lasky, with a Chyron System

Letters themselves are swept to the side and may suggest an arrow.

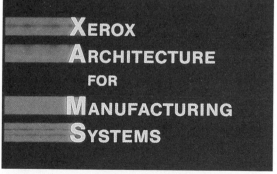

Courtesy, Pix Productions Inc.

A similar sweep effect can be achieved in a single plane by using solid filled bars coming in from the side of the space and meeting the first letter of the word.

Animation

You achieve animation with still slides by projecting them rapidly using two or more projectors so that one image fades into the next.

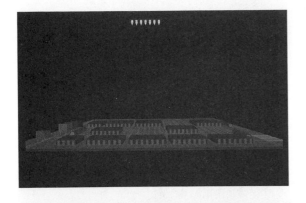
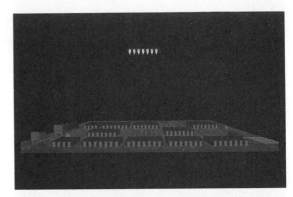

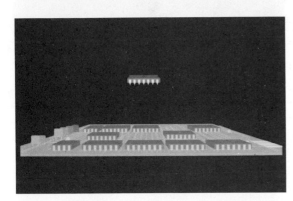
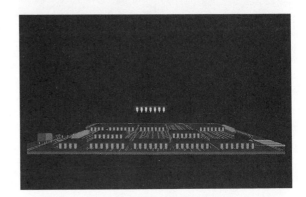

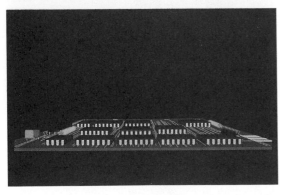
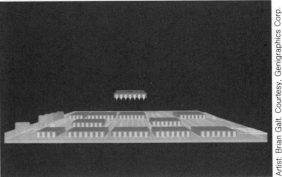

In this series of six slides, a chip is dropping onto a board. It is in place in slide 5, and in slide 6, the new chip is given a "glow" treatment.

The company logo with a framed picture is moved toward the audience by increasing the number of picture frames and moving each into another position for every subsequent slide.

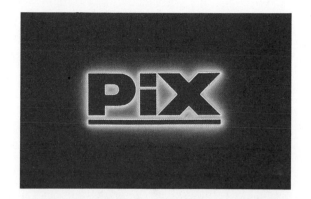 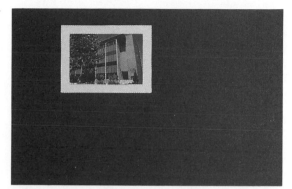

 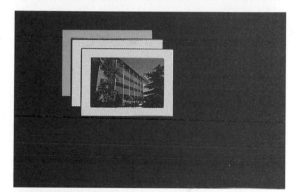

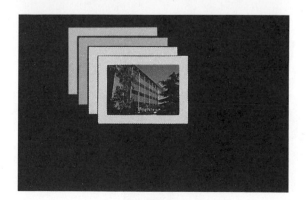 

[C] *(This slide is reproduced in color elsewhere in this book.)*

Superimposed Photography

A photograph showing the detail of an eye can be image processed, and another picture can be added within the eye. The potential of this work is limited only by imagination and equipment.

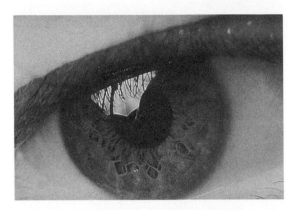

C *What the eye sees is now superimposed on the eyeball.*

C *A flower within.*

Digitizing and Superimposing

Artist Timothy Dempsey created a combination digitized image and computer-generated graphic for this series. He used the Sony Videotizer digitizing camera to take a picture of a circuit board to use for a background for a proposed artistic chart.

A photograph of a circuit board was taken with the Sony Videotizer digitizing camera. The picture was cut in half horizontally in the computer, then the top half was mirrored for the bottom portion.

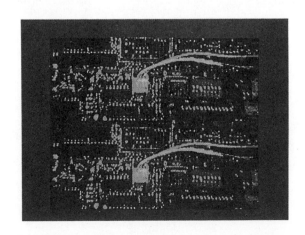

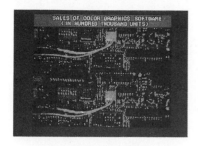

A title was added and placed across the top in a banner; the type alone on the circuit board was too busy and hard to read. This was saved to disk.

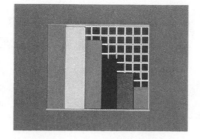

Next, the artist began creating the bar graph which was to include an illustration of a computer.

For the illustration, he used an image of a computer already stored on disk.

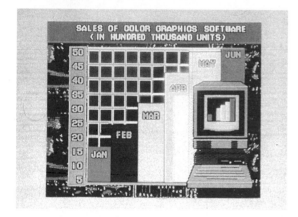

He assembled all the images but he wanted a little more artistry. He saved the picture to disk.

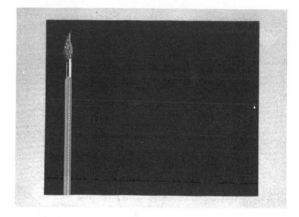

Next he created a paintbrush for the horizontal along the left-hand side. He drew the brush in another file but in the location planned in the final picture.

The final picture is the result of the previous steps with the paintbrush overlayed at left. It's too busy for the average boardroom presentation, but it illustrates a variety of techniques possible in a short time when one has all the right equipment.

The entire design represents approximately three hours' work, but that time can vary from designer to designer, with the software and hardware, and with the existence of previously stored images.

Artist: Timothy Dempsey. Courtesy, Sony Corp.

9

Presentations— Clear and Perfect

Overhead transparencies have been a traditional medium for presentations for many years. Their popularity has escalated as computers and presentation software have made them easier to produce. They can be generated quickly, almost at the last minute before a presentation is to be given.

Overhead projections are the preferable medium in some situations, but not all. They are an excellent choice when:

1. You want two-way communication.
2. You want an informal atmosphere.
3. The speaker wants control of the visual aids.
4. The speaker wants to add information spontaneously.
5. There is a relatively small audience (50 or fewer).
6. 35 mm slides or equipment may not be available.

The speed of making overhead transparencies has helped their popularity. It has also contributed to their abuse. People scribble on the transparencies, often thinking that informality is an excuse for making them "quick and dirty." However, once audiences are accustomed to well-done overheads, the presenter who uses hastily drawn, sloppy, colored marker visuals will lose credibility.

Computers make it easy to create well-designed text, business charts, illustrations, and logos. They save time; composing and producing visuals is faster than using lettering machines, press-on type, or typeset and pasted lettering. If you have a computer, you may as well use it to generate visuals. You may or may not need additional software and hardware.

Throughout the book, there has been an emphasis on using the same files or images in more than one medium. Files generated for 35 mm slides can also be used to create a transparency, hardcopy handouts, and reduced-in-size speaker's notes.

Transparencies can be created by three basic methods: (1) a slide service that uses a photographic or print process; (2) printed or plotted directly on film using in-house printers or plotters; (3) printed on paper, then transferred to film by photocopying. The Polaroid mini-transparency overheads can be made with a Polaroid instant camera and instant film.

THINK *like a* WINNER
TALK *like a* WINNER
DRESS *like a* WINNER

because

YOU ARE A
WINNER

A hand-drawn transparency used by an image consultant would not convey a very good image of the presenter.

C *The same message created with the software Applause II and imaged by MAGICorp would improve the image of the presenter considerably.*

Slide Service Overheads

All slide services will produce beautifully colored transparencies from the same computer files generated for 35 mm slides. These may be made with large 8 × 10 film recorders. There are also units that will produce prints directly from 35 mm slides. One is the Cibacopy System 120 made by the Ilford Photo Corp. (see

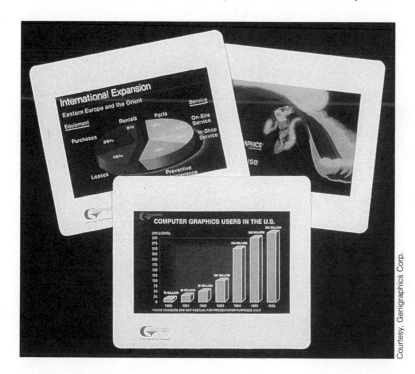

C *These same illustrations are shown as 35 mm slides elsewhere in the book. Reusing artwork for various presentations can stretch your graphics preparation budget over a wider application base.*

Courtesy, Polaroid Corp.

Polaroid's VideoPrinter Model 8 color film recorder is one of several systems marketed for obtaining instant photographic transparencies from a computer in the 8 × 10-inch size.

Chapter 14). Another is the QPS 101 Cycolor slideprinter from Noritsu. These are high-priced units; they cost from $10,000 to $24,000, so they are generally found only where high volume is required. Some services use ink jet or thermal printers, but these

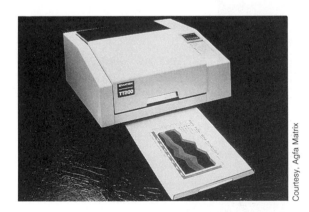

Courtesy, Agfa Matrix

The Agfa Matrix thermal transfer printer produces dense color on paper or film from several software packages.

Courtesy, Hewlett-Packard Co.

The Hewlett-Packard PaintJet printer produces color graphics and text. The ink jet containers are inserted under the lift-up flap at right. The inexpensive unit weighs only 11 pounds.

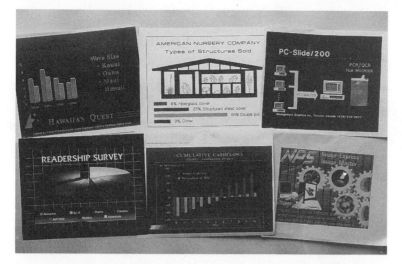

Print quality differs depending on the printer, the manufacturer, film type, and inks. Top row left to right: output from a Calcomp PlotMaster, Hewlett-Packard Plotter, Tektronix Color printer. Bottom row left to right: Ilford CibaChrome, CalComp ColorMaster, Matrix Thermal TT200.

do not produce as high a quality transparency as the other processes.

Overheads made by a service bureau will range from about $5 to $22, when generated from your files (see Chapter 14).

Color Printers and Plotters

Today's color dot matrix, ink jet, and thermal printers (Chapter 15) will produce full-color overhead transparencies directly on film. Color laser printers, still very costly at this writing, may be the unit of the future. Color intensity will vary by the type of printer used. Generally, you must use the proper film type for a specific printer. Film emulsions differ and are designed so that specific types of inks will adhere.

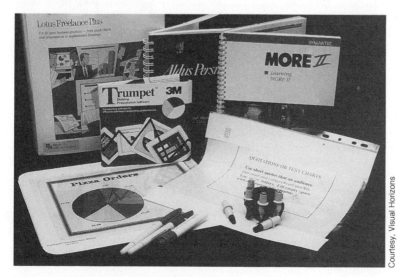

Lotus Freelance Plus, Persuasion, More II and most presentation graphics programs will produce high-quality overheads using a variety of output devices or slide services. Trumpet is specifically for overheads. A 3M Flip-Frame is shown at right.

Courtesy, Visual Horizons

Preprinted transparencies in vivid colors are available in sets that contain assorted headlines, borders, frames, etc. Print or plot your message on another sheet of film and place it behind the colored transparency or photocopy directly onto the film.

Plotters generally produce a denser color image than printers because the image is produced with felt-tip pens. Special transparency compatible pens are required; the pens used for paper will not produce the ink intensity required. They may not even write on film.

Black and White Transparencies

The majority of transparencies made in house are black and white. A common procedure is to print the information on paper, then photocopy that print onto a sheet of transparency film. The film used must be compatible with the photocopy machine. Toners differ in chemical makeup and adhere differently to different transparency emulsions.

When you make prints that will be transferred to film, allow for format differences. The overall usable image area for a transparency is 7½ × 9 inches compared with an 8 × 10 usable area on paper. When a paper print is too large, reduce it when you photocopy onto the film.

Adding Color to Black and White

Black and white transparencies can project the illusion of being colored. Photocopy your black print onto a light blue or light green sheet rather than a clear sheet of film. The result is a two-color transparency, and the blue or green will reduce glare that results when a clear film is projected. Colored copy, logos, and illustrations can be photocopied with a color photocopy machine directly onto transparency film.

Visual Horizons sells packages of film with preprinted colored borders, cartoons, and simple messages. When you photocopy black copy onto the open space of these prints, you'll have an instant color overhead attractively enhanced.

Software Simplifies and Improves the Process

The same software files you use for generating 35 mm slides can generate overheads. Software offers output options to a wide variety of printers, plotters, and film recorders.

There are packages designed with specific templates for overhead transparencies. They may limit the number of lines you can use and provide type sizes that can be read easily from a distance. Usually these packages are lower priced and do not have as many features or output choices as full presentation packages.

If you've generated files in color and output them to a black and white printer, you may have to rethink color elements. Software drivers vary in how they treat color as gray scale. Light colors,

Courtesy, 3M Audio-Visual Division

Presenters can quickly create computer generated transparencies with almost any peripheral, but the proper film must be used for the specific device and inks. It will differ for ink jet, thermal, laser, or dot matrix printers, plotters, plain paper copiers, or infrared transparency makers.

such as yellow, blue, and pink, may drop out and become white in the print and you may lose letters or data. Ideally, a program will convert light colors to gray scales, but not all printers will print those grays.

For basic overhead transparencies with text and simple graphics (about 80 percent of all overheads consist mainly of text), your existing MS DOS or Macintosh word processing software may do the trick. Desktop publishing programs such as Xerox Ventura Publisher and Aldus PageMaker excel at producing overheads that have a typeset appearance. They can import graphics, too.

When you have only a general word processing program and no large font output capability, you can still acquire usable word charts if you use a little ingenuity. Boardroom quality overheads (and 35 mm slides) can be made from word processing files by a slide service such as Brilliant Image (see Chapter 14).

Most presentation programs have a feature for displaying each slide on-screen. Those screens can be timed to change automatically, or they can be advanced manually using the space bar or return key. This feature can serve as a rehearsal tool. You can set the time it takes you to talk about each visual. You can rearrange their order as necessary and determine how you want to pace your talk. When everything is as you want it, you can output files for hardcopy up to minutes before your presentation.

Mini-Transparencies

Polaroid has developed a 3¼ × 4¼ inch transparency, called the Small-Format Colorgraph or a "mini-transparency." It can be made with Polaroid's Turbo Palette Film recorder using a Polaroid

The Polaroid Bravo Zoom projector has a sliding image tray and a 180–350 mm zoom lens that can enlarge standard size overheads. When the transparency is raised, a larger, brighter image will result.

The Bravo Portable overhead projector has a folding lens/mirror and a side-mounted handle. It has a 5-inch square adapter with a magnifying lens to display Polaroid type 691 mini-transparencies. Both are a low-profile design, lightweight, and offer silent, bright, even image projection.

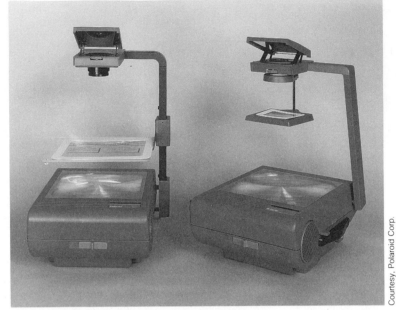

Courtesy, Polaroid Corp.

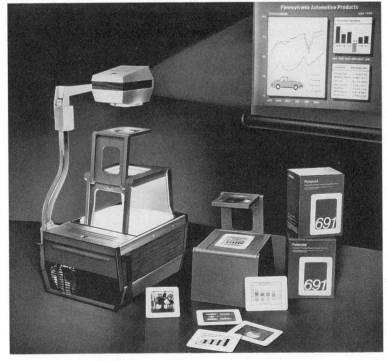

The Polaroid Overhead Enlarger is a portable folding platform for a standard overhead projector. The Overhead Enlarger magnifies the 3¼" × 4¼" transparencies 2.3 times, resulting in a nearly full-screen image.

Courtesy, Polaroid Corp.

3¼ × 4¼ inch camera back or in the BRAVO! Slide Maker. The Colorgraph 691 film is instant. That means that a mini-transparency can be taken and processed in four minutes. The peel-apart film comes eight to a package and includes cardboard mounts.

A mini-transparency can be projected using a traditional projector. The mounted film should be set in a template that will block out the light around it when using the basic light platform. Make a template by cutting a rectangle the size of the transparency from a sheet of dark heavy paper or cardboard. Without a template, it's possible to show four slides at once. They might be different views of a building, several solutions to a problem, or a comparison of data in different charts.

Polaroid has developed a line of projectors that accommodate the standard transparency, and also has a platform for the mini-format. Polaroid and other companies market an attachable platform that will hold the mini-transparency above the light stage so no templates are needed. They have a magnifying glass so the image will project large.

The advantage of the mini-transparency film is its compact size. A show consisting of 40 mini-transparencies weighs much less and is smaller and easier to carry about than 40 large, framed transparencies. The resulting image is comparable, and projection size is ade-

A flat, compact, and easily portable overhead projector has a triple lens, a built-in lamp changer, and convection cooling.

Eiki International's Portable Overhead Projector (POP-1) is a self-contained unit that you set up for use with three easy motions. Weighing in at 15 pounds for "show on the go" use, it has a three-element lens and will magnify in a range from 4X to 8.5X for versatile positioning.

The Dukane PRO 600 is a one-piece unit that fits into an attaché case and under the seat of an airplane. It weighs 17 pounds and has a 300 mm zoom lens.

PRESENTATION POINTERS

- **Short sentences**
- **One thought per line**
- **Six words per line maximum**
- **Six lines per slide maximum**

Software choices deal with frame and bullet styles, fonts, and layouts.

HOW TO CRITIQUE A VISUAL

- Too many lines on one slide
- Lettering is too small
- **Spacing is poor**
- Sentence lengths are not ordered
- Too many words and thoughts mixed in one line so text spills onto second line
- Mixture of fonts and colors can contribute to confusion.
- *Italics are hard to read for entire sentences. Use them to emphasize a word or thought.*

Regardless of the limitations built into a program, it's still easy to create bad slides by flouting all the rules.

QUOTATIONS OR TEXT CHARTS

Use short quotes that an audience can read and comprehend quickly. Use large letters. Fill empty space with an appropriate graphic.

Layout is awkward, with too much white space between title and text.

QUOTATIONS OR TEXT CHARTS

Use short quotes that an audience can read and comprehend quickly. Use large letters. Fill empty space with an appropriate graphic.

The answer is to move the text up and use an illustration or a logo.

quate for small audiences. There is also the same size color print film, called the 669, which is perfect for use in preparing handouts for customers.

Overhead Projector Considerations

Projector technology has improved tremendously as people use projectors more and the market grows. A projector purchase requires several considerations: the light output, ''throw light'' distance, and size and weight of the unit.

The amount of light needed depends on screen size; the larger the screen, the more light required. Light falls off in proportion to the area covered on the screen. The more ambient light, the more light your projector will have to overcome, so it needs to be brighter.

The ''throw light'' is the distance the light must be thrown from the projector to the screen. Most projectors have fixed focal-length lenses. The only way to change the size and focus of the image beyond a few inches is to move the projector in relation to the screen. There are wide-angle units for short throws to a larger

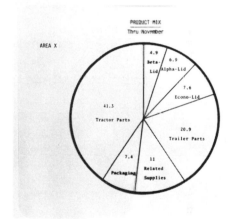

A typewritten table of statistics on an overhead transparency is hard to read; if it must be used, it should be offered to only a few people sitting close to the screen.

For an informal presentation, the same tabular data can be converted to an appropriate chart which compares the information more quickly. Even this type size would be hard to read at a distance.

To make the chart effective at a distance, the smart presenter would use simple, large, bold letters and heavier lines for the chart.

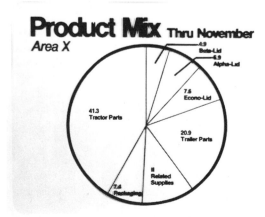

Artist: Bonnie Stewart. Courtesy,
3M/Bay Business Products, San Diego, CA

screen, but then the images will be too large for a smaller screen at a longer distance. Measure the usual throw distances required and choose a unit accordingly, or buy an accessory lens that can compensate for different focal lengths.

Manufacturers are designing units for any situation; some are portable and small enough to fit beneath an airplane seat. Larger units are compact, lightweight, and transportable, and heads fold down for easy storage.

Portable units may have the light in the head and produce a reflective image; nonportable units have the light in the base, which shines through the film and projects it onto the screen. A unit with a base light source is required when using an LCD flat panel display (Chapter 10).

Other features to consider are the heat generated by the bulb, the presence and efficiency of a cooling fan, how easy it is to change a bulb, storage of a spare bulb, and the availability of replacement bulbs.

Transparencies Have Their Rules, Too

Because the overhead transparency is a larger format than a 35 mm slide, presenters are tempted to cram more information onto it. Once projected, a busy, overloaded transparency can be as hard to read as an overloaded slide. Even worse, a slide with text that is typewritten is usually too small to be read by anyone more than a few feet away from the projector. The same rules for designing 35 mm data slides and entire presentations apply to transparency shows.

The preferred format for a transparency is horizontal rather than vertical. Information on vertical film may extend too low on a screen and accentuate keystoning.

Here are some rules for producing transparencies:

Text slides:

1. Allow six words per line maximum.
2. Allow six lines per slide maximum.
3. Allow 30 words per slide maximum.
4. An image or a logo may be added.

Fonts:

1. Use solid, block lettering.
2. Use no more than two or three fonts.
3. It's OK to use uppercase letters for titles.
4. Use larger size type for titles than for text.
5. Use upper and lowercase letters for all copy.
6. Use underlines, color, bold, or italics for emphasis.

Layout:

1. Use centered or left-justified text on all slides
   in a single presentation.
2. Use at least 18 and 24 point type for word charts.
3. Text and image should fill about three fourths of the space.
4. Place same-sized logos in the same position on each slide.
5. Order text lines; go from shortest at top to longest at bottom.
6. Avoid running letters vertically; they are hard to read.

Color:

1. Use color to group different ideas.
2. Use only two or three main colors.
3. Use bright colors to emphasize a word or a line.
4. Use color pens to add notes interactively as you speak.
   (Write on a clear sheet overlay to avoid ruining the slide.)
5. Position a framed colored blank sheet on the light platform;
   all sheets placed over it will look framed and colored.

Color Schemes

The color scheme you select will depend upon how you generate the transparencies. With printed output, test to evaluate how black or colored inks print on film and how they appear when projected. Also test photocopied color and black prints. Some photocopy machines print red, green, and blue, but the toners may not produce color dense enough to withstand the projector's brightness. Even a red or blue line of text that looks bright to the eye can easily be washed out and appear gray, or be lost completely. Some toners are opaque, and even though they print red or blue, they will project as black.

Generally, select either black or bright intense colors for text and apply the psychology of color. Contrasting colors can be used to suggest contrasting concepts. Colors on the red end of the spectrum are emotional and exciting. Colors on the blue end of the spectrum are cool and rational. That's one reason why blue is considered a "banker's" color.

Avoid reds for numbers and balance sheets; they suggest debits. For female audiences, use high, bright colors such as red, purple, green, yellow. For male audiences, use more subdued colors: dark blue and black, with green and yellow for accents. Avoid red/green color combinations for male audiences; many men are red/green color blind and the combination may appear muddy brown to them.

Colors selected for overheads made on office printers work best when the background is light and lettering and charts are bright and in dark colors.

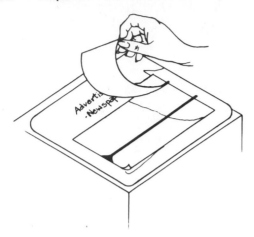

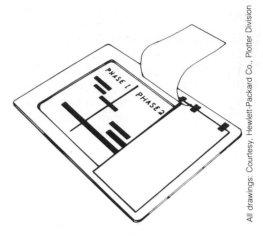

All drawings: Courtesy, Hewlett-Packard Co., Plotter Division

For a "reveal," tape one edge of rectangular pieces of opaque paper to the edge on the frame, as shown. Lift one strip of paper at a time to reveal the current topic.

Or hinge the paper at the top. The transparency should be mounted in a frame.

Overheads purchased from a slide service can have dark backgrounds with light lettering. The lightest colors come forward the most. White text, yellow title and bullets on a dark background are always a safe choice. Red accents with dark backgrounds show up better on overheads than on 35 mm slides.

Reveal and Build Techniques

Reveal and build techniques work a little differently on an overhead than on a slide. With 35 mm, you need at least three slides to show a four-line build. You can do an effective reveal or build with only one transparency.

To use the reveal technique on a transparency with four bulleted lines, print all the topics on one transparency and mount it in a frame. Then cut three pieces of opaque paper the width of the frame. Cut them so that one paper covers the second line, another

Tape the transparency to frame edges. The frame can hold notes, frame numbers, computer file numbers, references, and arrows to indicate right side up and frontward.

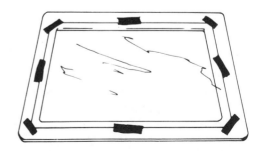

An "overlay" can be another sheet of blank film set up so you jot notes on it without ruining the original transparency.

Use special transparency felt-tip pens (they come in colors) to add information spontaneously. For a dramatic touch, use 3M's Color Hi-Lite Write-on Film. The blue film turns yellow where it's touched by an accompanying special white felt-tip pen.

Use up to three or four overlays for a build. Each may be hinged at a different side so it can be lifted on and off. Each overlay can hold an additional bit of information that lays in exactly where you want it when you flip it down.

This line chart will have a second data line in another color added with the first overlay, then a third line added with the next. Each line represents a sales projection for a given time period. Building a chart as you go is an effective presentation technique that keeps your audience looking and listening.

All drawings: Courtesy, Hewlett-Packard Co., Plotter Division

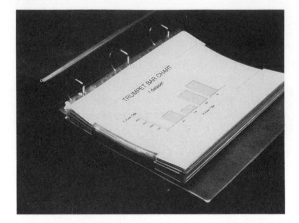

Courtesy, 3M Audio-Visual Division

3M Flip-Frame transparency protectors are a three-hole-punched sleeve, or sandwich, with a narrow strip of white sturdy paper on each side. Lay the whole *sheet, with the transparency inside, on the light stage and flip back the papers to form the frame. They're lightweight, easy to carry, and efficient.*

covers the third, another covers the last line. Tape them at the side of the frame as a hinge; one lower than the next. Then lift each piece of paper as you introduce each topic to "reveal" that topic. This procedure is easier and neater than using four transparencies or sliding a piece of cardboard down the light stage.

The same technique works well for discussing table and organization charts. Cover one part, then reveal the others one at a time as you discuss them by simply lifting the hinged paper.

TYPES OF INFORMATION

Data vs. Documents
Stable vs. Volatile Information
Text vs. Graphics
Raster vs. Vector Graphics
Color vs. Gray Scale
Centralized vs. Distributed
Machine Readable vs. User Readable

TYPES OF INFORMATION

Data vs. Documents
Stable vs. Volatile Information
Text vs. Graphics
Raster vs. Vector
Color vs. Gray Scale
Centralized vs. Distributed
Machine Readable vs. User Readable

Choose readable fonts that can be easily seen at a distance. In this example, the words are too small and the layout is worthless with all words condensed at the top of the sheet.

Use large letters. Avoid script text and lines that are thin. Bold, dark letters work best.

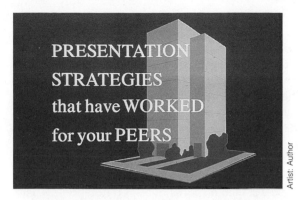

Artist: Author

C A title slide made with Applause II.

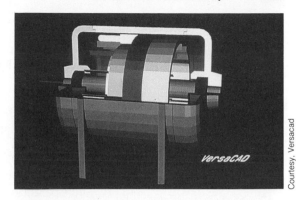

Courtesy, Versacad

C A CAD transparency made with Versacad.

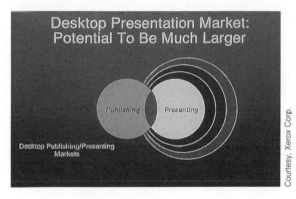

Courtesy, Xerox Corp.

A diagram chart made with circles using Xerox Presents.

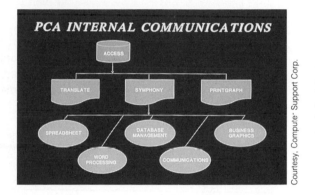

Courtesy, Compute· Support Corp.

An organization chart made with Arts & Letters.

Overheads made photographically, or converted from a slide to an Ilford print, will project dynamically. The backgrounds are dark and smooth, with lettering and messages that get attention. It's almost impossible to achieve this same quality from a printer. Find the top two transparencies in the color inserts, and you'll get the impact of the difference color can make.

For a build slide, begin with a basic transparency, place the next bit of information on another transparency in the position it should be shown, then tape it on the frame and overlay it on the original. That's smoother, and more effective, than using a new transparency for each addition.

Preparing the Frames

Finished transparencies should be mounted in plastic or cardboard frames to prevent creasing or rumpling. However, they can still get scratched, so they should be protected if you plan to reuse them.

Several types of sheet protectors are on the market. The most efficient is a Flip-Frame sheet from 3M. It sandwiches the unframed transparency; then it has two flip-down opaque white paper strips on each side. The transparency is laid on the light stage in the holder, and the strips fold out to form the frame and to eliminate edge glare. In addition, the sheets are hole-punched for easy storage in a standard 8½ × 11 inch notebook. They add no appreciable weight or bulk.

There are clear plastic protectors large enough to cover framed transparencies; these will fit in a special oversized notebook. There are clear plastic, three-hole-punched protector sheets into which you slide the unframed transparencies. Use the clear, not the frosted, if you plan to project through them.

Besides protection, here's how frames can be helpful:

1. Number frames for quick sorting.
2. Use the cardboard frame borders for notes.
3. Use colored frames to group slides by topics.
4. Notch frames at top right. When notches line up, you'll know they're all in the right position.

Position yourself to the side of the projector where you won't block the view of anyone in the audience. Use a pointer or pencil and place it on the transparency when you want to emphasize your topic; there's no point in walking up to the screen and in front of the projection light.

The flat-based portable 3M model 2010 can be placed directly on a table for sit-down presentations in an informal situation. Notice that the unit is very low compared to the screen, but there is no keystoning because of the adjustments possible in the light head.

Courtesy, 3M Meeting Graphics

Ⓒ*In a small to medium-size room with 10 or more people, place the screen at an angle in a corner of the room. Speaker and projector are centered.*

5. Note the computer program, date, and file name used should you have to update the slide.

6. When you plan to jot data onto a slide with a felt-tip pen, overlay a piece of clear film on the original and write on that so as not to ruin the original. The overlay can be taped to the frame for convenience and to prevent it from sliding.

7. Prepare one frame with a colored sheet and tape it to the light stage. Then all other clear, unframed sheets will appear colored and framed.

Readability and Projection Tests

Always pretest visuals for readability. Overheads work best with small audiences, under 50 people or so, in an informal environment in a lighted room. When you know the size of the room and the placement of chairs, you can estimate the distance of the last row from the screen. Create a sample transparency, put it on a projector in a large room, and determine from how far back it can be read.

Another method is to print the slide on paper and place it in a window. If you can read the copy when you stand 10 to 12 feet away, it's probably OK. If you can't, redo the slide with larger, bolder type.

Audiovisual experts figure the maximum viewing distance as six times the width of the projected image. If the image fills a 4-foot-wide screen, the last row for seating should be 24 feet away. That's assuming the slide is made with large, bold images.

Avoid keystoning, which occurs when the image appears wider at the top than the bottom. It can distort text by making a square appear trapezoidal and a pie chart appear oval. Focus the projector, then tilt the screen until it's in the same plane as the projector. Most screens have an extension bar at the top with notches so the screen angle can be adjusted.

Your Interaction with a Projector

1. Position yourself and the projector so neither is in the view path of the audience. You usually stand next to the projector when showing transparencies. If you tend to walk about, be careful not to walk between the projector and the screen. The light will blind your eyes, and you'll block the screen image.
2. Keep the image high enough so people in the back can view it over the heads of people in front rows.
3. Don't read exactly what is on the slide. Pause and give the audience time to read it, then elaborate on each point.
4. Face the audience when you speak. If you've arranged your transparencies carefully and have them framed, there's no need to double-check placement by looking at the screen. You'll save time, and transitions will be smooth.
5. When you finish explaining a specific visual, remove it from the screen. If you want to continue talking, use a piece of cardboard to block out the projector light glare. Or, when using transparencies, keep a sheet with your logo handy. When using an LCD, revert to a screen with the title or a logo. (Turning the projector on and off is not wise because the bulb should be fan cooled before shutting down the projector.)
6. Carry extra film and pens.
7. Carry a spare projector bulb.

Sources for Information[*]

Agfa Matrix
One Ramland Road
Orangeburg, NY 10962
914   365-0190

Arkwright, Inc.
Main St.
Fiskeville, RI 02823
401   821-1000
800   942-5900

Bell & Howell Video Systems/Eiki Intl.
6800 McCormick Blvd.
Chicago, IL 60645
312   673-3300 or 312   675-7600

Buhl Industries, Inc.
Audio-Visual Equipment
1401 Maple Ave.
Fairlawn, NJ 07460
210   423-2800

Dukane Corp.
Audio-Visual Equipment
2900 Dukane Drive
St. Charles, IL 60174
708   584-2300
800   634-2800
800   356-6540 (in Illinois)

---

[*]See Chapter 10 for LCD flat panel display manufacturers; see Chapter 15 for printer/plotter manufacturers.

Eiki International
Audio-Visual Equipment
27882 Camino Capistrano
Laguna Niguel, CA 92677
714   831-2511

Folex, Inc.
6 Daniel Rd. E.
Fairfield, NJ 07006
201   575-4500
800   631-1150

Hewlett-Packard Co. (Plotter Division)
16399 West Bernardo Dr.
San Diego, CA 92127
619   487-4100

Ilford Photo Corp.
West 70 Century Rd.
Paramus, NJ 07653
201   265-6000
800   631-2522

Noritsu America Corp.
6900 Noritsu Ave.
Buena Park, CA 90622
714   521-9040

Polaroid Corp.
575 Technology Square
Cambridge, MA 02139
617   577-2000
800   225-1618

3M Audio-Visual Division
Building 225-3N-01
St. Paul, MN 55144
612   733-3319

Transilwrap Company, Inc.
2515 N. Paulina
Chicago, IL 60614
312   528-8000

Visual Horizons
180 Metro Park
Rochester, NY 14623
716   424-5300

Xerox Corp.
Xerox Square
Rochester, NY 14644
716   423-3539
(also contact local centers)

10

Making Points with Desktop Slide Shows

Some presenters go from auditorium to boardroom carrying a carousel of slides or a stack of overheads; others carry only a floppy disk or two. They use the computer as their display tool.

Desktop slide shows, also referred to as on-screen slide shows, floppy disk shows, or video presentations, depend on the computer screen to display a presentation to an audience of one or of many. The entire show-on-a-floppy is popped into a computer where it can run with the presenter's help, by the viewer, or all by itself.

A presenter can augment a show or work with a program interactively. A viewer may look at a disk that demonstrates a product, a service, or a concept. A disk can take the place of a hardcopy handout or serve as sales support, an introduction, or an example of what something can do.

Desktop slide shows are becoming more popular and increasingly sophisticated. Of 45 top presentation and charting programs, more than half have slide show capabilities with some special effect features. Procedures for assembling shows have been simplified. Faster hardware speeds up a presentation, and higher resolution screens improve images.

The acceptance of LCD (liquid crystal display) flat panel presentation units, and the lower cost of RGB projectors, are helping, too. With these systems, a show can be projected directly from computer to large screen for sizable audiences.

Animated Presentations

Presentation and graphics programs are designed for preparing visuals; traditionally, that has meant 35 mm slides or overheads. Now, the same screens you design for traditional shows can become the show when stored in the computer or on a disk. That show can be colorful, lively, and animated, with special effects that grab and hold the attention of your audience.

That's a big order. If the disk must also serve as a stand-alone persuasive medium, it must hold a carefully prepared dynamic presentation. That requires design know-how, an understanding of how to use fonts, colors, special effects, pacing, and timing. It will also need a run-time module to run the disk without the host program. For commercial distribution, a license may be needed from the software company.

In some programs, each screen appears in a timed sequence. Originally, this feature was there to help the user proof screens and rehearse a presentation. Then a few programs appeared that allowed the user to change the timing on each screen.

Soon special effects were discovered and the picture really changed. Presentation software companies realized they could incorporate several of these effects in their programs. Initially, programming them was a chore, but simpler procedures evolved. Now it's not unusual to put a disk in the computer and see each screen, or portions of it, fade, sweep, scroll, dissolve, and fragment. Images can show fingers moving on a keyboard, a wheel rotating, balls bouncing, a horse running, or boats disappearing into the sunset.

The Origin of Disk Shows

Early charting software packages had utilities that would sequence computer images and play them back in order, much like a single projector slide show. Their purpose was mainly for proofing. Playback could be timed for up to 60 seconds per screen, or a screen could be changed manually by pressing a key. Many programs still have only that capability.

Then, two programs introduced the desktop slideshow concept: ShowPartner F/X from Brightbill-Roberts & Co. (originally called Grafix Partner), and IBM Storyboard which was updated to IBM Storyboard Plus. Immediately, one saw timed shows at computer conventions with special effects that moved messages on and off screen like television commercials.

Software Choices

Soon screen transitions based on those in ShowPartner F/X and IBM Storyboard Plus appeared in presentation programs, including Harvard Graphics, ExecuVision, Freelance Plus 3.0, 35 mm Express, and in paint programs such as Dr. Halo and PC Paintbrush. The features were added to new versions of older programs. Paint, chart, and graphics packages included either timed or special effects show capability, or both. Some also added sound and the ability to spill the show onto a videotape if necessary hardware was available.

Grasp (Paul Mace Software) appeared: it was more of an animation program editor than another presentation module. It showed what really good animation could look like. Other programmers quickly learned traditional animation techniques and applied them in new ways.

Sales promotions, customer information, and training are among uses for demos on a disk. They are often designed so packaging, labels, and logos are integrated.

Photo: Author

Macintosh presentation programs such as Cricket Presents, More II, and StandOut! included additional techniques and simplified menus for assembling shows. They also let the user sort slides using a thumbnail reproduction of each slide on-screen. You can move any slide about until the order is exactly as you want. That Macintosh facility was carried back into the MS DOS world with Xerox Presents.

Xerox Presents characterizes the simplicity of using the features in current programs. You can call up a screen, pull down a dialogue box, then select the timing and transition effects. A "play" command runs the show. Any slide, any sequence, can be revised for content, running time, and transitions.

While the presentation programs have a bevy of special effects, each movement requires a new screen. The base screen can remain and only a sentence added for a build sequence, for example. ShowPartner F/X, IBM Storyboard Plus, and to some extent Xerox Presents enable you to segment the screen and have one effect on a group of images in one part of the screen. They give you greater flexibility than moving full screens only.

How Are Shows Used Effectively?

You may see animated slide shows on a monitor in your bank detailing new services. There may be one at the entrance to an art museum detailing the events of the day, times, and locations.

You've probably received "demo" disks that illustrate how a program works. Demo disks used as sales promotions must be

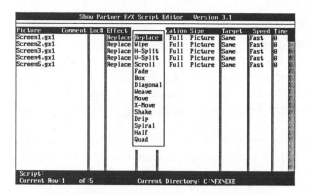

Different software approaches programming the slide show differently.

Above: Screen from ShowPartner F/X. A list of files is at left. Using a series of pop-up menus you can select and assign a different location, special effect, speed, and length of time to each screen. Any number of files can be highlighted and played back to see how the animation looks.

The slide show form in Lotus Freelance Plus 3.0 has a different type menu, but selections are made in a similar fashion. There are fewer choices but the program is not dedicated to a slideshow as is ShowPartner F/X.

targeted to an audience with computers and the correct operating system and disk size. That may require an inquiry mailing and a write-in so people can request the correct disk. Companies with national dealerships may distribute disks through dealers.

Ashton-Tate has used desktop presentations in dealer showrooms to familiarize customers with the virtues of dBASE and of Byline. The customer can take a disk home. These demo disks are created by a company that specializes in designing desktop presentations. Graphics designers may use a variety of movielike animation and transition effects.

Animation can demonstrate how a product works or how an operation proceeds. In the Byline demo, the multiple chronology of the software modules is shown through animation. For an engineering application, a mechanical part inserted and rotated within another part could be animated.

Viewer interaction, especially in a training situation, has proven effective. In one promotion/training disk, a user was enticed to request additional information by filling in his name and address on the last screen. The information was output to a printer. The user only had to fold the paper, then stamp and mail it.

Ford Motor Co.'s Lincoln-Mercury Division had a "mail-in-for" demo disk offer that was well received. The viewer could simulate a test drive of a Merkur car and interactively calculate the cost of the model and accessories he was considering.

Making the Point

A successful presentation involves performance principles and organization. If it is to have special effects, it can begin with the slides prepared for any other presentation; then the animation and transitions would be added. The best method is to use a storyboard and plan the effects before you select them on-screen for each slide.

Design rules that apply to 35 mm and overhead slides apply to screens: keep them simple, use short sentences, don't crowd a screen with too many ideas, colors, or typefaces. Use professionally drawn images and fonts. Keep construction and layout principles consistent throughout the presentation.

Vary timing of the movements so those at the beginning are on long enough to read and to acclimate the viewer to the medium as your topic is introduced. Then make your points with each slide but change the timing. Leave some slides from 3 to 10 seconds, others for 10 to 20 seconds. Move interior messages on and off screen quickly. (Give the viewer the option to manually speed up or slow down the show.) Plan visual effects so they aid the consistency. Perhaps all those that introduce a new subject will have a curtain open from the left; when that subject is over it will be "pushed" off screen or "disintegrated."

The total presentation should be between two and five minutes. Test every show on several viewers and observe their reactions.

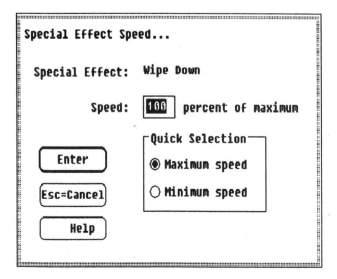

In Xerox Presents, the image you're working on is on-screen. The pop-up menus appear and you can select the effect and preview it immediately rather than working from a file list.

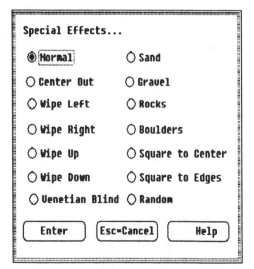

To select a special effect in Xerox Presents, place the cursor on the bullet and it's done.

If they begin to clean up a desk or do something else while the show is on, reduce the show's length.

If your current presentation, chart, and paint programs do not have animation and special effect features, you'll need a program that does. Many programs can import files from other programs. Or you may be able to grab screens you've designed with a special "screen grab" utility and export them to the slide show program (see Chapter 15).

The best way to learn how desktop presentations are assembled is to collect disks distributed by various companies and study them for content, pacing, and technique. First, outline a disk so you see how the topic is organized. They probably follow the same concepts for preparing a verbal presentation: use a catchy title, state the objective, set up the points to be made, then make them. Finish with a summary and a request that the viewer write, call, act, or whatever is appropriate for your presentation.

Screen Show Design Suggestions

1. Decide: What should the show accomplish? Who is the audience?

2. Plan: Sketch each frame and the movement to take place on that frame. Decide what effect to use to exit one frame and enter the next.

3. Typefaces: Select no more than three typefaces and use them consistently throughout. Use the same font for titles, another for subtitles, another for bullets and text. You can use a smaller size but the same type style for tagging charts.

4. Colors: Use them consistently in similar areas. Use drop shadows to make a word or object appear to stand away from the screen and get attention. On screen, use bright colors on light backgrounds.

5. Introduction: Each subject of one type could be introduced with the same special effect. When you present a new major topic, use the same style sweep, for example. Use a different style consistently for minor topics. You might use one shaded, or gradated, background, then move the topics on and off the same background. Gradated backgrounds may not appear as smooth as you would like on low resolution systems and they take too long to redraw.

6. Pace: Show slides at different time intervals. Start slowly to get your premise across; then speed up as you pound the points home. The major topics can be on-screen longer, then different timing for the points to be made. Present the conclusion; make it short and succinct. Finish with a contact name, address, and so forth. Leave that on long enough for someone to copy it or print it with a screen dump.

7. Start and stop help: Try to have a screen early in the presentation that tells people how to proceed and how to stop or end the show. Some presentations are completely interactive so the viewer can control the timing.

8. Reveal and build series: They are a perfect technique for adding sentences and images, then summarizing them. They're a good excuse for animation.

9. Avoid the "too" concept: Too much on-screen. Too many fonts. Too many colors. Too many effects for the sake of the effect and not the message. Too long.

Several companies specialize in creating disk presentations. They may develop and design the show, and arrange for quantity duplications. They can design and print matching disk labels, disk folders, and mailers. For names of these companies, write to the author in care of the publisher; please include a stamped, self-addressed envelope.

Special Effects Tools

Each program lists about 16 special effects. It may seem like more because they can be combined and moved in different directions. Their names and descriptions vary among programs. Experiment with each one to see how it can be used. Identify them in other programs to learn how they're applied. Check the following list against those in a program to learn which and how many effects are included and whether or not they will serve your needs.

Blinds: Opens the screen in vertical or horizontal strips.

Close: Closes the screen in a vertical line to the left and right simultaneously or in a horizontal line to the top and bottom simultaneously.

Diagonal: Moves from one corner to another.

The wipe effect: The new picture overlays the old in a specified direction.

The v-split effect splits the screen in half on the vertical axis.

The drip effect moves the picture onto the screen one row at a time so it appears to be "dripping" towards the specified direction.

In the fade effect, the new picture overlays the old in a random pattern.

The weave effect appears when the new picture crosses the old one off in two directions simultaneously. Even lines are pushed to the left, odd lines to the right.

The diagonal scroll replaces one picture with another; the new one appears along a straight diagonal line that proceeds towards one corner of the screen. Any corner may be selected.

Drip: Moves a picture onto the screen one row at a time so it appears as though the image is "dripping" in the direction specified.

Fade: A new screen disappears as though disintegrating into little dots.

Half: Shrinks the next screen to half-screen size and places it at top, bottom, left, or right half of screen.

Iris: Closes in on the screen from all sides toward the center or opens out from the center towards all sides.

Open: Opens the screen in a vertical line to the left and right simultaneously or in a horizontal line to the top and bottom simultaneously.

Overlay: Displays the slide element by element. It appears to overlay a previous slide if it has not been erased.

Quad: Shrinks the next screen and places it in one selected quadrant of the screen.

Rain: Appears to shatter the screen in small dot patterns. Also called gravel; larger shattering may be termed "rocks" or "boulders."

Random: Appears to have no set pattern, but it's similar to rain in a random fashion.

Replace: The simplest of the screen effects; it replaces one screen with another by a direct overlay as fast as your hardware allows.

Scroll: One screen appears to wipe off another. In and out scrolls can occur within a frame.

Spiral: The spiral effect replaces a picture by moving a new picture onto the screen in a circular direction, either clockwise or counterclockwise.

Square to center: Moves from four corners to inside in a square pattern.

Square to edges: Moves from square in center to outer edges.

Weave: Moves a picture onto the screen from two directions at once, converging at the center to present the whole screen.

Wipe: Causes the new picture to overlay the old in any direction: left, right, up, down, in, out.

Additionally, some, but not all, transitions can be designed to enter from the left, right, up, down, or in and out. They can then exit using the same or another effect.

LCD Units—The Ultimate Transparent Transparency

LCD units are based on a liquid crystal display technology. With this system, whatever is displayed on the computer screen is simultaneously displayed on a large screen in the same way an overhead transparency would be displayed.

An LCD unit is a panel about 2½ inches thick and works with an overhead projection unit. The unit sits on the light stage of an overhead projector and is connected to the projector and to a computer. It consists of a transparent area and a frame that contains necessary circuitry, such as cables and an electric connector. Some units have a remote control device.

Advantages of LCD units are:

1. They are portable and lightweight.
2. They are inexpensive, efficient, high tech.
3. There's no need to generate transparencies.
4. They can interact dynamically with screen images.
5. They are software independent; you can use any program.

6. A "what if" question can be answered instantly. A self-running demonstration can appear animated.

There are some disadvantages:

1. Color is limited, and what is there is not brilliant.
2. Resolutions are low—640 × 480 pixels at best; images are grainy compared to a transparency or a 35 mm slide.
3. LCD projectors require both an overhead projector and a host computer.

LCDs are ideal for teaching and marketing situations. They are proving invaluable for hands-on training. Students can use their own computers to interact with procedures projected from the trainer's computer. LCDs can be used with noncomputer types of training, too.

The units are being used in boardrooms where the presenter

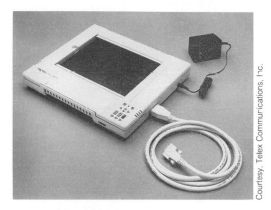

The Telex Magnabyte Model 5040 is IBM/clone compatible.

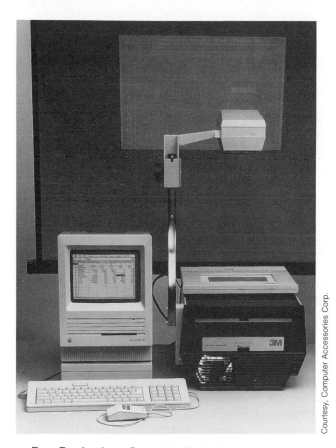

Data Display from Computer Accessories is one of three Data Display units. This Model A 342 is compatible with several Macintosh computer models.

Sharp Electronics QA–50 displays color images in eight shades of gray. It has a six-button remote control unit.

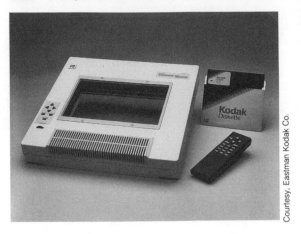

Courtesy, Eastman Kodak Co.

Courtesy, Eastman Kodak Co.

The Kodak DATASHOW HR Projection Pad has an 18-button remote control unit. DATASHOW units are available for the Macintosh and IBM systems.

The hand remote unit works in tandem with a small box attached to the computer. The hand unit must be roughly lined up with the infrared unit. Slides can be accessed randomly as well as serially.

can dynamically work with spreadsheet, project planning, and other systems that may benefit from instant updating and "what if" answers.

Designing for LCD Projection

The first LCD units on the market were designed only to project in black and white (and gray shades) and in low resolution from the PC. The next wave consisted of units that could project some color and higher resolutions. Almost all companies are now designing systems for the MS DOS, EGA, and VGE systems and for the Macintosh and Apple II computers.

A few units, such as those by In-Focus Systems, include a megabyte of memory. That means it's possible to load a program into the LCD unit and play it without a computer connection.

Most LCD panels are easy to carry in a case; they're about 12 × 15 inches. They weigh under 13 pounds, though the plug-in unit can add 3 pounds. They are inexpensive, with prices ranging from about $700 to $5,000.

There are problems with these systems that developers are striving to eliminate. They can overheat unless a fan, or other technology, is built in to cool the system during a long projection period. Some tend to deteriorate the image after the unit has been on 45 minutes to an hour, so they must be shut down to cool for 10 or more minutes.

True color is a problem in projection. Some manufacturers claim 16-color projection, but reality is a picture of 16 different shades, which are pastel-like hues. They help distinguish different bars on a chart, slices of a pie, or color changes in a bullet chart. If a color image is to be projected in black and white, it must be designed carefully because gray scales interpret the colors differently, and sentences or bars of a chart may drop out of the picture.

Green, brown, blue, and white will project as white. Black, red, and magenta will project as black or gray. Green lettering on a white background will show as all white, and the letters will disappear.

Colors of objects can be affected by background color. An exploded slice of pie in magenta may disappear against a black background—or it may show up as gray. Light-blue bars against a white background may vanish in monochrome. When a color is lost, reversing the screen color from black on white to white on black may solve the problem.

Presentation software such as Lotus Freelance Plus 3.0 and HOTSHOT Presents can convert color palettes to a wide range of grays or let you select gray scale for colors. They work especially well for producing LCD projected shows. Animation programs such as FantaVision on the Apple IIe and the PC, Autodesk Animator on the PC, and Macromind Animator on the Mac are good for animation.

"Using a computer screen or projecting the show will probably never replace traditional presentation media," says Stephen Brightbill, president of Brightbill-Roberts & Co. "However, the computer screen is another viable delivery device that has become one more way for you to make points with presentations."

Sources for Information
Desktop Slide Show Software

The following software includes slide show features with special transition effects, and/or animation and sound. Please refer to the software list in Appendix B for addresses.

Software	Company
35 mm Express	Business & Professional Software
Autodesk Animator	Autodesk
Cricket Presents	Cricket Software
Dan Bricklin's Demo II	Peter Norton Computing Co.
Dashboard 2.0	Bridgeway Publishing Corp.
Dr. Halo III 3.0	IMSI
Executive Picture Show	PC Software of San Diego
Freelance Plus 3.0	Lotus Dev. Corp.
Graph Plus	Micrografx, Inc.
Grasp 3.1	Paul Mace Software, Inc.

Software	Company
Harvard Graphics	Software Publishing Corp.
HOTSHOT Presents	Symsoft, Inc.
IBM Storyboard Plus	IBM
MacroMind Director	MacroMind, Inc.
MORE II	Symantec Corp.
Panorama 1.0	AT&T Graphics Software Lab
PC Paintbrush Plus	ZSoft Corp.
PCEMCEE	Computer Support Corp.
PC-Key Draw	Oedware
PictureIt 2.4	General Parametrics Corp.
Presentation System	SML Services, Inc.
ShowPartner F/X	Brightbill-Roberts & Co. Ltd.
Slide Presentation	Truevision, Inc.
StandOut!	Letraset
SuperCard	Silicon Beach Software, Inc.
VCN Concorde	Visual Communications Network
Video Works II	MicroMind, Inc.
Xerox Presents	Xerox Corp.

LCD Flat Panel Display Units[*]

Bell & Howell Video Systems/Eiki Intl.
6800 McCormick Blvd.
Chicago, IL 60645
312   673-3300 or 312   675-7600

Buhl Industries, Inc.
Audio-Visual Equipment
1401 Maple Ave.
Fairlawn, NJ 07460
210   423-2800

Chisholm
910 Campesi
Campbell, CA 95008
408   559-1111

Computer Accessories Corporation—Proxima
6610 Nancy Ridge Dr.
San Diego, CA 92121
619   436-4395, 457-5500

Dukane Corp.
2900 Dukane Dr.
St. Charles, IL 60174
708   584-2300 or 800   356-6540
800   634-2800 (in Illinois)

Eastman Kodak Company (DATASHOW)
343 State St.
Rochester, NY 14650
716   724-3313
800   242-2424

Eiki International
Audio-Visual Equipment
27882 Camino Capistrano
Laguna Niguel, CA 92677
714   831-2511

In-Focus Systems
7649 S.W. Mohawk St.
Tualatin, OR 97062
503   692-4476
800   327-7231

nView Corp.
11835 Canon Blvd. #B–107
Newport News, VA 23606
804   873-1354

Sharp Electronics Corp.
Sharp Plaza
Mahwah, NJ 07430
201   529-8741

[*]See Chapter 16 for large screen data/video display units.

Telex Communications, Inc.
9600 Aldrich Ave. S.
Minneapolis, MN 55420
612   884-4051

Toshiba America
1101A Lake Cook Rd.
Deerfield, IL 60015
708   945-1500

Visualon, Inc.
3044 Payne Ave.
Cleveland, OH 44114
800   321-3860
800   362-3108 (OH)

11

A Gallery of Art and Advertising Designs

There are millions of ways to communicate as many ideas and more than one way to communicate a single idea. In any field that deals with images, the computer can be the latest tool in the artistic paint box.

The computer, as medium, has features unparalleled by previous "new" media such as temperas, oils, and acrylics when they were introduced. Here is a tool that enables the artist to select from hundreds of possible choices that he may never think of on his own. Those choices can be displayed in a few minutes. The same picture can instantly be "tried" in different colors. The same lettering can appear in different sizes, be moved to a new layout, or change shape in seconds. The artist still must make the esthetic choice; the artist still is in control of the images that are produced.

What is another reason for artists to embrace computers as tools? Computers reduce the time required to achieve a finished work of art. They eliminate much of the repetitive drudge work that requires more tenacity than creativity.

The microcomputer is rapidly appearing on terrain where only big systems dared to tread previously. James Hance of James Hance & Associates, an advertising and graphic communication company in San Diego, uses a Macintosh to create and present ideas. He says:

> The graphics software, MacPaint, allows free form illustration to be accomplished on the computer with an enormous supply of tools and special effects. MacDraw lets the artist manipulate shapes and view art as large as 4 feet × 8 feet. An entire 48-page publication can be created and viewed on-screen at one time or zoomed for each page layout. MacVision adds the visual power of a video camera to the computer's arsenal. Three-dimensional objects can be digitized to create art, then further altered and arranged on the computer. In my line of work, this means I can easily create tight photo composition layouts for photographers to follow, or "camera ready" art for advertising or publications when the particular effects of the MacVision system are appropriate.

We have assembled a potpourri of computer-generated art used in advertising campaigns, book jackets, record covers, labels, logos, greeting cards, packaging, wallpaper design, prints, fabrics, menu covers, and annual reports from every industry where images are used to attract, illustrate, and sell. Several were winners in contests sponsored by software or hardware companies.

These examples are offered as a gallery of design ideas for typefaces, layout, images, textures, subject areas, mood, and application. Observe that often a low resolution slide can be as appealing and effective as one with high resolution; the dots themselves become texture and pattern.

The slides support the theory that little more need be said when the image tells the story.

C   *Show and tell. The slide combines several picture elements the company can use to produce slides for clients.*

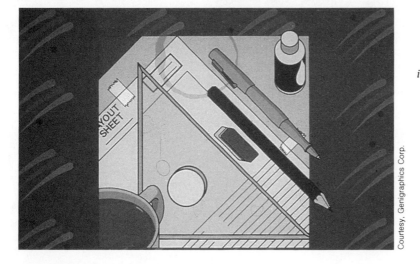

The old, cleverly and realistically interpreted by the new.

Artist: Marilyn Abers. Courtesy, Jones Photocolor, Inc.

Courtesy, Genigraphics Corp.

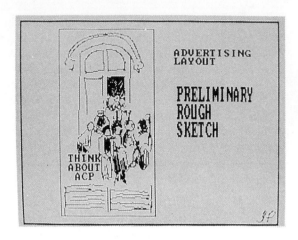

From rough idea, through preliminary sketch, to final layout. Each step can be captured and retained for reference. The final layout is a build-up of the subsequent sketches.

Step 1

Step 2

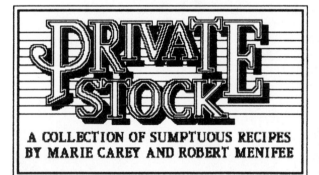

A book cover design project. The letters are designed, then tested in different type styles. Pushing a few buttons is easy compared to tracing and redrawing when hand work is required. The computer affords scores of "test" designs in a few minutes for type size, layout, background, and framing. All are easily and quickly printed as near finished art for presentation to a client and, with final touches, for production.

Final Art

Alternate Shape

Three designs for fashion illustrations. The computer is capable of many techniques from sketch, to outline, to fill, and color. Each figure can be isolated and kept on file; the next time the shape is required, it doesn't have to be completely redrawn. The image can be processed and reprocessed as the concept for the ad requires.

[C] *(Two of these photographs are reproduced in color elsewhere in this book.)*

Nature captured

Courtesy, Dicomed Corp.

Courtesy, Dicomed Corp.

Courtesy, Dicomed Corp.

Courtesy, Genigraphics Corp.

Courtesy, Genigraphics Corp.

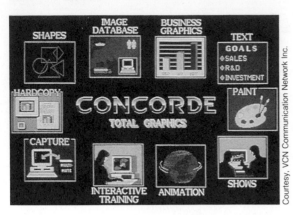

Courtesy, VCN Communication Network Inc.

Artist: Coleen Sterling. Courtesy, VCN Communication Network Inc.

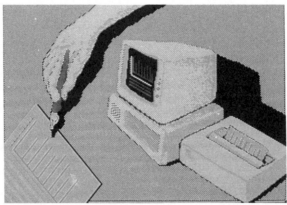

Artist: Kirk Rose. Courtesy, VCN Communication Network Inc.

Artist: Alfred DeAngelo. Courtesy, VCN Communication Network Inc.

Artist: Stacy Eisenbrey. Courtesy, VCN Communication Network Inc.

The photo at top left illustrates the type of output available in VCN Concorde software. The other illustrations were developed as potential bookcovers. Several images have been scanned and then edited.

*Created on a Dec Pro and
photographed with a Celtic image camera.*

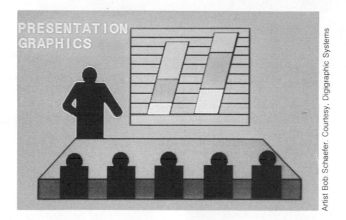

Created on an Apple IIe.

*Created with the PenPad by Pencept and
photographed with a Celtic image camera.*

People

Courtesy, Genigraphics Corp.

Courtesy, Dicomed Corp.

Courtesy, Management Graphics, Inc.,
Minneapolis, MN

Places

Courtesy, EIDOS

A computer-generated scene for a theatre stage set.

C *(These three photographs are reproduced in color.)*

Courtesy, Genigraphics Corp.

Artist: Bonnie Pelnar. Courtesy, Genigraphics Corp.

Vehicles

Artist Bonnie Pelnar. Courtesy, Genigraphics Corp.

Courtesy, Genigraphics Corp.

Chromatics Image. Courtesy, Dunn, Inc.

C

Courtesy, Management Graphics, Minneapolis, MN

C

Artist: Scott Lewczak. Courtesy, Artronics, Inc.

Products and textures

Courtesy, Genigraphics Corp.

Courtesy, Dicomec Corp.

Artist: Ellen Rosenthal. Courtesy, Brilliant Image, Inc.

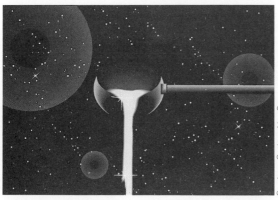

Courtesy, Genigraphics Corp.

Courtesy, Genigraphics Corp.

Logos

Courtesy, Decision Vision

Artist: David Lapidus. Courtesy, Brilliant Image, Inc.

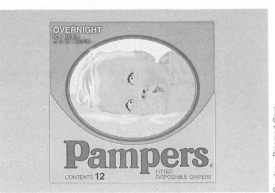

Courtesy, Management Graphics, Minneapolis, MN

C

Courtesy, Digigraphic Systems

Courtesy, Dicomed Corp.

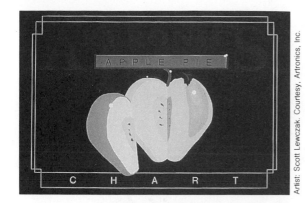

Art is everywhere

Artist: Conrad Dunton, using PC Paintbrush. Courtesy, IMSi

Artist and courtesy, Scott Daly

Artist and courtesy, Scott Daly

Courtesy, Genigraphics Corp.

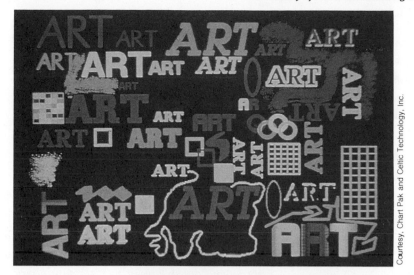

C

12

Software that Generates Presentation Visuals

There are several truisms about any graphics software package:

It will probably not do all you expect it to.

It will probably do some things you never expected it to do.

It is not as easy to learn as you hoped (or as advertising claims).

If something doesn't work as the manual says it should, it isn't necessarily your fault. Manuals are often ambiguous or wrong.

No matter what you buy today, it will be improved and updated next week.

Prices do not reflect program capability. A $49 package may do as much, or more, or perform better in some areas than a $400 package.

The choices are perplexing.

You can undoubtedly add to this list as you plumb the depths of graphics programs. To the newcomer they present a set of puzzlements that have little basis in previous experience. After you have muddled through one or two graphics programs, subsequent ones are easier. You become familiar with terms, routines, different modes, icons (or symbols) that show a line, an eraser, a save, and so on.

Graphics software runs a wide price gamut in the microcomputer market. Everything is available from public domain packages for the cost of a disk (through a user's group library or electronic bulletin board), to a mid-price range of $350–$500, and on to the $1,000–$2,000 range. Software for workstations and minicomputers is generally more expensive. But prices are constantly being revised and reduced. If you are not sure of your needs or what a program might do for your business, select a low-price program to become familiar with terms and routines. When you know what one program can or cannot do, you'll have a set of standards by which to judge others. Selecting and learning about graphics is no different than challenging a word processing, spreadsheet, data base, or other program.

With this empirical knowledge, you can begin to evaluate your needs and the available commercial software. Several features of a program will be obvious from the advertising, an analysis of the table of contents in a manual, and the help card (by the number and type of commands). Refer to current reviews of programs in computer publications. Ask other people what they use and for what purpose. Write to software companies for literature about their products.

Purchasing Problems

Potential problems exist with software purchases in the microcomputer marketplace. Often, you can't see or try the program in a real situation. A computer software store may have a demo disk to show off the program's best points. That will introduce you to the features of a program and give you an insight into commands and routines. Still, you can never be sure how the program will work in actual use.

Another problem is that shrink-wrapped packages thwart perusing manuals and prompt cards. Don't let that stop you. If a program costs a few hundred dollars, you should be able to test-drive it. (Some stores have shrink-wrap machines in a back room for redoing those that have been opened.)

A company that is a potential buyer of several copies of a program should expect a vendor to demonstrate it for the people who will be using it. Those people should work with the program for several hours for each application it purports to accomplish as well as for creating, saving, outputting, and retrieving—especially retrieving for an on-line slide show. One package tested worked magnificently until the slides had to be retrieved for a show; then it required using the company's compatible word processing software, keying in codes, and writing a program routine. Colors selected were not saved by the program; they had to be called by line commands.

Many graphics programs are copy-protected and require a system disk to function. If you have a hard disk drive, this means that you may also need to use the floppy disk to initialize and run the program. If something happens to the system disk, how long will it take to receive a new backup? What will the charge be?

Protecting Your Purchase

There are a few ways to exercise a "buyer beware" credo. One is to choose programs that have a 30-day guarantee. Put them through their paces in those 30 days. Know who stands behind the guarantee—the software company or the store.

Another way is to charge a purchase on a credit card account. If the software does not meet your needs or standards, or if it is not mature and bugfree, write an "intention to return" letter to the dealer explaining why you are returning the software. Write

A sampling from over 90 software packages reviewed for this book. They include presentation, chart, paint, draw, design, desktop publishing, and accessory programs that can be used for generating quality visuals on film and on paper.

Photo: Author

to the credit card company and enclose a copy of your letter to the dealer. The credit card company will investigate the charge; you have a 60-day grace period during which time you will not be assessed a late charge. But this must be in *writing*. Read the fine print in your credit card agreement for specific procedures.

It is possible to borrow a copy from the software dealer to try for a day or two. A two-way trust must be established: you trust the software store to sell you what you can use; they trust you not to make an illegal copy.

Support

Technical support should be available from the software company and the dealer. It would be unrealistic to expect a retail vendor to know the intricacies of each program sold for a variety of systems. Software companies almost always supply technical support. If that is so, it may not matter whether you pay full or discounted prices. Some software companies offer "extended" support, which they may term differently. They contract to provide telephone support for a limited number of calls, or for unlimited calls over a period of time for a basic support fee.

Software vendors who support workstations offer a thorough briefing and ongoing support. This will vary by vendor and can range from free to fee contracts.

Programs for Different Purposes

Software serves different purposes and industries. (See Appendix B for a listing of programs and vendors.) Several programs have evolved that are specifically for presentations. They combine an astounding number of features culled from many programs.

There is a broad range of software applications that can be used to generate presentation visuals. Software will produce word charts, data charts, organization charts, diagrams charts—all the examples throughout this book. Many contain drawing and word processing capabilities. Others will only generate charts and graphs. Some are only draw programs; some are for draw and paint. Generally, more specific programs have more features for their particular applications.

There are programs that concentrate on sophisticated designer tools or animation. There are many programs for computer-aided design and engineering. Integrated spreadsheet programs have chart capabilities. Word processing programs can generate text for slide making and for overhead transparencies. The choices are infinite.

It's hard to judge all the features you'll need until you use a program over a period of time. You can read reviews and watch a demonstration. Sometimes you can test a program at a conference or in a dealer's showroom. Still, until you apply a program to your specific needs, it's like breaking in a new pair of shoes. It's hard to evaluate where it feels good and where it pinches until you break them in. Even if they pinch a little, you get used to them and wear them anyway.

Feature Leapfrog

Software developers seem to play feature leapfrog. New programs with expanded features enter the market constantly and new features are added to updates of existing programs. In the MS DOS world, programs and their interfaces differ greatly but many accomplish similar tasks. People begin to think about how they like to work with a program as well as what the program will accomplish.

Several programs work with Microsoft Windows. That results in a more standardized user interface than DOS. Windows use icons to establish a Macintosh-like environment.

Many programs retain the command line menu structure and they are efficient and excellent. Lotus Freelance Plus is a good example. Others are SlideWrite Plus, Graphics Gallery, and Image-Builder. Several have mouse support; with others you navigate about the program with the keyboard.

Macintosh Software Is Stunning

When the Macintosh II appeared with color, five major companies introduced presentation software. New features were added.

Entire slide shows of 16, 24, or more slides can be lined up on screen, studied, and sorted. Speaker notes and handouts can be printed in different formats. Slide files can be generated from text outlines; a word changed in the slide image is automatically updated in the text outline.

Adding, moving, deleting, or editing any line, color, or single element in a chart can be done with a quick movement of the mouse. The user can generate and store templates so slides can be consistent. If a presentation requires updating, an added or amended slide will match the originals without reselecting fonts, sizes, and colors.

Hewlett-Packard's Graphics Gallery software collection illustrates a menu from Charting Gallery that contains icons at the left of the screen and a command line at the bottom, with a work area in the center. It's compatible with MS DOS systems.

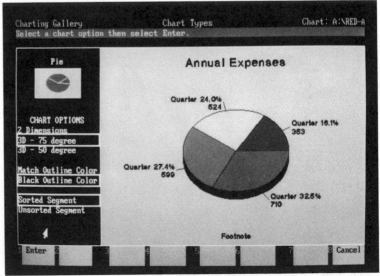

Courtesy, Hewlett-Packard Co.

MS DOS Software Takes on Mac Characteristics

MS DOS developers continued to evolve additional concepts and adopted features initiated for the Macintosh. Xerox took its cue from Mac programming and offered similar features for MS DOS in Xerox Presents and Xerox Graph.

More new features appeared in well-established programs such as 35 mm Express and Harvard Graphics. Lotus Freelance retained its menu-driven user interface and piled new features into each new version. Applause II brought in menus adopted from its workstation look-alike and a new type of interface was born.

Micrografx's Draw and Designer, Computer Support Corporation's Arts & Letters, and Corel Draw, all working under Microsoft Windows, incorporate ways to manipulate portions of a line using Bezier curves. These programs can be used for presentations but require more artistic talent than just filling in form sheets to generate charts.

The programs have predrawn library images that can be mixed, altered, and individualized. These images are indispensible for people who do not have inherent art ability or training. Trained graphics artists use them, too, because they are time savers.

General Programs Begin to Tout Presentation Capability

Companies with nonpresentation software programs in specialized areas want to hang on to their users. AutoCAD, for example, includes drivers to the Agfa Matrix image recorder, which most service bureaus have so users can generate slides directly from AutoCAD. Until the driver was available, several software gyrations were required to obtain a slide.

Even word processing programs are in the act. Several slide companies will convert word processed files into boardroom quality text and bullet charts. No graphics software is needed.

Choices—Choices—Choices

Now the user has many choices. When it comes to high-quality, high-resolution visuals, it doesn't matter which program is chosen, as long as it contains film recorder drivers. With Mac software, often only a coordinating or bridge program is needed. Your software choice will be based on several points within three areas:

1. Features:
   a. If you need special features, does the program have them? Perhaps chart formats for scientific data? Demographic data for mapping?
   b. Does it support your printers and other output devices?

2. Which user interface do you prefer to use?
   a. There are pull-down menus, Lotus-like menus, and a combination of both. How well are the menus implemented?
   b. What type of input device? Some programs work only with keyboard input; others support keyboard, a mouse, and a digitizing tablet.
3. Lumped into the third area would be:
   a. Program cost and training time.
   b. Hardware available including system memory and disk space.
   c. What slide service or image recorder will be used? Not all software is imaged by all slide companies at prices one wants to pay (see chapter 13).

Beyond that, users should investigate output quality and a software company's reputation for support.

Keystroke Testing

When you begin to evaluate programs you can get an idea of a program's efficiency with a keyboard (or mouse movement) test. Compare a few procedures in one program against the same procedures in another.

For example, how many keystrokes or mouse button clicks are needed to input the same line of text, add a bullet, resize the line, move it to a new position, change color, change font size, then save the file?

How to Assess Your Needs

Before you buy a software package and necessary hardware (if you don't have it) how do you know what you want? That can be a problem when you don't know what programs have to offer.

Analyze the chart output you now use. What kind of data is involved? Must they be shown as bar, pie, or line charts? Are they report graphs and charts for in-house use? Promotions for out-of-house? How sophisticated (or crude) are they now? If they are not up to the examples in this book, it's time to improve. You can be sure your sharp competitors will already be using quality graphics.

Do you need overhead transparencies? 35 mm slides? Do you have a use for on-screen slide shows? Do you use graphics for advertising or designing? Desktop publishing?

When you have clearly defined your current needs, try to anticipate how you might want your visuals and output improved and supplemented. A reason for using these packages is to expand beyond your present limitations, to burst through constraints and take advantage of new opportunities.

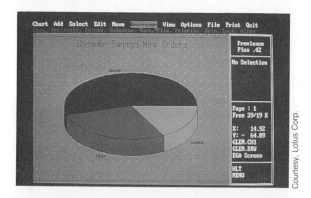

Courtesy, Lotus Corp.

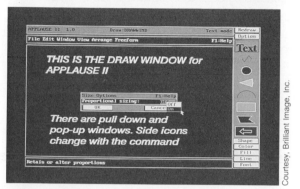

Courtesy, Brilliant Image, Inc.

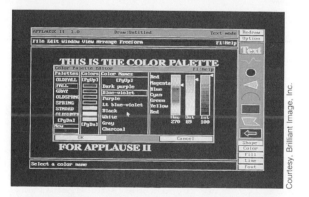

Courtesy, Brilliant Image, Inc.

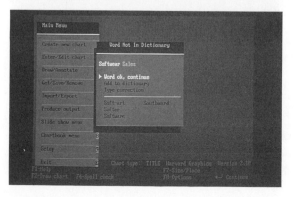

C   *Lotus Freelance Plus 3.0 uses a command line menu; the commands are words along the top of the program from which you choose action. Different levels appear when a new type command is selected. Choices can be made by typing the first letter of a command, or moving the cursor to the word with an arrow key or a mouse. In different menus you can use chart entry forms or work directly on the chart.*

Applause II offers menus with icons at right, pull-down menus at top, and help comments at bottom. A data or word chart made in its appropriate menu can be brought into the draw menu for enhancement and fine tuning. Images from the 750 pictures in the library are easily added.

C   *Default color palettes are provided in all presentation software. However, a program should offer the option of altering the palettes easily. Applause II shows colors in the current palette at left, then uses a sliding color scale for adjusting colors, shown at right.*

Harvard Graphics uses overlapping pull-down frames in the main menu. Once selections are made, another series of menus appears on each screen. They differ depending on the screen information that is entered into forms. Then the chart can be previewed, and elements can be altered in a draw module.

Table 12–1 (at the end of this chapter) will help you understand features in graphics software, what is available, and what you may need or want. Place a sheet of paper over columns 2 and 3 to evaluate additional packages. Or photocopy the pages and use them to evaluate as many programs as you like.

Column A: This is a compiled list of features in many programs. (No one program has them all.)

Column B: Check items you are now using. Any blank spaces will give you an idea of what's available that you may not know about or have access to in current software.

Column C: Estimate what you must have now.

Column D: Estimate what you may want to use in the future. Compare columns B, C, and D; then look for software that will give you the improvements desired.

Columns E, F, and G: Software packages (programs).

Filling in the chart will familiarize you with terms and features and give you an understanding of what a program may have. When you see a term or procedure you don't understand, focus on learning what it is. Several features may be filled in by studying the documentation, noting the table of contents and index in the manual, or working with the demo. Features not listed may not be in the software.

Evaluating Software

Programs have as many variations as there are programmers who write them, yet there are general similarities. The table at the end of this chapter provides a checklist of features culled from all programs reviewed. No one program will have them all. Features listed in a program today would be obsolete next month, and again in six months. New versions appear frequently; often updates appear within a version and these may be offered to registered users free or at a minimal charge.

The following discussions are keyed to the headings and roman numerals in the "feature" column (A) in Table 12–1. Watch computer publications for similar checklists. Look for software reviews. Study ads. Write to the companies for information. Phone technical support departments to clarify any points not covered in your research.

I   Software Information

Before you purchase software from a dealer, it's wise to call the software company and learn the number of the latest version. A dealer may have old stock when a new version is introduced.

You could easily buy software that is months behind new releases. Companies do offer updates, but that can take time and extra charges. Usually someone in technical support or marketing will have the answer.

If the vendor is selling the current version, find out when the next release is due. Ask about the update policy. It may pay to wait a week or two.

A list price and discounted prices can vary by as much as 10 to 40 percent. Dealers who discount a program heavily may not offer after-purchase support. If you pay list price, you're entitled to some support. Know what to expect. Training sessions? Telephone support during what hours? If several packages are purchased for a department, will the vendor supply a training session in-house?

Don't expect support when you purchase mail order. If you get it, consider it a bonus.

Some software companies provide a trial period for the software, usually 15 or 30 days, to see if you like it.

Every software package includes a user agreement before you unseal the disk container. Some warranty disks if they're defective; often they must be returned within a given time period after purchase. You may have to show a bill of sale.

It's wise to register your software when a registration form is supplied. A company may provide newsletters and update information to registered users. Unfortunately, many also provide your name to allied services and you may begin to receive unsolicited mail.

If you see product reviews, clip or photocopy them, note publication and date, and file them. Use a code to indicate a comparison rating, perhaps 1 to 10 or A to D.

II Hardware Requirements

What system is required to run the program? There's no point in reviewing a program for a DOS system if you're running a Macintosh or Amiga.

As programs become more sophisticated, memory and disk space requirements increase. Many DOS programs now require a megabyte or more of memory over the initial 640K. They may take up to 3 to 5 megabytes of hard disk space if you load tutorial, templates, and slide libraries along with the program. Be sure you have ample memory and hard disk space before you invest in a program. Or plan to buy it if you don't.

DOS software may also require an EGA or VGA board for color. Mac programs may require the Mac II hardware series. Many will work in monochrome also; output colors are assigned to elements by a numerical code provided by the slide service.

DOS programs may require an AT or OS/2 class machine; they

will not function on an 8088. They may need a high-density disk drive to load software. Programs may ship with either or both high-density floppies and 3½ inch floppies. If you have only one or the other, be sure to select the proper format. Most heavy memory programs also function best on a machine with a 10-megahertz or higher speed. Slower machines will redraw screens very slowly.

Can you use only the keyboard? Will a mouse or digitizing tablet make the system more efficient? Will it accept scanned images? If you have these peripherals, will the program support the ones you have? Most support a Microsoft and Mouse Systems mouse; others are usually compatible with these installations. This may not be true with digitizing tablets, light pens, or all scanners. If the program doesn't support scanned images directly via a TIFF (Tagged Interface File Format) file, you may be able to bring them into another package and save them in a format the program can read.

III   User Conveniences

The user interface requires more careful consideration than most people have been led to believe. Entire seminars are conducted on how programmers should design menus. Menus can be graceful or clumsy or a combination of both. They're graceful when actions you need to perform with a mouse, for example, are close together in the order you will most likely use them.

A light table or slide sorter feature is shown from Aldus Persuasion. Reduced sizes of each file can be viewed simultaneously and studied for sequence, consistency, and content. They can be moved about and repositioned on-screen. Several Macintosh programs have this feature.

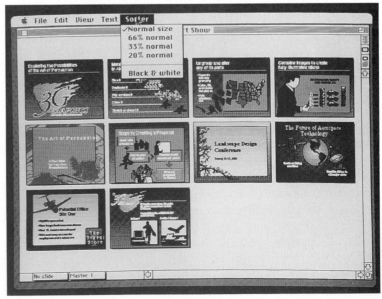

Photo: Author

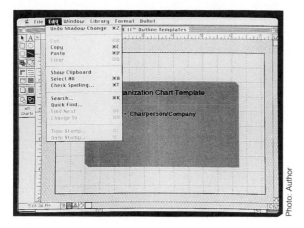

Photo: Author

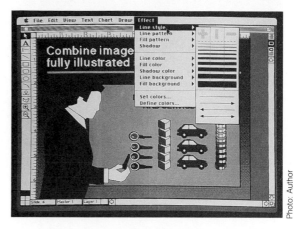

Photo: Author

A menu from More II illustrates the consistent Macintosh user interface. But each program has a unique set of tools at left. More II generates word slides from a text outline; then each chart can be individually enhanced. More II has a spelling checker.

Aldus Persuasion also illustrates the consistent Macintosh top menu line. However, it has a different set of drawing tools than those in More II. Shown are clip-art images that have been combined. Pull-down menus provide additional tools.

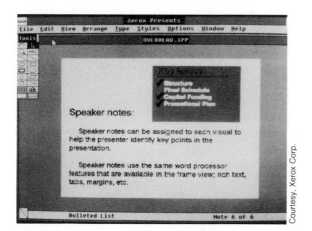

Courtesy, Xerox Corp.

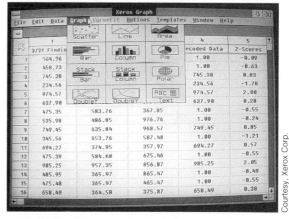

Courtesy, Xerox Corp.

Xerox Presents for MS DOS systems works through MicroSoft Windows. Almost all the presentation software provide a feature that lets you generate speaker notes. The slide is printed small with space allowed for text.

Xerox Graph is a sister program to Xerox Presents. It also works through Windows in the MS DOS environment. It provides more chart types than Xerox Presents. After data is entered, or transferred from a spreadsheet program, you select the chart type from the graph menu.

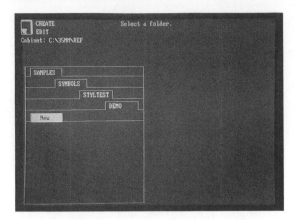

A series of steps and the menus from 35 mm Express for MS DOS users. The user interface has both command line and icons. A new folder is highlighted to open a new file.

Text and data are filled into a chart form.

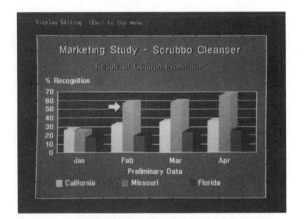

The chart is instantly generated for preview. Additional editing can be accomplished directly on the chart by pointing to an element and indicating the change required when the editing menu is selected.

To select colors for any element in the chart, or for the whole chart, a pull-down menu offers the choices.

Pull-down menu interfaces may be used with a mouse, but they should have alternative keyboard menus. Programs with command-line menus (as in Lotus 1–2–3) along the top of the screen should be accessible by typing the first letter of the menu word, and by moving the cursor using the keyboard or mouse. Each menu level should be different enough from another level so you always know where you are. There should be an on-screen explanation of the chosen command.

Pop-up menus should be movable. If not, they shouldn't pop up on top of an area where you're working. They should be well outlined or framed so they are easy to read on a busy screen.

Graphics programs rely heavily on tab, escape, space, alt, function, and arrow keys, plus the enter key. A keyboard is used gracefully when consecutive commands use logical key sequencing. Your hands or fingers should not have to fly all over the mouse pad or keyboard. The program should also use the same keys for the same kind of functions in different menus.

Does the program provide form sheets or worksheets to fill in data for charts? Can it import files from Lotus and other spreadhseet software? Are commands easy to carry out? Can you make choices for layout purposes? Can you place tags on axes? Values on the tops of bars? Change line thickness of frames and grids?

Is what you see on-screen the same as the output image on film or paper? That is the WYSIWYG (What You See Is What You Get) feature.

Can you work directly on the chart? Or must you return to a template to edit items and then repreview the chart?

If there are changes, must you go back to the form sheet? The ability to work directly on the chart is an advantage.

IV Chart Types

Templates are predesigned formats for charts. By using well-designed templates the user may not have to make design decisions. He only needs to provide the information and the program will produce visuals in a proper format. All slides within one presentation will be consistent regarding color, fonts, and layout. Many programs provide a couple of dozen templates. They have additional templates for color, backgrounds, and so forth so that some mixing can be accomplished.

Templates are fine when they're well done. Their formatting should be flexible so you can customize or create new ones.

A global reformat feature first appeared in Macintosh software. If you create a presentation with several slides and decide to change font, background color, title size, or another element, changing it on one slide can affect the change on all slides. Without this feature, you would have to redo each slide individually.

Most presentation and charting software will generate several chart styles from text or data. Draw, paint, and design software packages may not. Then charts have to be constructed or grabbed and brought in from another program.

The variety of type fonts, chart styles, and variations is probably the most important reason to accept or reject a program. You

Courtesy, Aldus Corp.

Aldus Persuasion provides attractive templates. Each type of chart is spilled into the template so titles and other elements are consistent. Yet the user can edit and change any element.

In Applause II you select a template and then fill in the chart or text data and it will conform to the template layout. Any element can be changed or rearranged by working directly on the chart in the draw window.

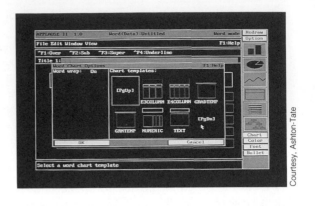

should also observe how and where tags are placed and if they conform to the good design principles stated in earlier chapters.

Word Charts.   With word charts making up 70 to 75 percent of all presentations made, it's imperative that the program provide the tools to do them well. There should be text style sheets so that bullet charts, for example, will be composed instantly as you type in words. You should be able to select the layout. You should have options for justifying text left, right, or center.

How many fonts are provided? Two fonts can become boring quickly; five is a good number. More is better providing you don't use all of them in one slide. There may be options for downloading other fonts to a laser printer and using those. You should be able to emphasize a single letter or number, or a word, and to use underline, bold, or italics. These manipulations should be accomplished easily and not require several different entry procedures.

Does the program generate word charts automatically from an outline? Does the program let you create that outline? If you make a change in the outline when you're working on the slide, will that change appear in the original outline?

Many presentation programs have a spell checker and also search and replace capabilities. They're like mini-word processors within the presentation package.

The above criteria apply to other charts that need copy: title and text charts, organization charts, and so forth.

The next question is: does the program generate those types of charts easily? Title and text charts offer no problem, but in some programs, organization chart boxes must be constructed with box drawing tools. In others, they're generated; but when they're generated, you may forego some flexibility. If you need software for organization charts, be sure to see how easily the organization chart happens before you buy. How many levels are supported, and can you disassemble the chart and move elements about individually?

In many programs, you select the chart type from a thumbnail picture of the chart. This is from Graph-in-the-Box.

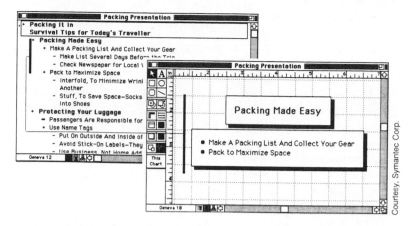

The outline and a resulting bullet chart from the selected levels. The chart is generated automatically when a format is chosen from the icons at the bottom of the screen. This also illustrates several tools in the MORE II tool box, at left.

Courtesy, Symantec Corp.

Within all chart styles you should be able to choose different textures, outlining, and three dimensions. Some programs will let you separate and move individual elements, others will not.

Bar Charts. There are many variations of a basic horizontal or vertical bar chart: clustered, stacked, overlapped, three dimensional, bar/line, bar/pie, step graphs, and more. Most programs provide these basics, but if you need formats for scientific, weather, or other specialized applications, look for a program that provides those formats.

How much chart customizing can you do? Can you eliminate frames or portions of them? Change tag locations? Change colors of elements? Add grid lines in different weights and spacing? Is there a limit to the number of bars you can have?

Pie Charts. There should be a maximum number of pie slices allowed to prevent you from overdoing a pie. The order entry for pie charts should be flexible so you can decide how you want

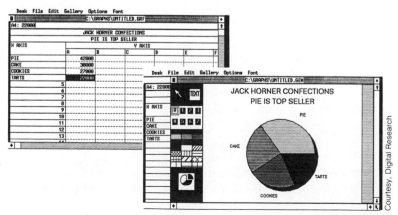

GEM Graph is one of many programs in which you fill in a form with the data, then preview it. In this screen, a pull-down menu shows the chart style, slice numbers and textures, and other elements that may be selected for a given slice.

Courtesy, Digital Research

the slices to fall and where you want the largest segment to be. The default slice should begin at the 12:00 position and others should move clockwise. You should be able to explode and change the textures and colors of slices.

How many pies are allowed per chart? Four should be maximum. You should be able to tilt a chart and have it retain its perspective and proportions. A 3–D effect and a drop shadow add to the professionalism.

Line and Surface Charts.   In these chart styles you need formats that will let you generate a chart style that will best interpret your data. Are there different line styles, including dotted, dashed, and solid lines in different weights and colors? What is the maximum number of data points, data sets, and markers per line?

Other Graph Types.   If you need a high/low/close graph format, you'll want to see what data variations are possible. The same is true with bubble charts.

Specialty Charts.   Gantt and PERT charts do not appear in most presentation software packages. If you need them, look for a chart package that does have them; be sure the programs have drivers to the output devices you'll use. That is true with maps, too. Some programs will include maps, but often they are predrawn contour maps of the United States or sections of Europe and other countries. You can tag these maps and use them to show locations. However, they do not generate mapped data from statistics; that requires special mapping software.

Analysis.   Does the program only output charts? Or does it provide analytical capabilities? For what types of charts?

V   Drawing Tools/Free-Form Graphics

Today's programs include an incredible array of enhancement features along with automatic chart generation from data. The basics are lines, boxes, rectangles, ovals, and circles. Some will have arc and freehand curve drawing features; boxes can be sharp or round cornered. Triangles, diamonds, parallelograms, polygons, and other geometric shapes can be drawn easily. Objects can be moved, copied, sized, stretched, shrunk, filled, and hollowed. Bit-mapped images can be changed to object-oriented art using a feature called "autotrace."

A 3–D feature will let you angle text and perhaps shapes. Bar and pie charts with a third dimension can add variety and interest. Usually the third dimension is like a shadow rather than true three dimension, unless it's a CAD program.

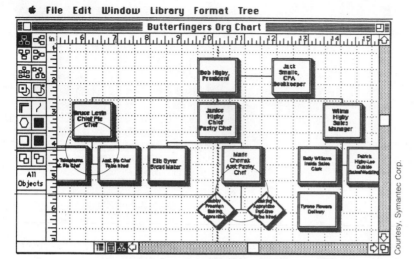

In More II for the Macintosh, a tree chart appears on screen as you work. Copy is generated in an outline, then chart type is selected from the menu at screen bottom. Icons of chart styles are in the toolbox at top left. Boxes can be clustered as the user prefers.

Depending on hardware, and operating systems, a drawing can be moved from one slide to another and from one file to another. Objects can be sized, stretched, rotated, flipped, and mirrored. Portions of objects can be manipulated using Bezier curve features.

A clipping path may be called by other terms in many programs. The principle is that you establish a curved line, then lay text or another image next to the curve and it will assume the same curve as the line. In some programs, this path can be any shape you like, not necessarily a curve.

In a Microsoft Windows environment in an MS DOS program, usually data is filled in on a worksheet (upper left), a dialogue box offers options while the chart is selected (upper right), and the chart is generated (lower left). Another dialogue box is used to select additional formatting options (lower right).

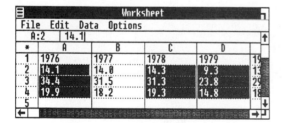

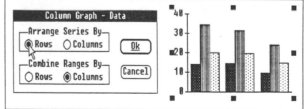

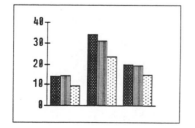

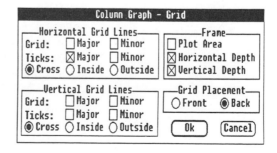

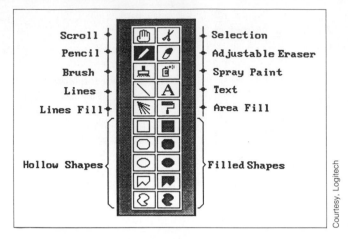

Scroll — Selection
Pencil — Adjustable Eraser
Brush — Spray Paint
Lines — Text
Lines Fill — Area Fill
Hollow Shapes — Filled Shapes

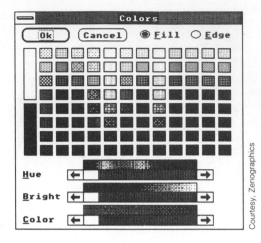

A paint, draw, or design program will have any combination of tools represented as icons. They are for creating geometric shapes, painting, cutting, erasing, filling in, and scrolling. Another set of icons will show line sizes and textures. There will be editing, file, and other options in pull-down or pop-up menus.

The color selection window in Pixie has sliders at the bottom for changing hues, brightness, and shades of color. When the sliders are moved, the associated boxes change colors accordingly.

Other features include a library of borders or frames or the ability to zoom into a section and edit it pixel by pixel. You'll want to use gradated backgrounds for a professional touch and distributed lettering.

Autotrace automatically outlines an image that may be entered as bitmapped, then changes it to an object-oriented image. It can be manipulated, then saved as a library image.

A calligraphy pen, an image hole cutter, and a blend tool all help make it easier to create special effects.

Color Selection. Are colors easily changed with a palette on screen? How are those colors selected? Can you mix to achieve a different hue, saturation, and intensity?

Clip Art. Does the program provide library images? You'll quickly tire of as few as 100. Can the images be unlinked, or the parts separated, so you can change them? Can you use only portions of them? (See Chapter 11.)

Are there industry specific optional symbol libraries? Are more available? What will they cost? In what format are they saved? You'll want to know this if you plan to convert them to other formats for use in desktop publishing.

Under the clip art category, you'll want to know if the program contains a "grab" utility. This is a RAM resident program that

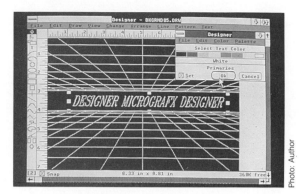

Photo: Author

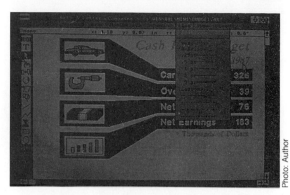

Photo: Author

C Draw and design tools are so easy to work with that a nonartist can achieve spectacular results by using a little imagination. A library grid pattern in Micrografx Designer (using Windows) was sized, then copied and rotated 360 degrees to achieve the upside down grid. The title was added and stretched to fit the space, then colors were selected from the pull-down menu.

C In Arts & Letters Composer, many elements can be combined. Here are a diagram chart and images from the image library combined with numbers added. Pull-down menus from the top and icons at left are used to design the chart. The program requires Microsoft Windows on an MS DOS system.

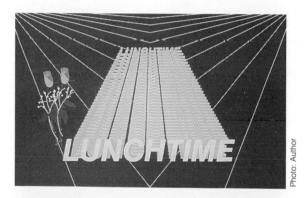

Photo: Author

C Distributed lettering in Applause II is combined with library images of the linear background and the rose.

(The slides on this page are reproduced in color elsewhere in this book.)

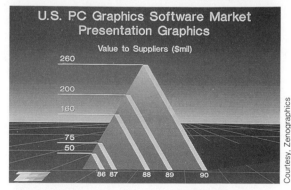

Courtesy, Zenographics

Courtesy, Visual Business Systems

C Mirage has tools similar to those one would find on a workstation program. It has always been a pacesetter, with many less expensive programs trying to accomplish the same effects.

C Visual Business Systems No. 5, working on the Macintosh, has added a three-dimensional feature that rotates a chart or line of text so it is in perspective as true three dimension.

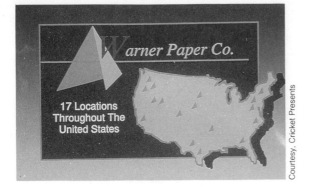

Courtesy, Cricket Presents

C Gradated colored backgrounds are a capability within most high-end graphics programs in Macintosh and MS DOS software. This example is from Cricket Presents. Colors will appear much smoother on a slide than on-screen due to the differences in resolution and computer terminal colors versus film colors.

Courtesy, Genigraphics Corp.

C Programs that support scanned image formats can bring in photographs and combine them with computer-generated text, backgrounds, formats, and images.

Slideshows that have special effects such as wipes, scrolls, fades, and so forth expand the potential of a software package to animated desktop presentations. A diagonal wipe is shown.

Photo: Author

will grab screens from other software to use in presentation software files. A "convert" utility should also be included so that files with one format can be converted to another.

VI   Data Import/Export

Select this for a DOS or Macintosh System. Does the program support the file types you'll need for greatest flexibility? Can ASCII files be imported from a word processor for text slides? This is crucial if the presentation package lacks a word processor or outline processor. If you've prepared your notes in a word processor, and spell-checked them, you shouldn't have to retype them for slides.

TIFF files are brought in using a scanner. They can be imported directly into some programs. Otherwise, they must be converted to a format the program can read, so a conversion utility is necessary.

HPGL is the Hewlett-Packard graphics language; it's a language for output to plotters. Files can be saved in the HPGL language and converted to compatible programs such as AutoCAD. Conversely, AutoCAD files can be brought into a presentation package that accepts HPGL files.

CGM stands for Computer Graphics Metafile. This is a format advocated as a standard for slide making systems.

PCX files are created in PC Paintbrush and convertible or importable to different programs.

PIC files are Lotus-based and can be imported into some programs.

PICT/PICTII, which are MacPaint files, include images saved in the Macintosh that can then be printed or imaged on a variety

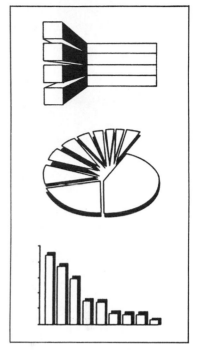

Clip art, also called library symbols, stock images, art gallery, and so forth, have become an essential feature of many programs. You can usually disassemble the parts and customize them, then reassemble them. Or use any portions. You can also create new symbols and store them as library images.

of printers and film recorders. That is true of Clipboard and Scrapbook files for the Macintosh.

Postscript is another file exchange format that, at this writing, is being pushed as a standard format for the future.

.DIF stands for Data Interchange Files. These files can be brought from spreadsheet packages into presentation and chart packages.

.WKS/.WKS1 files are extensions from Lotus 1–2–3, and, like .DIF files, can be imported into presentation and chart programs.

VII   Miscellaneous

Slide shows that run one screen at a time appear in most programs. You should be able to forward them manually or time them in 1- to 99-second increments. More programs are including transition effects such as fades, wipes, or scrolls (see Chapter 10). How many different effects does the program have? How easy is it to program these effects?

Is there a macro feature? Macros are keystroke sequences that you can program for frequently used input routines.

Does the program create speaker notes? Can you set the layout and the number of images per page? What are the limitations?

Does the program output handouts and change slide colors to gray scale for output to printers?

Some programs will print name tags and table number seating labels.

Sort lets you rearrange slides on-screen either by icon or by a line of text.

VIII   Output Devices

What printers, plotters, and film recorders does the program support? If you buy a program and discover it doesn't support your peripherals, check with the company's technical service. Often they have drivers available for additional peripherals but may not include all with the master program. That happens with new software and old equipment. A company may have drivers to older model printers. Check with technical support.

IX   Slide Services

Which slide services are supported directly with drivers? (See Chapter 14.) Does the program contain a telecommunication module that automatically dials up the selected service?

Which services? Read Chapter 14 for information about slide services and prices. Note which services are supported by the software. Compare the export files supported, such as CGM and PICT.

What kind of documentation accompanies the program? The more the merrier. There may be manuals, color cards, slides that show colors, help cards, demo disks, keyboard overlays, or audio and video instruction tapes. The program may also have on-screen help.

Photo: Author

If the program has these, you may use any slide service that can image those files.

X   Documentation

Try to look through the manual and determine the type of instruction. Look for a tutorial on disk, in a training guide, or within the manual. Color charts, either printed or on 35 mm slides, may be included. A few programs include a videotape showing how the program proceeds. They can be very good . . . or very bad. Try to preview a disk or tape to learn what the program does and how it works before you buy it. A reference card for commands is a big help. So is on-screen help if it's good.

Are there schools or individuals in your area who can supply independent training if you need it for yourself or for a department?

Worksheet

Table 12–1 is a list of presentation program features compiled from all programs in DOS and Mac environments. Use the list as a worksheet to help you determine the program's features and how the program compares to others. Fill in as much as you can for each program based on ads, brochures, reviews, and demos. For "other" in the graph entry, add any styles you must have that may not be listed. Decide which features are important and which are not, then make your decision. Don't expect any one program to do everything.

Table 12–1 Presentation Program Features

(A) Feature	(B) Now Use	(C) Must Have	(D) May Want	(E) Program 1	(F) Program 2	(G) Program 3
I Software Information*						
Program name						
Current version no.						
Date						
Company						
Address						
Phone						
Contact person/dept.						
List price (source)						
Discounted price(s) local						
Mail order						
Support policy						
Trial period?						
Warranty/guarantee						
Registration						
Update policy						
Support policy						
Reviews/rating						
Source/Date						
Source/Date						
Source Date						
II Hardware Requirements						
System						
RAM						
Hard disk space						
Color/b&w						
Monitor required						
Input devices supported						
Mouse						
Tablet						
Keyboard						
Light pen						
Scanner						
III User Conveniences						
Line menus/fill-in						
Templates						
Pull-down menus						
WYSIWYG						
Work directly on chart						
IV Chart Types						
Templates/forms						
Flexibility						
Global reformat						
Word charts						
Spell checking						
Search and replace						

* Software is listed in Appendix B.

Table 12–1 *(continued)*

(A) Feature	(B) Now Use	(C) Must Have	(D) May Want	(E) Program 1	(F) Program 2	(G) Program 3
Thesaurus						
Outline processor						
Number of fonts/faces						
Table charts						
Organization charts						
Bar/column charts						
Clustered						
Stacked						
Maximum data sets						
Overlapped bars						
3–D bars						
Pictographs						
Bar/line graphs						
Step graphs						
Other?						
Pie charts						
Maximum slides per pie						
Maximum exploded slices						
Two or four per graph						
3–D						
Line charts						
Scatter plots						
Maximum line types						
Maximum line markers						
Maximum data points per line						
Maximum data sets per graph						
Area graphs						
Other graph types						
High/low/close						
Bubble charts						
Gantt charts						
PERT charts						
Semilog charts						
Organization charts						
Maps						
Also . . .						
Data analysis						
V Drawing Tools/Free-Form Graphics						
Text						
Free-form lines/shapes						
Curves (freehand)						
Arcs						
Ellipses/ovals						
Rectangles/boxes sharp cornered						
Rectangles/boxes round cornered						
Triangles						
Diamonds						
Parallelograms						
Polygons						

Table 12–1 *(continued)*

(A) Feature	(B) Now Use	(C) Must Have	(D) May Want	(E) Program 1	(F) Program 2	(G) Program 3
Other geometric elements						
Select all elements						
Copy/move between files						
Drop shadows selectable for position/depth						
Line weights selectable						
Flip/rotate objects						
Mirror objects						
3–D text						
Bezier curves						
Clipping paths						
Image hole cutter						
Blend tool						
Undo command						
Rulers/grids						
Borders or frames						
Zoom feature						
Linking/unlinking images						
Gradated backgrounds						
Distributed lettering						
Color selection						
Clip-art						
How many images?						
Industry specifications						
Extra available?						
Convert program						
Grab program						
VI Data Import/Export						
ASCII						
.WKS1 (Lotus 1–2–3)						
TIFF						
HPGL						
CGM (Metafile)						
PIC						
PCX						
.DIF						
PostScript						
MacPaint						
PICT/PICT II						
Clipboard						
Scrapbook						
VII Miscellaneous						
Slide show						
Timed (timing increments)						
Automatic/manual						
Special effects						
Self-running						
Macro capabilities						
Speaker notes						

Table 12–1 *(concluded)*

(A) Feature	(B) Now Use	(C) Must Have	(D) May Want	(E) Program 1	(F) Program 2	(G) Program 3
Name tags/labels						
Sort show on screen						
VIII Output Devices						
H–P PaintJet						
H–P LaserJetII+						
H–P HPGL compatible plotters						
Xerox 4020 color printer						
Matrix Pro-Color						
CalComp Color/Plot Master						
Tektronix 4693D						
Matrix QCR/PCR/Pro-Color						
Matrix; other units						
Matrix SlideWriter						
Mirus FilmPrinter						
PTI ImageMaker						
PTI Montage FR 1						
Polaroid Palette, Palette+, Turbo						
Epson dot matrix and compatibles						
Other						
IX Slide Services						
Autographix						
Genigraphics						
MAGICorp						
Management Graphics (Indep's)						
Stokes						
Independent						
Telecommunications module						
Other						
X Documentation						
Quality of manual						
Tutorials?						
Demo disks?						
Video tape						
On-screen help						
Quick reference cards?						
Independent training?						
Overall elegance						
Scale of 1 to 10						
Keyboard test results						

Notes:

Other observations/features/recommendations not covered above:

13 Capturing the Image with a Camera

You've developed your presentation, polished your notes, and designed your visuals. You're ready to make your 35 mm slides. Now you must ask: What quality slides do you need? How will they be produced? Tied in with those questions are the following:

1. What do you want to accomplish?
2. How persuasive must you be?
3. Who will produce the visuals?
4. How fast do you need slides?
5. How many slides do you use monthly?
6. What hardware/software is available?
7. What is your budget?

When you watch a presentation, you generally concentrate on content, not quality. Yet slide quality has an effect on how a presenter is perceived and how well he accomplishes his goals. If a slide color is bad or resolution is poor, it can reduce the speaker's effectiveness. It's as though he attended a fancy party wearing the wrong clothes. He makes an impression . . . but it's negative.

The quality slide you need may also depend on your audience. If you're out to sell a product or service, you want the best quality slides possible. If you're showing the results of a study, or this week's sales figures, to a group of five peers in your office, that quality may not be as critical.

Slide quality is intricately woven in with how the image is produced on film. There are two possible procedures: using a film recorder that takes images from the computer file, or photographing the screen or hard copy with a camera. There are several options and techniques within these two categories.

Generally, this discussion will concentrate on slide making. Color print and black and white photography require the same set of questions, film information, and equipment.

Film Recorders

In the current market, computer-generated 35 mm slides used by professional presenters are usually made with a film recorder. To

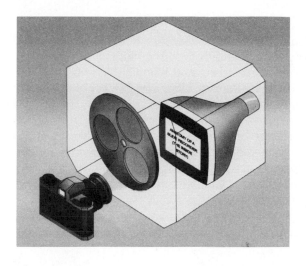

C Most slide recorders consist of a 35 mm camera that takes the photo through a red, green, and blue filter of an image projected on a small picture tube.

most people, converting a low-resolution computer image from your screen into a high-resolution 35 mm slide is mysterious. In practice, it's not much different from outputting the same file on paper using a printer. Think of a film recorder as another peripheral device that requires specific software drivers.

Film recorder prices range from $1,800 to over $100,000. Many companies have high-priced film recorders in-house for use by a graphics arts department. Low-priced digital units are in a desktop category and cost under $9,000. When volume justifies the investment, businesses bring them in-house quickly. The alternative is to use a slide imaging service (see Chapter 14).

How Do Film Recorders Work?

A film recorder, also called an image recorder, looks like a box with a 35 mm camera at one end. There are desktop and floor-standing models. Many film recorders can be outfitted with different cameras for different film types. These include instant cameras in two sizes and an 8 × 10 camera for larger format film and for photographic overhead transparencies. A few will accept 16 mm movie film.

Desktop units vary in size. They may look like a large, elongated toaster oven, or like a microwave oven. Larger models are floor-standing and are about the same height as a washing machine but half the width and depth.

Units vary in the time they require to produce an image on screen; this is called "throughput." Generally, the more complicated the image and the more colors it contains, the longer the throughput. This can range from seconds up to several minutes and more. It's possible for an inexpensive recorder to take from 5 to 30 minutes to image one complex file.

A film recorder transfers the image you see on your computer monitor onto a small, black and white, high-resolution CRT within the recorder. When the camera is triggered, the image is exposed sequentially through a red, green, and blue filter, producing a full range of saturated color on the film. Lines and shapes are smoothed by special software that drives the recorder.

Some systems require a film recorder controller (a board installed in a host PC or software on the Mac) that electronically separates a color slide file into its red, green, and blue components. It then displays each separation in turn in black and white on the slide recorder's picture tube. The camera makes a triple exposure, once for each color; the color wheel is timed to have the correct color filter in place for each exposure.

There are two types of film recorders on today's market, analog and digital.

Analog Film Recorders

An analog film recorder generally delivers a slide that has about the same resolution as your computer screen. A digital recorder increases resolution considerably. The Polaroid Palette, which can be credited for putting slide making capabilities on office desks, sells for about $1,800; its output depends on your computer hardware. With a CGA quality screen on your MS DOS computer,

The Polaroid Palette Plus Computer Image Recorder delivers full-color 35 mm slides, instant prints, and overheads from an IBM compatible computer system using an EGA board or CGA board. The unit comes with software, an automatic 35 mm camera, a Polaroid Instant Film back, the PowerProcessor, a slide mounter, cables, software, and manual.

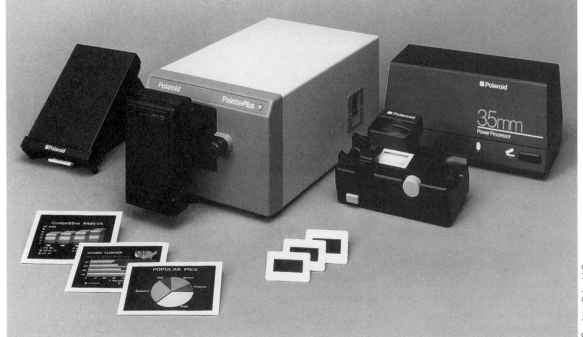

Courtesy, Polaroid Corp.

the slide will have only a slightly higher resolution. A 320×200 display screen will appear as a 640×400 display.

The Polaroid Palette Plus Computer Image Recorder, at a list price of $2,995, also depends on your computer hardware for slide resolution. It is CGA or EGA compatible. Maximum addressable resolution is 640×350 pixels for slides, 700×640 for hard copy. Each frame is exposed very fast, under a minute per shot, because images are sent to the recorder all at once. Low-priced digital devices can take 5 to 30 minutes or more to shoot one complex image; digital files are sent to the recorder pixel by pixel instead of all at once.

These two Polaroid film recorders include either the AutoProcessor (hand-operated) or the PowerProcessor (electric) unit and a device to mount the slides. Using Polaroid's PolaChrome or Presentation Chrome color film, you can shoot a roll of 12, 24, or 36 shots, then process and mount the film at your desk within half an hour or so. For speed, the film can't be beat. The Presentation Chrome projects as bright and clear as any other film. Images appear very sharp with only a little softness around letter edges.

The same film and processing can be used with any other camera or recorder. Conversely, any other type of film may be loaded into the unit. Film speeds are set through the software, not the camera. Polaroid has several types of instant 35 mm slide film. (See Table 13–1 later in this chapter.) An Instant Polaroid print camera may be used interchangeably with the 35 mm camera.

Before you buy a Polaroid system, be sure your software has a Polaroid driver. Call Polaroid technical support for clarification.

Agfa Matrix makes the MultiColor analog film recorder recommended for use with a monitor that offers between 800 and 1,550-plus lines of resolution. CAD/CAM applications use such monitors. Often medical X rays are digitized, then low-contrast areas are enhanced and imaged onto film. At analog resolution, hard-copy slides or prints reveal things that are barely distinguishable on a normal X ray. They may be used in diagnosis or during an operation to document the procedure. They're invaluable for low-resolution testing of an animated sequence in filmmaking. Every second or third frame is imaged to test for continuity, flow, color, and image quality. Prices for the units range from about $6,500 to $25,000, depending on film and camera requirements.

N.I.S.E., Inc., makes a Renoir 3600 F analogue film recorder for 60 Hz noninterlaced video signals, color graphic slide, and print cameras.

Digital Film Recorders

Almost all other film recorders on today's market are digital. They work in a similar fashion to analog devices. They have an internal

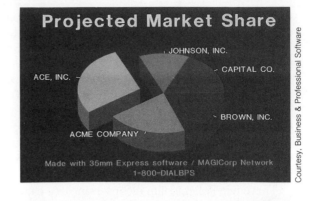

C A low-resolution slide imaged on a Polaroid Palette. Note the jagged edges on curved letters and the circular pie edge. Letters are not proportionately spaced or kerned; it's most obvious in the title, where the r, o, and j are evenly spaced. In kerning, the o would tuck under the r and the j. The same spacing appears between the e, k, and t in "Market."

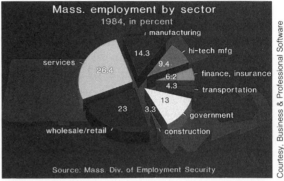

C In this example, letters are proportionally spaced; each is allotted only the width necessary so that an i takes up much less space than a w, for example. However, they are not kerned. Note the distances between the o and y in "employment," and the t and o in "sector." If kerned, the o would tuck in close to the y; and the o would be closer to the t. No jagged edges are apparent because the slide was created with a 4000 line Agfa Matrix film recorder.

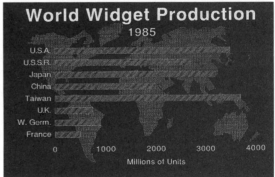

C A high quality film recorder, such as those used by Genigraphics Slide Service, produces a 4000 to 8000 line resolution slide. You won't see jagged edges on angled or curved letters. Serifs—the little tails at the ends of letters—are used and they are crisp and sharp. Serif fonts are usually avoided in low-resolution slides because they exaggerate jagged edges. Compare the appearance of letters in this title that has proportionally spaced and kerned letters with those in the examples above.

black and white CRT and pass light through a color wheel that has a red, green, and blue filter. In a digital recorder, each image sent to the CRT is built up pixel by pixel, line by line, from digital information and changed to analog information. That accounts for a longer throughput, or exposure time required, compared with analog computers.

Digital recorders may require adapter cards and software drivers to send and receive information. Software must have the drivers necessary for specific film recorders. Before you purchase software or a film recorder, be sure they are compatible. (That holds true if you plan to send software files to slide services; the service must be able to read, or interface, images from your software to its film recorder.)

The problem of hardware/software/film recorder interfacing is an important issue in the graphics community. It has led to the establishment of a standard called Computer Graphics Metafile (CGM). A CGM driver in software will generally mean that files can be imaged by film recorders that support the standard.

Resolution and Slide Quality

Slide resolution and, ultimately, slide quality will depend on the film recorder used. The film is not a significant factor. Almost all film will yield a quality slide, though some may be slightly more blue than others.

Comparing film recorder output quality is tricky. Usually, slides are referred to in terms of "line resolution" such as 8,000, 4,000, 2,000 lines or less. The highest resolution is 8,000. Most recorders produce slides in the 4,000 line category. Only the expensive units produce an 8,000 or 4,000 line resolution slide.

Resolution is measured as the number of horizontal and vertical pixels (or points of light) on a screen and the 2,000 or 4,000 numbers refer to a square format. Since 35 mm slides have a 1.5 to 1 ratio of width to height, a 2,000 line slide consists of 2,048 by 1,366 pixels, and a 4,000 line slide has 4,096 by 2,733 pixels.

However, manufacturers grade film recorders by "addressable resolution." This refers to the number of minute points on the screen where data can be placed and the precision with which the electron beam of the internal CRT moves across the tube's face. A 4,000 line means you can position and focus the beam with a precision of 1 in 4,000 spots (spot size), or points, across the CRT. That is different from optical resolution, which is the sharpness of a visual image.

Several issues affect optical image quality. These involve the number of addressable points combined with the grains of phosphor, their quality, consistency, and the spot size of the CRT. On better recorders, tube quality is higher and spot size is smaller and better controlled, resulting in a sharper picture.

When the size of the beam of light is too big, the final slide may show "fringing" or "blooming." These are a color change where two primary colors abut and overlap slightly. Placing a red circle inside a green square will result in a yellow line around the circle in all but the most expensive digital film recorders.

Even among film recorders advertised as having a 4,000 line

resolution, the quality varies. A 1989 test report by *PC Magazine* of seven recorders under $15,000 deemed the ProColor from Agfa Matrix Instruments as its editor's choice, followed closely by the Lasergraphics LFR and the Agfa Matrix PCR. It noted that the ProColor slides are of a slightly lower quality than those produced by the other two. However, the ProColor offers a 2K or 4K addressable resolution and a palette of over 16 million colors. The ProColor is also supported by drivers in a wide number of software packages. It is less expensive than the other two units.

In other testing reported by *Publish Magazine,* the Lasergraphics Mac/LFR was rated "thumbs down"; the general quality of its slides was no better than that of less-expensive recorders.

Different film recorders require different lengths of time to photograph the image. High-priced recorders such as a Celco, Crosfield-Dicomed, Genigraphics, and Matrix QCR may be able to shoot almost any slide in 45 seconds. Others may require from 1 minute to 45 minutes to shoot a single slide, depending on its complexity and number of colors.

How to Detect Differences in Slide Quality

You can evaluate slide quality if you know what to look for. When a slide is projected large, observe the edges of letters with curves and angles: *B, C, D, G, O, P, Q, R,* and *S.* In a low-resolution slide, jagged edges that look like stair steps will appear. In a high-quality slide, edges will be smoother and sharper (see p. 220).

Letter bottoms should line up perfectly on an imaginary base line. Spacing between letters is a clue to quality, too. Letters should be proportionately spaced and kerned.

Proportional spacing means letters are allotted only the space they need; *I* and *W* would each use only enough space for the letter. Nonproportional spacing would give each letter the same amount of space, resulting in an awkward appearance when letters are placed next to one another.

Kerning moves some letters closer together to create a more attractive, easier to read word. Rather than a *T* and *i* using only their necessary space allocation, the *i* would fit closer to, and tuck slightly under, the crossbar of the *T.*

Lettering, however, should not be squeezed so closely that the lines are not clearly legible from a midrange distance. Lettering should be the same as, or as close as possible to the fonts used in the software program. Different film recorders interpret fonts differently.

Color saturation and quality are also functions of the film recorder in tandem with the film type used. "Fringing," or "blooming," mentioned earlier, occurs if colors overlap at text edges, for example, and appear to be another color. That means spot size is large and slide quality is poorer. Red text on a green background that produces yellow at the edges is an example of overlap.

If you make a starburst pattern on a slide, the lines are farther apart at the edges and converge in the center to form a white area. The smaller the white area, the higher the quality.

Slides with gradated background colors will appear differently in low and high resolution. The gradations in a low-resolution slide may appear in linear steps. In a high-resolution slide, that background will appear smooth and each shade will blend beautifully with the next.

Courtesy, Management Graphics, Inc.

Courtesy, Agfa Matrix, Inc.

The Solitaire Image recorder from Management Graphics shoots 4K and 8K resolution slides at high speeds and with more than 16 million colors. Prices begin at $35,000. It can accept files from Macintosh and PC software and produce them in brilliant color and resolution. Many slide bureaus have adopted the Solitaire.

The Agfa Matrix PCR Film Recorder is at the high end of lower-priced film recorders, around $14,000, depending on configuration. It is judged well worth the price difference compared to its lower-priced competitors because it produces superior resolution and color in slides. It is on wheels and is portable.

Software Compatibility

Before a film recorder can create a slide, it needs to access a software file. Not all software has drivers to all film recorders. Either select the software you want to use first and learn which recorders it supports, or select a recorder and buy compatible software.

Remember that a business chart or artwork that appears one way on your monitor may not appear the same on film. You're dealing with two different media—a lighted screen and film and a process that requires considerable converting between. Except for analog units, the hardware used has no effect on slide quality; that's dictated by the film recorder. Several recorders support either or both Macintosh and DOS operating systems.

Software companies are scurrying to make their programs WYSI-WYG (What You See Is What You Get), but there are so many variables that it is not always possible. You can achieve color slides from a black and white system by designating color numbers for design elements. However, if you assign the wrong number to a symbol or to a line of text, the slide may not be exactly what you expect. It may need to be remade. Your fault, your cost.

Slide colors generally will be a great improvement over the 4-color CGA or 16-color EGA computer system, considering that film recorders can utilize millions of colors. Text styles may differ because there may be variations between your software and the drivers that output your files to the film recorder. These are conditions you learn to work with given the software and film recorders you use often.

In digital film recorders, the computer has no bearing on final

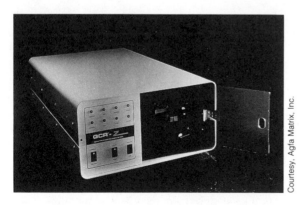

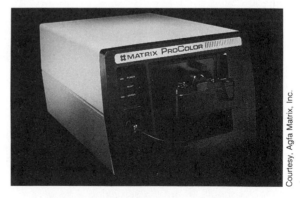

The Agfa Matrix QCR-Z is probably the unit used by a majority of commercial slide services and in-house art departments. It is priced in the low $20s, a mid-price range between the low and high-priced units, and it's output is dependable and excellent.

The Agfa Matrix ProColor was introduced in July 1988 and quickly became a top-rated desktop unit. It is half the price of the PCR and one third the price of the QCR. Slide quality at 2K or 4K resolution is almost on a par with the PCR.

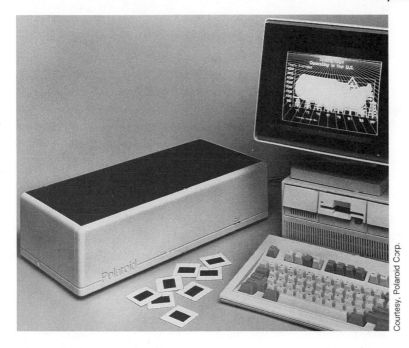

Courtesy, Polaroid Corp.

Polaroid markets the high resolution BRAVO! SlideMaker. It's a digital unit with an 8,000 line resolution and up to 16.7 million colors. It uses an advanced digital technology.

slide quality. A file created on an 8088, or an 80386 MS DOS system, on a CGA or a VGA board will yield the same results from a film recorder.

Wide Range of Film Recorders

Film recorders range in price from about $1,800 to well over $100,000. Output quality varies, too. Prices change dramatically in this industry. For updated information, contact the film recorder companies.[1]

The highest priced units are Celco, Genigraphics, Crosfield-Dicomed, and the Agfa Matrix Forté. These produce 8,000- and 4,000-line resolution slides. Large corporations and slide services generally use these cameras because their slide volume, speed, and the quality required justify the cost. That also explains why slide service bureaus generally provide high-quality slides.

Celco has a line of five units that range in price from about $50,000 to $250,000. They support 68 billion colors, have a 4,000 to 8,000 line resolution, and have a throughput of between 23 and 35 seconds per slide depending on the unit. They are considered the Cadillacs of film recorders.

---

[1] See film recorder companies in the list of vendors at the end of this chapter. Prices given are general at time of publication.

Crosfield-Dicomed has the D148S/A model, which supports 16.7 million colors and can be adjusted to a 4,000 or 8,000 line output. Throughput is 90 seconds. Its list price is $130,000. Another is the Captivator at $75,000.

Genigraphics' two Masterpiece models, priced at $44,900 and $70,500, support 16.7 million colors. Resolution varies from 2,000 to 4,000 lines and throughput is 10 seconds per slide.

The Agfa Matrix Forté film recorder was designed for large volume use in service bureaus and corporate imaging centers where compatibility to MS DOS and Macintosh platforms is essential. It can image a 35 mm slide in about 50 seconds at selectable 2,000 and 4,000 line resolutions. The 8,000 line resolution mode is generally used for larger formats. The unit lists at a base price of $45,000, plus additional costs for added cameras and film modules.

Cameras for in-house use can range from $4,000 to $40,000. The floor-standing $35,000 Solitaire film recorder is an 8,000 line system from Management Graphics, Inc. It has penetrated the expanding market quickly because of its superior resolution. Throughput is 43 seconds per slide in 2,000 and 4,000 line resolution, 79 seconds per slide in the 8,000 line, or up to 70 slides per hour.

Probably the best-known and most widely used film recorders are the Agfa Matrix QCR-Z and PCR models. The QCR for 2,000 and 4,000 line resolution lists at about $23,000. The PCR unit is about $14,000 or $15,000 depending on configuration. It is considered the top machine in this mid-price range with a 2,000 or 4,000 line resolution. Agfa Matrix advertises a 45 to 60 slide-per-hour

The Photometric Slidemaker is designed to work compatibly with VideoShow (see Chapter 16), a high-resolution presentation system; both are from General Parametrics. The unit will image files from about 40 software packages at 4K resolution. The unit works best when hooked up to a VideoShow system.

Courtesy, General Parametric Corp.

throughput for these units. Agfa Matrix also has the ProColor, an $8,000 desktop unit, which produces a slide of near equal quality; it is slightly slower than the PCR. There are compatible models for both MS DOS and Macintosh systems.

In addition, Agfa Matrix scooped the market in 1989 when it introduced the first PostScript compatible film recorder. Called the Matrix RIP, it has complete control over fonts that can be scaled and rotated. It allows the full power and flexibility of the PostScript page description language at 2,000 and 4,000 dot addressability. That means that any files established for other PostScript output, such as 300 dpi laser printers, can also be output to the Matrix PostScript RIP and be imaged at high resolutions. The unit lists at $17,900.

Several desktop units are rapidly gaining popularity. General Parametrics offers the Photometric (2,000 line) at $4,200 and the Slidemaker 250, (4,000 line) at $4,500. Both require a Colormetric board at $1,695 or a VideoShow Presentation unit. Another line of General Parametric products accommodates Macintosh files.

The Lasergraphics Film Recorder (LFR) at $9,950 uses a Rascol/II controller board to change the digital image to analog and send it to the film recorder via a high-speed parallel port. The board fits into a full-sized slot in your PC and comes with a megabyte of memory. The system uses either a Nikon N–2000 or Pentax PT 135 camera. Several file languages are supported, so it is versatile. It can be configured to output 2K or 4K resolution slides. With an optional interface it will support a Macintosh and an MS DOS unit.

Courtesy, Presentation Technologies, Inc.

The Montage FR1 film recorder from Presentation Technologies will generate a typical slide in three to four minutes with up to 16.7 million colors at 4,000 line resolution. The front panel holds the camera. A 35 mm camera can be interchanged with a Montage Color Transparency camera for making instant 3¼ × 4¼-inch overhead transparencies.

The Polaroid Turbo Palette Computer Image Recorder is an IBM PS–2 compatible version of the Palette Plus. It produces a 2,000 line resolution slide. There are drivers to this unit in popular PC software such as 35 mm Express and Harvard Graphics. Software must have specific drivers to the unit.

Courtesy, Polaroid Corp.

Courtesy, Lasergraphics, Inc.

The Lasergraphics PFR (Personal Film Recorder), at $4,995, will image Mac PICT files.

Courtesy, Lasergraphics, Inc.

The Lasergraphics MFR Mainframe Film Recorder System generates high-resolution, 2K to 6K images on film using any of today's popular graphics software packages.

Two versions of the Lasergraphics Mainframe Film Recorder (MFR) at $13,950 will output Lasergraphics Language or Hewlett-Packard Graphics Language. They are compatible with high-end graphics software such as DISSPLA, TELL-A-GRAF, SAS/GRAPH, Freelance Plus 3.0, Mirage, AutoCAD, and others. Several optional camera backs help make this unit versatile.

A third Lasergraphics model, the Personal Film Recorder (PFR), for both the MS DOS and Macintosh systems, lists for just under $5,000. There's also a Mac/LFR at $9,750.

Bell & Howell's CDI–IV, at $5,500, produces a 2,000 line resolution slide. The same technology is used in the new Polaroid Turbo film Recorder mentioned below.

Presentation Technologies has the 4,000 line Montage FR1 Film Recorder at $6,000 with MS DOS and Macintosh compatibility. The Montage uses the same Lasergraphics Rascol/II board as the Lasergraphics LFR and has the same versatility as the LFR. With proper software and configuration, it will image from PC files in a variety of formats and from the AT&T Targa board.

The Mirus FilmPrinter, priced under $6,000, offers resolutions from 2,000 to 8,000 lines. Initially it was introduced for Macintosh users, then followed by a unit for MS DOS systems. The FilmPrinter has a new technological approach: direct digital imaging. This means it has digital control over the computer interface, dot position on the internal CRT, and dot recording. It supports 35 different typefaces compatible with the Apple LaserWriter Plus. There is a trade-off. At the higher resolutions, it is slow. However, its 2K resolution is supposedly on a par with the 4K in other desktop units. Not surprisingly, in a comparison between the FilmPrinter's 8K resolution and that of the higher-priced Solitaire, the Solitaire slide was visibly superior.

The Polaroid Palette and Palette Plus are in the low-price category and produce a lower resolution slide. The Polaroid Palette at $1,895 images a slide just slightly higher than a CGA output and up to 640 × 400 lines. It will interface with IBM and compatibles, Amiga, and Apple computers. These are analog systems. (See Chapter 12.)

The Polaroid Palette Plus, priced at $2,999, offers either 640 × 700 or 640 × 340 lines, depending on drivers in compatible software. Jagged edges are apparent on letters and curves and color can be slightly washed out. Its low price makes it a practical unit where high-resolution slides are not required.

Polaroid also has the Turbo Palette film recorder with a 2,000- × 1340-line resolution that lists at $3,495. It uses the Bell & Howell Quintar 1080 graphics controller board; there are more color choices and shorter exposure times than with the two lower-priced units.

The Polaroid BRAVO! presentation system will produce high-resolution 8,000 line slides from either an IBM compatible or a Macintosh computer. This is a digital computer film recorder with a palette of up to 16.7 million colors.

Polaroid also offers a special film that makes its units a "complete system" for instant slide making. Instant 35 mm PolaChrome slide film comes with a processing pack. Exposed film and pack are placed in the PowerProcessor unit; film is processed in under four minutes, ready for mounting. A film-mounting device is included. Conceivably one could shoot a roll of 12 shots in about 36 minutes, develop them in 4 minutes, mount them in about 12 minutes, and have them ready for showing. From computer to slide tray in under an hour!

American Liquid Light has a $4,000 unit, the Still Light film recorder, for the Macintosh. The company also has an imprint interface card that links the Amiga computer to the Polaroid Palette.

It should be emphasized that lower-priced units can also produce negatives, overhead transparencies and instant prints, and 35 mm slides, depending on the camera and film used. Polaroid Instant film (for use with the Polaroid PowerProcessor) may also be used in any camera, providing the proper ASA film speed is set. Table 13–1 summarizes film recorder prices.

The BRAVO! Instant Slides from Hard Copy

Another innovative Polaroid system should be noted. The BRAVO! SlideMaker will produce 8,000 line slides or overheads from hard copy (not from a computer). The low-price unit, at $2,595, uses

---

Table 13–1   Film Recorder Price Categories

Price	Recorder
Under $7,000	Agfa Matrix ProColor
	American Liquid Light
	Bell & Howell
	General Parametrics Photometric and Slidemaker
	Lasergraphics PFR
	Mirus FilmPrinter
	Polaroid Palette/Palette Plus
	Presentation Technologies, Montage FR1
$7,000–$35,000	Agfa Matrix PCR, QCR, SlideWriter, RIP
	Lasergraphics LFR
	N.I.S.E. Renoir
Over $35,000	Agfa Matrix Forté
	Celco
	Crosfield-Dicomed
	Genigraphics
	Management Graphics

---

an instant camera to produce instant 35 mm slides, instant prints, and instant mini-overheads from any flat document. It can make a slide from computer printouts, illustrations, brochures, and photographs, even small three-dimensional objects such as circuit boards and jewelry. The BRAVO! SlideMaker looks and operates like a conventional desktop office copier. No photographic training or experience is required. Film is processed in the PowerProcessor.

The Polaroid BRAVO! SlideMaker produces instant 35 mm slides from hard copy (not from a computer). You could print a file, then make an Instant slide with Instant film and the PowerProcessor. It will make slides or mini-instant overheads or small Instant prints from any flat copy or small three-dimensional items.

Courtesy, Polaroid Corp.

When Is an In-House System Practical?

A film recorder used in-house offers confidentiality, flexibility, fast turnaround time, and control over the final product. When is a purchase cost effective? When enough slides are needed and when perceived savings justify personnel, time, and maintenance costs. There's another unknown that must be factored in. Having equipment available means more people will use it. The quality of presentations improves along with potential for increased business.

A person using a service bureau to generate slides from scratch could easily spend $7,000 or more for a 100-slide show—or an average of $70 per slide. That price reflects overhead costs of a computer and film recorder, a designer, proofing, finalizing, processing, mounting, shipping, rent, and so forth.

You can reduce that per-slide cost to anywhere from $4 to $20 per slide if the file is created in-house, then sent to a slide service. A 100-slide show would then cost $400 to $2,000 instead of $7,000. You must figure in software and someone's time to create files and send them to the slide service by modem or disk. It also ties up a computer.

The same slide made with an in-house film recorder would

Any Polaroid Computer Image Recorder can have the 35 mm camera interchanged with the Instant Film back. Some film types are peeled away from the back.

The Polaroid Palette interfaces with the PC. It was the first desktop film maker on the market. It is only CGA compatible and low resolution. The hand-operated AutoProcessor is shown.

cost an average of 60 cents per slide, or $60 for a 100-slide show. That reflects only the cost of film and processing. Add investment costs for equipment, maintenance, and operator time. Even so, a company that averages 100 slides per month could justify buying a $7,000 desktop unit. It would pay for itself in one to three months if slide cost alone reflected expenses.

Having the flexibility of a film recorder in-house doesn't mean you'll always save time. It can take someone two to three days, or longer, to create files for a 40 or 50-slide presentation. A machine can be tied up for several hours while slides are sent to the film recorder.

The average PC software package under $400 may not have as many fonts and features as high-end workstation software. Companies that produce a lot of presentations report that they may use in-house systems for simple word and graph charts. They may supplement them with the jazzier graphics for titles, transitions, and so forth, made by a custom service.

Confidentiality is another reason companies prefer in-house systems. They don't want to send proprietary information to a slide service. However, film still must be processed and, unless that's done in-house, too, that security is a moot question.

Key issues when considering purchase of a film recorder revolve around cost, quality, volume, flexibility, control, turnaround time, security, and personnel.

Slides from Front of Screen

Another way to make slides from your computer is to shoot the image from the front of the screen with a 35 mm camera. The result will be the same resolution as the screen. However, with

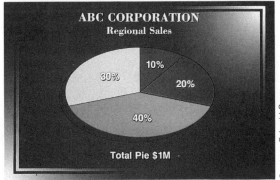

Taking a photograph of a screen, or of hard copy, using Polaroid's Instant PolaBlue 35 mm slide film will produce a slide minutes after it's been shot. The film is processed in a Polaroid PowerProcessor shown on page 230. The result is white letters on a blue background.

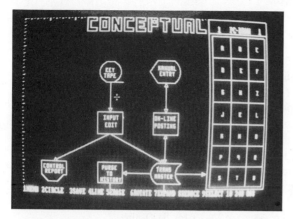

Flares appear around light areas when the screen is too bright. Horizontal lines are distorted because of screen curvature. Use a telephoto lens to flatten.

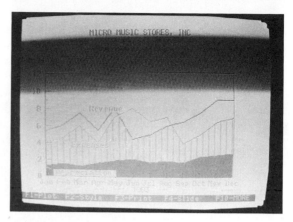

When too fast a camera speed is used, a portion of the image will be lost because of screen refresh rate. Try about a ¼th or ⅛th second shutter speed and adjust the f-opening accordingly.

Use a special silver "cropping tape" to hide distorted lines or a CRT frame. (See shaped, cropped overlays under Special Effects, Chapter 8.) They often can save a slide.

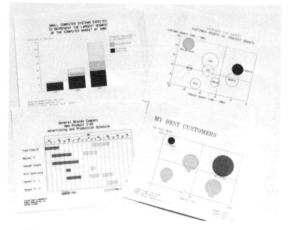

Photograph sharply printed hardcopy when you can't get a good screen shot. Color prints from a plotter or dense thermal print work well . . . if you're facile with a camera.

high-resolution color EGA, VGA, and MVGA screens, the slide can be acceptable for presentations where highest resolution is not so important. Nonglare and flat screens make photography easier and yield good results. None is as good as those that come from a 4,000 line film recorder.

Think twice if you imagine you'll save time by shooting a screen compared to sending files to a service. Remember, slide film has to be developed commercially (unless you have developing facilities in-house). Same day four-hour service is rare outside big cities. It may still take a day or two to get slides processed, and you're never sure how they'll come out.

Optimum equipment for shooting from screen includes a 35 mm camera with f-stops and time openings that can be set manually, a 70 mm or longer telephoto lens, a tripod, and a shutter release.

A 70 mm or longer telephoto lens will tend to flatten the screen image and minimize distortion from the screen and CRT tube curvature. Use a tripod to steady the camera. The camera must be carefully positioned and perfectly parallel with the screen. A shutter release will avoid camera movement. The camera's shooting speed will be slow, only about ¼th of a second at an F4, F8, or F15 aperture using ASA 64 or ASA color 100 film.

Use a slow 35 mm film, such as Kodachrome 64, Ektachrome 64 or 100, AgfaChrome, or FujiChrome 100. You'll get best results if you shoot in a darkened room with electric lights off. Electric lights can reflect in the CRT screen without your realizing it.

Take a light reading with a light meter **close to the screen** (room lights can be dimmed). Don't rely on a meter on camera or an automatic camera. Set camera openings, then turn off lights and shoot. Bracket each shot. That means set the f-stop so it is open one more aperture than the reading, then closed one more aperture than the reading. That will give a better chance of getting a usable shot.

Shooting at speeds other than ¼th of a second may result in a gray band through the film, or half screens, caused by the screen refresh rate. For the first one or two rolls you shoot, record the camera setting for each shot, then mark each finished slide with its setting. (Slides are usually numbered.) When you compare them, you'll discover that one setting is best for all slides. Expect to use up a roll or two for trial and error.

Here are problems you may encounter when shooting slides from a computer screen, why they happen, and solutions.

1. *Pictures aren't sharp.* This is probably due to camera motion or poor focusing. Use a tripod and a cable release on the trigger. Focus on a line or image on the computer screen. Be sure the camera lens is straight at, and level with, the screen and the monitor is straight and in line with the camera lens. When camera and lens are not parallel, the resulting photo can be in focus in the middle of the slide and out of focus at the top and bottom.

2. *Distortion.* Horizontal lines are curved because of screen curvature; letters and images appear elongated. Use a long lens, 70 mm or longer. The longer the focal length, the flatter the screen will appear. Short focal length lenses such as a wide-angle or even a 50 mm lens will show line distortion.

3. *Paths of light or reflections on screen.* Shoot in a darkened room with overhead lights off. Don't wear a white shirt. If you do, don't stand in front of or near the screen; reflections can throw off the lighting and appear on screen as a light shape. Keep a flashlight handy when you work in a dark room. You need it to see camera settings, to find the cable, and to avoid tripping on tripod legs.

4. *Halos or light flares around the edge of images.* Reduce screen brightness and take a new light reading. Try shooting at a couple of different contrast levels.

5. *Slides are smaller than the mount.* Try to fill up the lens when you shoot the screen. If you still have area around the film that you don't want to project, crop the slide using slide tape. Cropping can also be "dramatized" by using a slide mount or mask with a shape such as a trapezoid, a circle, or a keyhole. (See companies listed at the end of the chapter. Check for products at photo supply stores or request a catalog from the supplier.)

Hood Devices

Another option is to use a hood device that is made for photographing the terminal screen. Such devices fit snugly over the screen (they come in different sizes). The large, open end blocks out extraneous light, the other end has a camera attached. With lower slide costs from slide services and the popularity of desktop film recorders, these units are not as well known. However, they can serve a company's needs in the right environment (see p. 236).

The attached camera is especially adapted to shoot the screen at its preset distance, about 18 inches. An inexpensive unit is the NPC ScreenShooter at $189. The Camtron CopyVision MK1 also has a Polaroid Instant camera back. Models are available for 6-inch, 9-inch, and 12-inch CRT screens at about $589. The Tektronix C4 camera also has a hood and an Instant camera; it's available in 8½ and 12½-inch hoods.

DATACAM graphics recording systems, from Photographic Sciences Corp., are complete with a 35 mm single lens reflex or other type camera preset with a lens of the proper focal length. Six models are available for 12, 13, and 19-inch screens. Three units with instant print cameras are $545 to $595. The same three-size cones, fitted with 35 mm cameras, are $875 and $925. The company recommends the use of Instant film and the Polaroid PowerProcessor for fast turnaround time.

These low-priced units are practical for preparing and proofing a slide show. Take a shot of each screen in your show, then lay out the developed prints in the order you'll show them. You'll be able to determine the flow, proof it, and be sure colors or fonts are consistent from one slide to another. You can work with the

The NPC ScreenShooter has four rubber feet that help steady it against the CRT screen. It includes a Polaroid OneStep 600 camera, CRT hood, CRT hood adapter, diopter lens, and a 35 mm SLR camera bracket. All these device systems are used by positioning the hood to the screen, holding it steady, and taking the picture.

Courtesy, NPC Photo Division

The Tektronix C4 camera is available with 8½ and 12½-inch hoods and is complete with an Instragraphic camera.

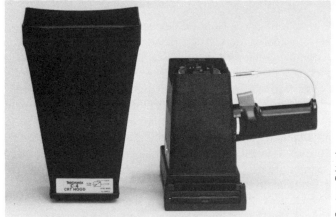

Courtesy: Tektronix

The DATACAM 35 (left) Graphics Recording System is complete with a 35 mm camera; the DATACAM I (right) is for instant prints. Two handles make the unit easier to balance than those without handles. A coordinated thumb trigger release is at the top of the right handle.

Courtesy: Photographic Sciences Corp.

proofs until the day you need to order the slides or print final overheads.

Several programs based on Macintosh and a few that work through Microsoft Windows let you view 16 or 32 slides (depending on the size of the monitor) on-screen at one time. You can print out the images on paper as "speaker notes" and use these for rehearsal and proofing so you don't tie up a computer.

Polaroid prints, or speaker notes, keyed in to a computer file name and kept on file can also serve as a record of slides available. Often slides from one presentation can be used for another.

Slides from Hard Copy

There is another option. If you can generate a sharp, clean, hard copy of a file from a plotter or printer, you can photograph that with a 35 mm camera. Of course, you can photograph brochures or anything made by any process; it doesn't have to be computer output.

This is the more traditional process used by art studios for generating slides. It's an alternative when you don't have computerized equipment and if you're adept with a camera.

You can get a blue and white slide from black and white copy by using Polaroid PolaBlue Instant 35 mm slide film; the background will be blue, the copy white.

Always set the camera on a tripod to prevent camera motion. Set the copy to be photographed on a copy stand, or tape it on a wall. Be sure edges are perfectly parallel in the view finder. If they are not, the lettering or image can be askew. You should bracket the settings as explained for shooting directly from screen.

Be careful when you mix computer-generated slides with those taken by direct photography. Maintain a consistency. You might use all computer-generated slides for word slides, photography for product shots. If you can scan photographs into the computer, it's possible to combine photos and computer output in one slide.

Sorting Out Film Types

Given the number of film types and brands, and their tongue-twisting titles, it's often hard to remember which film is used for what purpose and for which cameras. Use the film type information given in Table 13–2 for quick reference. Note that the same films are used for any of the photographic procedures mentioned. Generally, "any 35 mm camera" means one that is not fully automatic and that the user can set manually for speed and f-opening.

Table 13–2 Types of Film

For 35 mm slides

Instant film for use with PowerProcessor by Polaroid

ASA	40	PolaChrome: full color
	40	PolaChrome: high contrast full color
	125	PolaPan: black and white
	400	PolaGraph high contrast: black and white
	4	PolaBlue: blue and white from black and white originals

Conventional processing, color slides

ASA	100	Presentation Chrome
	64	Ektachrome
	100	Ektachrome
	400	Ektachrome
	100	FujiChrome
	100	AgfaChrome

For color prints

Polaroid Instant Prints: Polaroid Instant Print Cameras
Conventional print film: any 35 mm camera

For black and white prints

ASA	32	Panatomic X: any 35 mm camera
	125	Plus X: any 35 mm camera

For instant prints

Note: $3\frac{1}{4} \times 4\frac{1}{4}$ peel apart Polaroid film requires the instant camera
Type 669 Color print film
Type 691 mini-transparency film (see Chapter 9)

Polaroid PolaBlue is an instant high contrast 35 mm slide film that will produce white images on a brilliant blue background from black and white copy such as computer printouts, typed pages, charts, and graphs. Film and developing pack (right) are purchased in one package. After the film is exposed, both are placed in the Polaroid PowerProcessor or AutoProcessor.

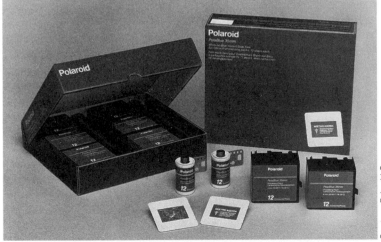

Courtesy, Polaroid Corp.

Products and Distributors/Manufacturers[2]

Film Recorder Companies

Agfa Matrix Division
1 Ramland Rd.
Orangeburg, NY 10962
914   365-0190
800   828-6489

American Liquid Light
2301 W. 205th St.
Torrance, CA 90501
213   618-0274

Aztek, Inc.
17 Thomas St.
Irvine, CA 92718
714   770-8406

Bell & Howell Co.
411 Amapola Ave.
Torrance, CA 90501
213   320-5700
800   320-5231

Beseler Film Recorder
1600 Lower Rd.
Linden, NJ 07036
201   862-7999

Celco
70 Constantine Dr.
Mahwah, NJ 07430
714   985-9868
201   327-1123

Crosfield-Dicomed Corp.
11401 Rupp Drive
PO Box 246
Minneapolis, MN 55440
612   885-3000

General Parametrics Corp.
1259 Ninth St.
Berkeley, CA 94710
415   524-3950

Genigraphics Corp.
PO Box 591
Liverpool, NY 13088
315   451-6600

Graftel (formerly Data Innovations, Inc.)
323 New Boston St.
Wilmington, MA 01887
617   933-8170

Lasergraphics, Inc.
17671 Cowan Ave.
Irvine, CA 92714
714   660-9497

Mirus Corp.
445 S. Antonio Rd.
Los Altos, CA 94022
415   949-5544

N.I.S.E., Inc.
20018 State Road
Cerritos, CA 90701
213   860-6708

Polaroid Corp.
575 Technology Square
Cambridge, MA 02139
617   577-2000
800   225-1618

Presentation Technologies, Inc.
743 N. Pastoria Ave.
Sunnyvale, CA 94086
408   749-1959

Hood Photographic Devices

Camtron Electronics International Ltd.
184 N. Main St.
Champlain, NY 12919
514   340-1125

NPC Corp. (NPC ScreenShooter)
1238 Chestnut St.
Newton Upper Falls, MA 02163
617   969-4522

---

[2] Write or call for current prices and models.

Photographic Sciences Corp. (DATACAM)
PO Box 338
Webster, NY 14580
716   265-1600
800   828-6489

Tektronix, Inc. (C4 Camera and Screen Hoods)
PO Box 500
Beaverton, OR 97077
503   627-7111

Special Effects and Mounts for Cropping[3]

Gepe, Inc.
216 Little Falls Rd.
Cedar Grove, NJ 07009
201   857-0171

Visual Horizons
180 Metro Park
Rochester, NY 14623
716   424-5300

---

[3] See Chapter 8.

Tapping Slide Service Resources

Slide services are booming and they are a boon to the presenter. A service that produces volume output can afford top-quality film recorders, printers, and other equipment. Using a service can eliminate, or postpone, your investment in a film recorder and color printer, and learning and training time.

In the beginning, there were only custom slide services that created a presentation from your written notes. They helped the presenter organize a presentation. Their artists designed and created the necessary visuals. With personal computers and do-it-yourself chartmaking, new types of slide services emerged. Their function was to create slides from files generated by the user from a variety of programs.

Service bureaus with artists on staff, graphics workstations, and heavy-duty film recorders are called "custom shops." Those that image your files are called "click shops." As you might expect, there's a difference in costs.

Software has advanced far beyond making basic charts. It includes an incredible array of features and is called "presentation software."

These packages are designed so the casual user can produce dynamic slides by following templates provided. Templates may allow only a certain number of text lines or chart elements. If you adhere to their limitations, the results will be very presentable visuals. Fonts and colors are preselected, and a library of graphic images is supplied for easy enhancement (see Chapters 8 and 12).

Despite all these aids, there may be times when you need outside help. Often a presentation will require 20 to 50 slides within a day or two and there's neither time nor staff to generate them. Sometimes special enhancements or photographic effects are needed. Then a custom service is the best solution.

Custom services may:

1. Enhance your slide file.
2. Design slides from your notes.
3. Design or scan in logos or special art.
4. Work with you to create a consistent presentation.
5. Generate overheads, color, and black and white hard copy.

6. Provide stock formats into which they will enter your data.
7. Provide color separation systems for your color print needs.
8. Assemble and transfer your slide presentation onto video tape.

Click shops will:

1. Accept the files you create in popular software.
2. Process and return them in four hours to four days.
3. Generate overheads, color, and black and white hard copy.
4. Some will provide a combination of click and custom services.

Turnaround Time

Regardless of the service you use, turnaround time (time required for your order to be processed and delivered) is a prime consideration. It may take from four hours to overnight or two to five days. Four-hour turnaround service usually has a premium charge. Slide files must be in the service's labs by a certain time of day. They need time to shoot, mount, and package the slides. They are picked up by an overnight messenger service such as Airborne or Federal Express for next morning delivery. Billing is automatic because invoices are printed or credit cards billed by computer when slides are processed.

Files may be sent by modem, by messenger, or by mail on disks. Mail or overnight express can take an extra day or two. It will depend on delivery times and how the service is set up to handle incoming mail.

Slide Prices Vary

Both click shops and custom shops quote prices for one slide in a cardboard or plastic mount returned by whatever standard turnaround times are offered.

Prices have dropped considerably since the first service was

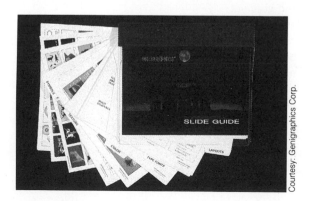

Courtesy: Genigraphics Corp.

Genigraphics' slide guide has hundreds of stock images that can be adapted to a variety of situations. Slides are organized in several categories: industry, textures, special effects, buildings, travel, symbols. They can be integrated with customized text or image slides designed by Genigraphics artists.

The procedure for developing a slide presentation via a service consists of designing rough drawings, entering the information in the computer, and generating each image. The client is shown proofs in black and white hard copy; he can view the color onscreen if desired. The images are OK'd after checking carefully to be sure there are no factual, design, or type errors. The finished slides are produced.

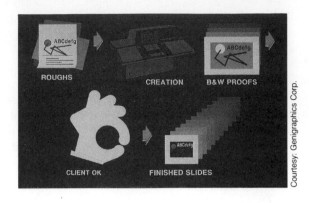

ROUGHS   CREATION   B&W PROOFS

CLIENT OK   FINISHED SLIDES

Courtesy: Genigraphics Corp.

introduced. Click shop prices per slide range from $3.50 to $22.00. Delivery may be extra.

Normal service may be a cardboard mount, although some services use a glass mount for all slides. Film that is sandwiched between glass cannot get scratched or dirty. In a cardboard (or plastic) mount, the film is exposed. The glass mount may exist in the telecommunications software as an option in your slide order. You may have to request the mounts in a note to the service if the option doesn't appear on-screen.

When estimating service costs, figure in long-distance charges if files will be telecommunicated. Plan to send files when phone rates are low. Macintosh files are very large; a single file may take as long as a half hour to send by modem. Several services offer toll-free transmission. Check carefully—some advertise a toll-free number, then charge for per-minute connect time.

Add delivery costs both ways. Delivery costs by overnight mail add $8 or more to slide cost. If you order several slides, the cost is amortized over all of them; but order only one or two slides and that charge increases the per-slide cost considerably. A local slide service, or a national service with a local bureau, may offer next-day service to a central shop. If you can pick up the slides, you'll save shipping charges.

Duplicate slides of the same file ordered at the same time as an original will cost less than two originals. Ask about a corporate discount if your company orders a certain number of slides annually.

Besides 35 mm slides, services usually offer overhead transparencies, color, and black and white hard copy from the same files.

Services Support Different Software

Every slide service does not accept files from every software package. It will depend on the film recorders they have and the software that supports it. When you first select a service, you'll have to know which software it supports. If you have software, you'll have to shop for the service that images it.

The industry is trying to standardize output to film recorders by using the ANSII Computer Graphics Metafile (CGM) standard (see Chapter 13). The aim is to image any software with a film recorder that can work with a CGM format. CGM isn't the final answer yet, according to experts, but it's a giant stride forward.

If your service uses the Agfa Matrix QCR and PCR film recorders, you may require software that has the Matrix SCODL format. Autographix, Crosfield-Dicomed, or Genigraphics film recorders initially required their own drivers. Eventually, they adopted CGM or another specific driver to effect compatibility with certain off-the-shelf MS DOS and Macintosh software.

Most major slide services support their own "front-end" software that is an entry to the complete services offered. They let you create a good graphic but nothing jazzy; for that you let the center spruce up the information. Most guide you every step of the way in fill-in-the-blanks worksheets. Their defaults try to prevent you from producing a bad chart (unless your data is wrong). The offerings are Autographix AutoVisual (Autographix), Graftime (Genigraphics), PC Chart (Aztec, Inc.), Personal Business Software (Management Graphics, Inc., Minneapolis), Presenter PC (Crosfield-Dicomed), Slideworks (Management Graphics, Inc., Canada), and Professional Image (Stokes Slide Service).

Photo: Author

Slidecrafters, Inc., and other independent slide-making services work through Management Graphics, USA (based in Minneapolis, MN). They supply Macintosh users with Easy Slider. The inexpensive program works as a "bridge" between several Macintosh programs and a film recorder.

When you work with the service, you receive the software, a set of slides showing all the background and colors, and another set showing how to develop a build series. There's a printed color palette and a manual. The color support is for people who work with monochrome systems. Colors are selected by numbers.

Sending Slides by Modem

You'll need a modem (modulator-demodulator) to send slides by phone lines. Most companies accept files transmitted at 1,200 or 2,400 baud.

Presentation packages make it as easy to send a file over telephone lines via modem as it is to save a file and send it to a printer. When telecommunications are built in to the software, the procedure is called "seamless." You fill in the necessary ordering information on-screen, your site code, and the telephone number, then hit the "send" button to transmit files. They are processed and sent. On-screen updates keep you informed of what's happening.

When telecommunications are not built in (nonseamless) you'll need a "bridge" or "link" program that will convert your files to the format required by the service. The slide service may require that you use specific software that may cost from $25 to $150. Very often, they will include an offer of free slides that will be worth the cost of the software.

A nonseamless procedure requires that you save the files in the necessary format, then upload them to the service via a general telecommunications program. A disk can also be sent to a service by mail or overnight courier.

One disadvantage of telecommunications is that it ties up a computer and a phone line during transmission. Those are two good reasons to plan to transmit at night, or to send files on disk. However, after you telecommunicate a few orders and get used to the idea, you may never want to put a disk in the mail again.

Workstations

Companies that manufacture mainframe and turnkey systems also have PC-based products that will generate slides for their workstations. Among them are Autographix, Aztek, Chyron, Superset, Genigraphics, Crosfield-Dicomed, Bosch, Computer Associates, Chorus Data Systems, Computer Graphics Laboratories, Pansophic, SAS Institute, Inc., Visual Business Systems, Wasatch Presentation Systems, and others.

These systems may be the same ones used by a service. They can accept your slides and enhance them, because drivers have become very efficient for transfering files from PCs to mainframes.

Courtesy, Management Graphics, Toronto

Management Graphics, Toronto, Canada, supplies PC Slide Slideworks as the front-end software to its service. Slides included show color schemes and layouts.

Other Hard Copy and Services

The same services that image slides will also produce overheads and color and black and white hard copy from your files. You may want to order only overhead transparencies or color prints, for example, and no slides. That's no problem.

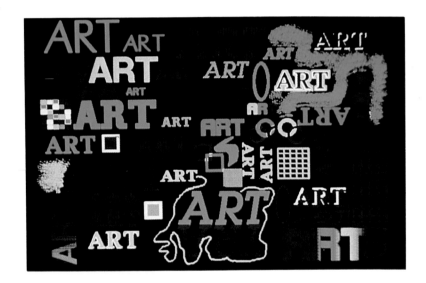

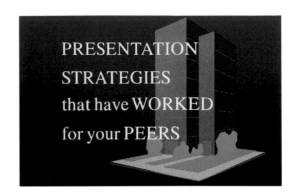

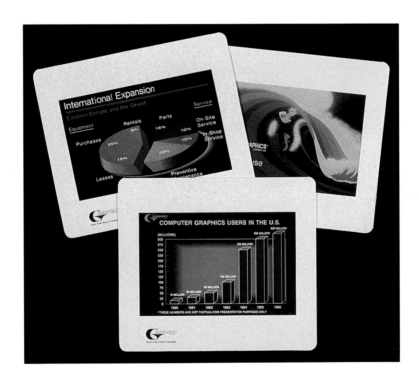

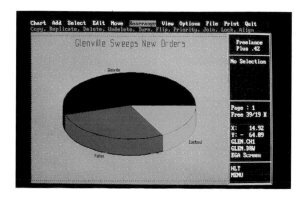

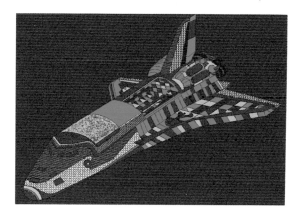

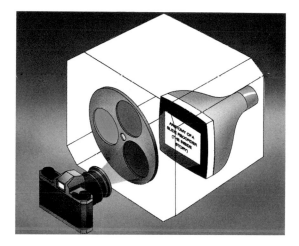

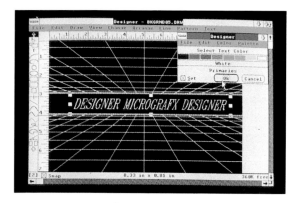

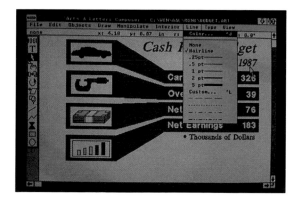

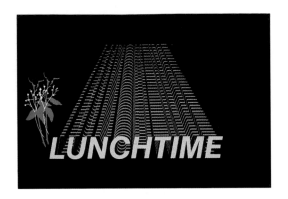

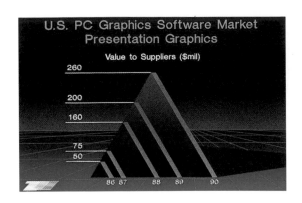

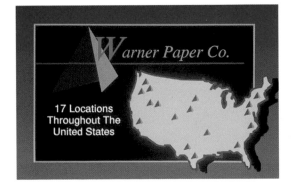

Photo Drop-ins

Color Photo..

...Scanned...

...Pasted

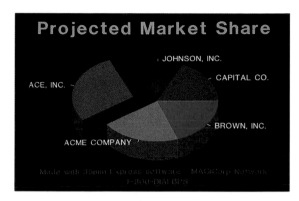

Projected Market Share

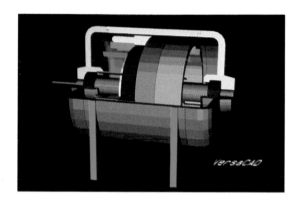

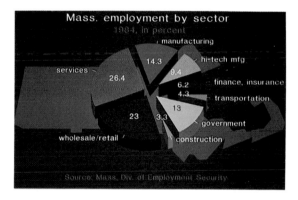

Mass. employment by sector

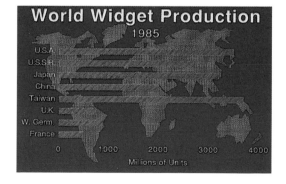

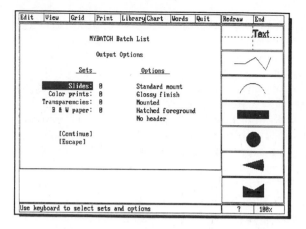

When you order slides by modem, you fill in the order form on-screen, and it accompanies your slide order. When ordering from Ashton-Tate slide service, the Draw Applause menu requests the number of slides, prints, etc. that you want. (A similar form appears in the Applause II program.)

The next screen is the work order; here is where you can add comments. The selected files are then processed in your computer. The phone connection is made and transmission occurs. The screen usually presents a countdown regarding files sent or how much of the order has been processed.

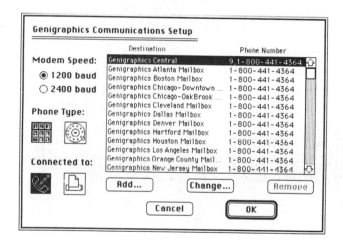

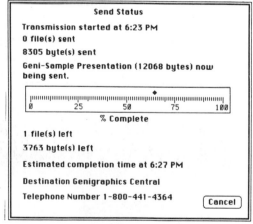

When using the Genigraphics service with PowerPoint, an 800 number is used to send slides to a central service. You select modem speed and phone type.

As transmission continues, the scale records its progress. You're told how many files and bytes remain to be sent and approximately when the transmission will be completed.

Overheads will cost from $9 to about $35 each depending on the service. As with film recorders, the advantage is that you don't need to invest in the printing or plotting equipment. Overheads generated by a service with special cameras are significantly better than those you can produce with most printers and plotters. Remember, they use a photographic process, not a print process, so colors are more solid and brilliant when projected. Backgrounds can be colored or gradated, as opposed to the solid blue, yellow, or clear of a transparency film.

The Ilford Cibacopy System, a unit that retails for about $23,000 with the slide making attachment, will produce color prints and overheads from a 35 mm slide. That means the service generates the 35 mm slide first, then makes the print. That also means that if you have a 35 mm slide and want to make a print or overhead film from it, the service can do that easily.

Another unit that produces beautiful prints from slides is the Noritsu Cycolor System, for about $10,000. It uses a "Mead Cycolor" system developed by Mead Imaging. It produces color images through a photosensitized, dye-transfer process. Called the QPS–101 Cycolor SlidePrinter, the prints are a full-color $7 \times 10\frac{1}{2}$-inch image on an $8\frac{1}{2} \times 11$-inch sheet of paper framed by a white border. The first print is ready in 35 seconds, then three per minute for subsequent prints. Each print will run about 60 cents maximum for supplies.

Many new thermal and ink jet printers can output excellent overheads that will project nicely. However, the photographically produced overheads are more color intensive and project so brilliantly that the presenter's image is enhanced by their quality.

Black and white laser print and color print prices range from $2.50 to $8.00 each.

Services constantly evolve new capabilities, so watch for their

The Autographix 200A Presentation Design system uses an IBM AT and a high-resolution monitor, a digitizing tablet, and an Agfa Matrix QCR film recorder.

Courtesy, Autographix, Inc.

announcements. Some services can make slides of a "screen dump." They provide a RAM resident software that can, literally, take a picture of any screen and store it as a file on disk. Send the files and have them imaged at the same or slightly higher resolution than the screen and with many more colors. That's perfect for people who need slides of menus, forms, and other screen images that cannot be brought into a presentation program easily.

Another service (Brilliant Image, Inc.) will make 35 mm slides and overheads from any file created with your word processor. The significance of that is that you can now generate word slides without the need of a presentation or graphics program. The company's procedure interpolates the typed text into presentation quality fonts.

What to Expect from a Slide Service

Sending your files to a service bureau takes only a little experience. You'll get that the first time you try it. You may make a few not-too-costly mistakes and you'll learn quickly. It's wise to begin with a small order.

Not all software is WYSIWYG (What You See Is What You Get) so the image you see on-screen may differ from how it appears on a slide. Almost always, the slide looks better than the screen, unless you've made a major design error.

Colors may appear different on your monitor than on the slide.

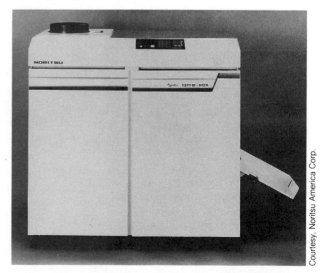

The Ilford Cibacopy machine will make a color print or an overhead transparency from a 35 mm slide in seconds. Colors are as dense and brilliant as those on the slide.

The QPS 101 Cycolor™ Slideprinter from Noritsu makes color prints from slides.

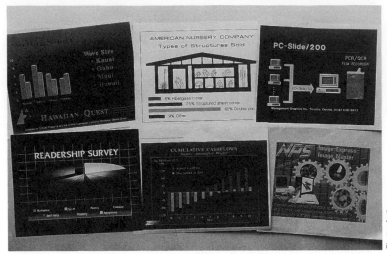

Photo: Author

Different printers will produce different quality and type of output. Top left and right are from ink jet printers; center is from a plotter. Bottom left is an Ilford print; center is from the CalComp Color Master; at right is a dot matrix output.

For example, in a color monitor the colors may not be properly adjusted. White, light blue, and pink selection squares may all look white. If you think you're selecting white for text, but pick the blue block, all your text may be blue . . . not what you wanted. If you vary the selection blocks, slides won't match in a single presentation. Remakes and extra delivery, maybe even rush charges, can add as much as 50 percent to your costs.

Remember that your monitor will show only a minimum number of colors, while image recorders can interpret those colors into millions of shades. Colored backgrounds on your monitor can appear linear with tiny crosses and zeros; on a slide that background will be smooth and evenly shaded.

When you send slides by modem, line noise and poor connections can be a problem. You may have sent a 25 or 30-slide order and then discover that the transmission has been aborted and you have to begin at the beginning. If static or interference occurred, remakes or retransmission may be necessary. Most likely, the service will detect that; they'll telephone you and ask for another transmission. A day could be lost in this scenario.

Ordering information on a modem module can be confusing at first. You may want one copy of some slides and duplicates of others. You group the order by numbers wanted and upload the first group, then the second. The process is automated, and the camera can't make decisions as it goes to shoot this file once, this one twice, etc. If you have any questions, call customer service and clear them up before you transmit your first order.

The combination of software and your inexperience in designing slides can result in surprises, too. Letters or lines that show up well on your computer screen may not be read by the service

Courtesy, Pix Productions Inc.

c *A multi-projector full presentation for a major client's annual function held in the hangar of the Spruce Goose, Long Beach, California. The slides were projected on a portion of the airplane used as a huge "projection" screen.*

bureau's software in the same way. A line you thought you erased in the file and replaced may mysteriously reappear on the slide.

Initially, you may have some mistakes and be disappointed in either or both the software and service. Worse still, you'll have unusable or less than perfect slides for your presentation. With experience, and some dialogue with a customer support representative, you'll learn to overcome the idiosyncrasies. Slide services are eager to retain your business and may write off the cost of remake slides during your initiation period.

Full-Production Companies

Full-production services are offered by audiovisual production companies and also by several of the custom slide service companies. Usually a corporation contracts with a service to develop an entire production or to supplement work that is done in-house. The service may be responsible for slides for all the lecture presentations, setting up the auditorium with the audio visual equipment required, and having someone available to run it.

Other services may include producing a television commercial or a fund-raising campaign, videotaping a conference, generating videotapes or videodisks from material used for the lecture, and so on. The service representative may work closely with the company's advertising agency and with a committee of top executives to develop the production. Their service may include scriptwriting or coaching the presenter.

Production companies can provide design services from creating a logo to a multi-image presentation for thousands of people. A production might involve still and motion photography, computer graphics, handmade art, and a sophisticated blending of all. Produc-

It's hard to believe that any image was neglected by Visual Horizons. Their catalog has an incredible number and variety of stock slides and formats for customized slides. They offer a multitude of services and equipment for every aspect of presentation: projection equipment, slide storage systems, flip charts, overhead transparency supplies and projectors, and viewing systems. The catalog is a compendium of what's available for anyone involved in photography, presentations, and allied fields.

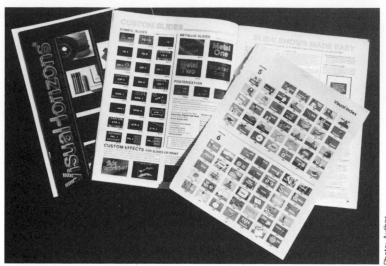

Photo: Author

tions may be synchronized with sound for television, training, or use at a convention booth. Charges vary with client needs and generally run into thousands of dollars for a complete campaign.

Stock Slides

A ready made stock slide is complete as is. Nothing is added. You order them by subject matter and they're ready to pop into your slide tray. These well-designed, general purpose illustrations are available with an incredible variety of messages from Visual Horizons and Wilson & Lund. (See source listing at the end of the chapter.)

Examples are: a slide showing an order pad with the words "Order Today" in bold bright letters; a dollar sign in a special sweep effect with the word "sales"; a message announcing "coffee break" or "lunchtime"; a finger pointing at you; a clock with the word "timing"; or the word "Goals" surrounded by neon lights. It might be a graphic only such as two hands shaking, a "no smoking" sign, or people working together. These may be purchased individually, or in sets. Some are available as 35 mm slides only; others may be purchased as overheads, also.

In addition, there are slide sets with humor, famous quotations, zany definitions, computer quips, and textures. Another group of slides is designed with borders or graphics so you can write your own message on the slide. Prices are only about $30 for sets containing 24 to 40 slides.

If the messages and colors of stock slides are not quite right for your needs, the vendor catalogs may suggest ideas you can use to create your own stock slides.

Slide Service Bureau Checklist

When you consider working with a slide service, here are points to check.

1. Software system supported:
   MS DOS
   Macintosh
   Other
2. Software packages supported.
3. Film recorder used.
4. Is a front or bridge program required to convert the files into recorder readable formats?
   Name/choice
   Costs
   Evaluate what they do
5. Do you need additional telecommunications software? If so, which packages and what cost?
6. Can you upload files by a telecommunication or electronic service you have now such as MCI, COMPUSERVE, or AT&T Mail?
7. Is there a toll-free number for uploading files? Is there a connect charge? (If not, what will your phone bill be for the approximate length of transmission?)
8. Charges for basic slide? Type of mount?
9. Charges with Wess (glass) mounts?
10. Charges for duplicate slides ordered at the same time?
11. Turnaround time options:
    Standard
    Rush
    Slower service
12. Delivery charges. Can you opt for next day or longer service?
13. Minimum order charge?
    Remake minimum?
14. Hardcopy prices:
    Overheads—How are they made?
      Photographically?
      Ink jet printer?
      Price when ordered without slides?
      Price when ordered with slides?
    Color prints:
      Single price
      Quantity price
    Black and white prints:
      Single price
      Quantity price
15. Corporate (quantity) discounts.

Directory of Services

Write or call for local or regional branches of major companies. For local services, check your telephone company yellow pages under "Photography" and under "Computers."

Artronics, Inc.
300 Corporate Court
South Plainfield, NJ
201   756-6868

Ashton-Tate Graphics Service
20101 Hamilton Ave.
Torrance, CA 90502
213   329-8000

Autographix, Inc.
100 5th Ave.
Waltham, MA 02154
617   890-8558 in MA
800   548-8558, ext. 1000
Image and service centers throughout U.S.

AVL, Inc.
56 Park Rd.
Tinton Falls, NJ 07724
201   544-8700
800   223-0213
TWX   710-772-9499

Aztek, Inc.
17 Thomas
Irvine, CA 92718
714   770-8406

Brilliant Image, Inc.
141 W. 28th St.
New York, NY 10001
212   736-9661

Chartmasters, Inc.
1750 Montgomery St.
San Francisco, CA 94111
415   421-6630

Crosfield-Dicomed Corp.
11401 Rupp Drive
PO Box 246
Minneapolis, MN 55440
612   885-3000
TLX 290837
Service centers in several cities. Check local phone book or write or call for service nearest you.

Express Slides
318 39th St.
New York, NY 10016
212   370-9275

Fox Photo
70 N.E. Loop 410, Ste. 1100
San Antonio, TX 78216
512   341-1616

Genigraphics Corp.
4806 W. Taft Rd.
P.O. Box 591
Liverpool, NY 13088
315   451-6600
Service centers in several cities. Check local phone book or write or call for service nearest you.

Ilford Photo Corp.
West 70 Century Rd.
Paramus, NJ 07653
201   265-6000
800   426-0781

Kinetics Presentations, Inc.
Distillery Commons 250
Lexington Rd. @ Payne
Louisville, KY 40206
502   583-1679
Service centers throughout U.S.

MAGICorp
50 Executive Blvd.
Elmsford, NY 10523
800   FOR-MAGI

Management Graphics, Inc., Canada
1450 Lodestar Rd. #1
Downsview, Ontario M3J 3C1, Canada
416   638-8877
Centers in Ottawa and U.S. Check phone book or write or call for locations.

Noritsu America Corp.
6900 Noritsu Ave.
Buena Park, CA 90622
714   521-9040

Pix Productions, Inc.
3843 S. Main St.
Santa Ana, CA 92707
714   957-1749

Slidecrafters, Inc.
777 Third Ave.
New York, NY 10017
212   546-1990

Slide Express
601 Madison St.
Alexandria, VA 22314
703   836-8320

Stokes Slide Services
7000 Cameron Rd.
Austin, TX 78752
512   458-2201

Visual Horizons
180 Metro Park
Rochester, NY 14623
716   424-5300

Wilson & Lund
1533 7th Ave.
Moline, IL 61265
309   762-7366

Hardware: The Hard Choice

There is a profusion of, and confusion about, hardware used to produce graphics. Add to that the volatility of the market, new systems, upgrades of older systems, new companies starting up, and old companies fading out. It's no wonder the new graphics user doesn't know where to start and what to buy. This chapter gives a brief overview of computer graphics hardware, with input and output peripherals. It will acquaint you with the choices and options to consider.

It's true in all computerdom that something you buy today will be changed and updated tomorrow. That shouldn't prevent you from making a decision and plunging in. Anything you purchase today will do a great job, and updating isn't always essential. Often updates are cosmetic rather than structural. It's more important for you to get started so you can realize the benefits that graphics can bring to your business.

Personal Computers

The meteoric rise of the presentation graphics market is a phenomenon associated with the personal computer and the lower cost of graphics hardware. So many other elements are so closely intertwined that sorting through them is like hacking through the vines of a liana plant. These include:

- The ease of telecommunications from the personal computer.
- Development of low-cost film recorders.
- Growth of slide-making services.
- Software with more features.
- More powerful computers.

Though presentation capabilities existed on workstations and large computer systems many years ago, the momentum picked up, and continues, thanks to the personal computer.

There are many hardware configurations one can use to run almost any popular presentation package. Higher-resolution boards, faster chips, and better monitors speed up the task of creating visuals and showing them. Software is friendlier.

The Macintosh, with its excellent graphics capability, is an exciting product that has helped propel presentation graphics to a top market position. Macintosh developers did a magnificent job of creating new formats for visuals, easier user interfaces, and more features than most people would ever dream of having at their fingertips.

Another phenomenon was evident. When a company brought in personal computers that could generate presentation materials, more people began to use visuals. Good presenters learned that visuals help persuade, help sell. Business improved.

Now people look for more creative applications for visuals, more effective formats, and higher-quality and easier-to-use programs. The ready-to-use templates in some programs help the presenter who has no design background to produce slides that can look as good as those made by a professional service.

Graphics Workstations

As more industries bring computer graphics in-house and the volume increases, they often bring in a graphics workstation. Graphics workstations appeared a few years ago, mainly for CAD/CAM, manufacturing, three-dimensional modeling, and animation applications.

Companies such as Apollo and Sun offered them usually as a dedicated system, which meant they were used mainly for graphics, not for word processing or spreadsheet work. The units, not much larger than a PC, are as powerful as many mini- and super-mini-computers. Other companies, such as DEC and IBM began offering desktop minicomputer systems as a workstation for graphics. The NEXT computer followed as a hybrid between a workstation and a PC.

Courtesy, Pansophic Systems, Inc.

[c] *Pansophic Systems StudioWorks Graphics Workstation.*

Raymond Lasky works with a digitizing tablet to touch up a seven-color electronic logo for a videotape and slide presentation at The Hartford Insurance Group. The logo is then stored and available for instant recall when needed. The system is the Chyron.

The advantage of a workstation is that it offers higher speeds, greater memory and storage capabilities, and more sophisticated programming than a PC. Usually there is additional circuitry and processors for the intensive calculations required for graphics. These systems generally use proprietary software or software designed specifically for a group of workstations with common formats. They may have PC compatibility so that files can be transferred back and forth.

Workstations often are teamed up with high-end film recorders. Conversely, companies such as Autographix, Aztek, Crosfield-Dicomed and Genigraphics assemble a workstation with their film recorder and bundle it as a system. Depending on the system, the capacities, and the peripherals, a complete graphics workstation, including a film recorder, can cost from $25,000 to $100,000 and up.

Special graphics conferences are your best source of information. Here you'll be able to compare several systems in one setting.

Input Devices

Before a computer can perform the myriad tasks it is designed to do, it must be fed the information it is to manipulate. This information feed is called input. Several devices enable you to input information: keyboards, digitizing systems, and optical scanners. Several manufacturers and distributors can provide each type of device.

The traditional keyboard is the most obvious and pervasive input device. Software requires the use of arrow keys and combinations of keys for directing lines and manipulating shapes. Keyboard input lacks the spontaneity and fluidity that can be achieved with

A trackball is like an upside down mouse. You manipulate the ball with the palm of your hand and push the buttons with your thumb; that activates the cursor.

other devices; however, not all software supports devices such as a mouse, light pen, or graphics tablet.

Mouse

The mouse has become a popular instrument for graphics input because it allows freer movement for drawing than a keyboard does. The push buttons act as the enter key would on a keyboard and perform other functions determined by the program. There are two types, an optical mouse and a mechanical mouse. The optical mouse requires its own pad; a mechanical mouse may be used on many surfaces.

Joystick

A joystick looks like a handle protruding straight up from a small box. Most people have used one to manipulate battleships and rockets in computerized games. But joysticks are also used to manipulate graphic images that appear on-screen as a result of data entered. (A joystick is pictured in the CalComp workstation photo.)

Trackball

Trackballs have been available for some time on large systems; they are only beginning to appear in the personal computer market. Instead of rolling a mouse on an electronic pad or the table top, one turns a ball with the fingers or the palm of the hand to manipulate the cursor. Input buttons act as the enter key on a keyboard.

Light Pen

A light pen allows the user to select an icon, which is an illustration of the task to be performed, by touching the pen to the screen surface. It is a stylus-shaped, photosensitive pointing device for interactive communication between the user and the terminal screen. The information it sends to the computer is the coordinate of the X- or Y-axis to which it is pointed.

Graphics Tablet

A graphics tablet may be called a digitizing tablet or digitizer. It is a flat tablet containing electronics that sense the coordinate position of a "puck" or "stylus" that a user may move across the tablet surface. Graphics tablets are typically more accurate than a mouse. They are indispensible in CAD applications, when existing hard copy drawings must be accurately traced and entered into a CAD data base. Graphics tablets used with a stylus are popular with

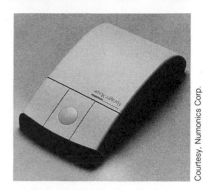

The Manager Mouse is shaped so the hand cups it naturally. This is a one-button "mechanical" mouse with a ball in the bottom. It is rolled directly on the desk.

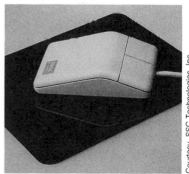

The ergonomically designed, two-button, high-end optical mouse requires a pad; the pad technology is calibrated to the screen at 2,000 counts per inch (CPI).

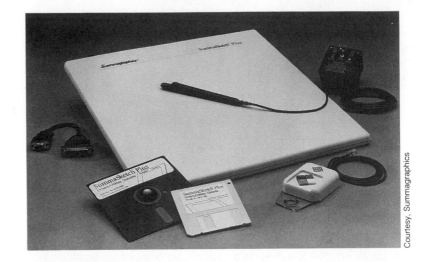

Courtesy, Summagraphics

The SummaSketch Plus is a lightweight, easy-to-use digitizing tablet designed to interface with a variety of PC presentation and design software. It comes with a stylus, or digitizing pen, and a four-button puck that has a cross hair at the top for accurate position selection.

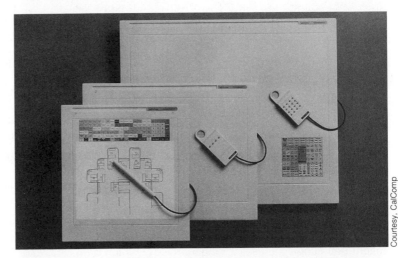

Courtesy, CalComp

For CAD and mechanical applications, CalComp has a series of DrawingBoard digitizers. Templates are available free for popular CAD software.

Courtesy, Microtek Lab, Inc.

Microtek MS-200 unit (center) is an image scanner that accepts documents up to 8½ × 24 inches, digitizes the image at 200 pixels per inch resolution, and transfers the image to the host computer memory for subsequent manipulation with compatible software and printing. The unit can scan text, pictures, and mixed text and pictures.

paint programs. In a typical graphics application, the cursor on the display screen moves proportionately with the user's hand movements on the puck or stylus along the tablet.

Image Scanners

A scanner will read graphics or text from hard copy into the computer. The resulting image can be manipulated, redesigned, and altered as if it had originated in the computer.

An image scanner can read line drawings and halftones into the computer by scanning the images dot by dot and recording them digitally. Images can then be manipulated, combined with text, read by a presentation package, or sent to a printer or other output device.

Most scanners that read images will read text only as if it were an image. It can only be altered as if it were an illustration, not edited as in a word processor. Some scanners can be used to read both graphics and text when appropriate circuitry and software exist.

There are small handheld units that can scan an image up to about three inches wide; these are in the $150–$800 category. Several narrow images can be combined. You can bring them into a paint program and perform necessary drawing changes to meld edges using a pixel-by-pixel color change.

There are page size scanners and larger units that will scan full-size CAD drawings. Scanned images can be read by several presentation software packages, providing the format conventions are consistent. These are usually a TIFF (Tag Image File Format) for a PC, or a PICT (Picture) format for a Macintosh.

If the presentation package can't read a file directly, there are several roundabout paths to take. The scanned image is usually compatible with a paint program, where it can be saved and then converted to a format the presentation software can recognize. Or, if the paint package has drivers to a film recorder, visuals can be made directly from that package.

About 45 companies market scanners at this writing. The technology is constantly changing. Consult current magazines, watch for the units at computer conventions, and ask your dealer about them. Often one manufacturer will make a scanner for a variety of vendors. The name and design will vary, but the circuitry may be the same. These are referred to as OEM (Original Equipment Manufacturer) arrangements.

Video Capture Systems

A video camera combined with the computer's necessary graphics cards and software can photograph a live image, or a hard-copy

The PERCEPTOR, an electromechanical, three-dimensional digitizing device, inputs coordinate information directly from a physical three-dimensional object by means of a movable arm that measures the dimension. It can acquire 3-D points at the rate of seven X, Y, and Z coordinates per second and send them over an RS 232 interface to any computer accepting serial input.

A high-resolution Image Scanner.

image, and enter it into the computer. The image can be cleaned up with a paint program, colored as desired, saved in a necessary format, and brought into a presentation program for output as a slide or overhead. The image can also be combined with titles, text, and so forth in a slide. It's another scanning method.

Screen Capture Utilities

A screen capture utility is software, not hardware, but for this discussion it may be considered an input method. Graphics software usually contains a screen or image capture module. Generally, you load the capture module into memory, then run whatever program you like. You invoke the capture keystrokes and the screen image is saved to a file. That file can then be read by another program or, if necessary, converted to a format the program can read.

Hijaak, by Inset Systems, Inc., is an efficient software package designed specifically to capture screen images and convert files to a variety of other formats. With it you can grab a drawing from the library of one presentation software package to use with another. You can create line drawings on vector-based software, then import them into pixel-based paint software for paint editing. It gives you the best of two worlds: the precision, resolution, and scalability of vector graphics and the more artistic, free-form, and expressive features of a pixel editor.

The same files can then be saved into a CGM (Computer Graphics Metafile) format and output to a film recorder for high-resolution slides. It works like a universal graphics editor.

A slide service company, Brilliant Image, was the first to introduce the capability of making 35 mm slides, overheads, and color and black and white prints from a screen capture program without requiring any conversion on your part. You get its screen capture utility, then send the captured files to Brilliant Image by disk or

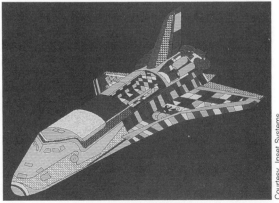

[C] *A wire frame image with its many intricate curves was constructed in AutoCAD, a vector package. Hijaak converted the file to a pixel format, and it was painted and detailed in PC Paintbrush file. Then Hijaak again converted the file to a PCX format so it could be merged with a word processor file. Finally, it was printed on the Hewlett-Packard PaintJet printer (ink jet) in bright colors against a dark-blue background.*

Courtesy, Inset Systems

modem. The company will create the hard-copy output. The slides will not be the same 4,000 line resolution as slides made by a presentation package, but they will be significantly sharper than front-of-screen photographs. You'll have no distortion or screen refresh problems. You'll save a lot of time, frustration, and aggravation.

These methods may seem boggling. Once you sort out what you need and go through the steps required, it's not as roundabout as it seems when you read it. In the Macintosh, screens from one program are easily pasted into a screen from another using the clipboard. Many of these procedures can be used to bring images into desktop publishing software such as Xerox Ventura, Aldus PageMaker, Ashton-Tate Byline, Springboard Publisher, and others. The process will probably be simplified as more people demand it and as software companies perceive these transfers as a marketable utility.

Pixels (picture elements) appear as dots on the screen and as print elements of a dot matrix printer.

Output Devices

Output refers to data that is sent from the computer for display. The device might be a monitor, a printer when the output is hard copy, a 35 mm slide, or a video display. A floppy disk is both an input and output agent—input when it provides data to the computer, output when the computer reads data to it.

Monitors

The monitor, containing the CRT (cathode-ray tube), is the initial output device that displays images and text. Several manufacturers provide a range of models with various attributes and price tags.

The CalComp System 25 interactive design workstation illustrates input and output devices. Keyboard, joystick, and digitizing tablet may be used for input during a single project; two monitors are used for output: one for data, the other for the image.

Courtesy, Calcomp

Important aspects are whether the monitor will interface with a particular system and color board, the resolution, styling, convenience of controls, performance, color rendition, and dealer support.

Integrated workstations generally include a monitor interfaced and correct for the system. Often there are two monitors, a black and white for viewing input data and a large color unit for viewing the image.

All CRT monitors work the same way. Phosphors painted on the CRT's screen are made to glow by a beam of electrons scanned across the tube's face from left to right (a raster) and from top to bottom. The beam's intensity illuminates the phosphor to varying degrees of brightness, which results in images formed on the screen.

Color monitors are generally low- and high-resolution, composite, or RGB (Red, Blue, Green). With composite video monitors, all color and synchronization information is carried to the monitor on one conductor as a combined signal. With RGB monitors, separate conductors are used for red, green, and blue color signals.

In the MS DOS world, there are several standards for color monitors that tie in with the graphic board used, from the low-resolution CGA to the higher-resolution EGA and VGA signals. A VGA board is generally downward compatible with CGA and EGA.

However, another type of monitor was introduced by NEC. Trademarked as the "MultiSync," the monitor is compatible with any current standard and adaptable to future standards. That means the monitor will support any graphics board. Users didn't have to upgrade a monitor when they upgraded a board. Other manufacturers followed and introduced multisynchronized monitors under different names such as the Sony MultiScan, the Mitsubishi Diamond Scan, and the Princeton Graphics UltraSync. The "sync" monitors

A high-resolution monitor.

Courtesy, Princeton Graphics Systems

The Mitsubishi Diamond Scan is a multi-sync monitor with a 14-inch diagonal measure and a 600 × 800 resolution.

Courtesy, Mitsubishi Electronics America, Inc.

Table 15–1

Monitor	Resolution	
CGA	320 × 200	4 colors
	640 × 200	2 colors
EGA	640 × 350	16 colors
VGA	720 × 400	Text resolution
	640 × 480	16 colors
	320 × 200	256 colors

are slightly more expensive than the single-standard monitors. Monitor capabilities are summarized in Table 15–1.

The color monitor requirements of the Macintosh II are not so varied because Apple standardized the output.

Large-size monitors are popular in some applications such as CAD/CAM and for displaying output to several people. For the average presentation application, a 12 or 14-inch monitor is preferable. A large monitor may not add to the amount of information on screen; the size only enlarges the information. The image will appear grainy and less sharp, though. It's like blowing up a 35 mm photo to a large picture.

Printers and Plotters

Printers and plotters are the devices that produce hard copy on paper from graphics systems. As the market has matured, the number of printers and plotters from which to choose has become staggering. Which is the best choice for you depends on your needs. Many offices require both a printer and a plotter.

Printer technology has expanded, and prices have dropped, so high technology is in an affordable range. A magazine recently reviewed 167 dot matrix-type printers for one issue. The reviews covered letter quality, ink jet, thermal, and laser printers. The dot matrix printers were categorized by price range: under $800, $800–$1,200, $1,200–$1,999, and $2,000 and up.

Dot matrix printers producing black and white images have been the backbone of graphics printing. Each character formed by a dot matrix printer is composed of tiny dots grouped to match the way the character appears on the display screen. Matrix printers are considered "impact" systems because they employ fine wires mounted in the printhead which strike through a ribbon that places ink on the paper. Speeds range from about 60 to 400 characters per second. Because each dot is the result of a single hammer strike, an infinite variety of images can be formed. A letter quality

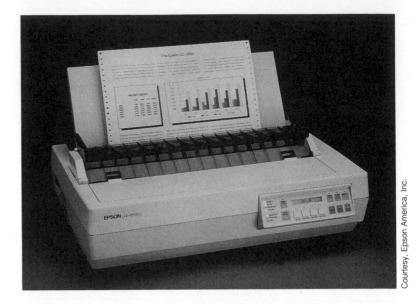

Courtesy, Epson America, Inc.

A 24-pin, dot matrix printer that outputs color copy by using a four-color ribbon. Several passes are made over the ribbon to mix colors.

printer can produce only minimum graphics because preformed letters are used.

The new ink jet printers (as compared to impact printing) work in a "spray paint" fashion to place dots on the page. Sometimes special coated paper is required to prevent the color from spreading or splaying. Thermal designs use heat to burn dots onto specially treated paper.

Color Printers

Initially, people were happy to have any kind of print output for their computers. Now that color is available at a modest price, color printers are becoming as popular as color TV did in the early 60s.

Dot Matrix Color Printers.   Dot matrix color printers have multicolor ribbons in either red, green, blue, and black or magenta, cyan, yellow, and black. The technology is the same as that for a matrix printer that has only a black ribbon. The difference is that software controls the ribbon position so the hammers strike that portion of the ribbon required for color output. By multiple striking through two or more colors, tertiary colors result. Because of multiple strikes, color printing is a slower process than monochrome printing.

Thermal Printers.   Thermal printers have been on the market for some time. Pins in the printer's printhead are selectively heated in the pattern of a particular character. The heat burns off the coating of a specially treated paper in the shape of that character, allowing the ink to adhere to the paper only in that shape. Therefore, the printhead never touches the paper, and printing is silent. The print quality is good, but speeds are slow, and images can fade over a period of a few months.

Ink Jet Printers.   Ink jet printers do not employ an impact system, so they provide a quiet operation, with none of the clatter that results when the matrix hammers hit the papers. Ink jet printers cannot produce a carbon. Instead of the hammer device, they have ink-filled channels that spray liquid ink either in a continuous stream or one drop at a time, depending on the system.

Newer, low-cost ink jet printers are based on the "drop-on-demand" technique. Ink cartridges feed the ink into several nozzles. When pressure is applied selectively to each nozzle, a drop of ink is ejected and deposited on the paper.

Technology involved in ink jet printers is constantly improving. The problems? A high-quality, slick-surface paper must be used for best results. The paper is designed so that the ink will dry quickly before the next color hits the paper, thus avoiding color bleeding. Multiple passes to produce different colors are not practical because the more ink sprayed in one place, the more likely that colors will bleed. Normal bond paper cannot be used because it encourages the ink to spread and appear fuzzy at the line edges. Ink jet printer nozzles tend to clog, although this problem is being tackled and minimized. High altitudes can affect ink pressure.

On the positive side, ink jet printers have fewer moving parts to wear out than do matrix printers. The image is always the same intensity, whereas ribbons used with impact printers tend to produce

Courtesy, CalComp

The CalComp ColorView thermal transfer printer with a color video controller. Together they provide full-screen resolution hard copy completely independent of the software used.

increasingly lighter images as they wear out. Ink jet printing is more suitable for multicolor printing than ribbon base printing; it is easier to mix ink dots than it is to overprint with multicolored ribbons for different color tones.

Laser Printers

Ever since laser printers were introduced in 1984, their popularity has increased. The quality of text and graphics available with a laser printer is unsurpassed by other technologies. They are fast, quiet, and versatile. They are more expensive than other types of printers but significantly less than they were initially.

The laser printer, in combination with the Macintosh's ability to do desktop publishing, and the right software at the right time, set the whole industry in a new direction. In a short time, about 50 companies began to manufacture laser printers.

A laser printer uses a toner to produce ink on paper; it's the same principle as a photocopy machine. Usually, laser printers produce only black ink on paper. In 1988, the first color laser printers were introduced, but prices were high.

A laser printer uses either a Hewlett-Packard-based language or a PostScript language. Companies are developing modules that will make a Hewlett-Packard compatible printer accept PostScript files.

Plotters

Plotters are a granddaddy of graphics output. They have been used in CAD/CAM environments for years. Their resolution and ability to draw fine detail far exceeds that of most CRTs or printers

The LaserPro Gold Express eight-page-per-minute laser printer has a cartridge-based PostScript compatible interpreter system, ProScribe, so that the printer can accept PostScript language files.

Courtesy, Oasys Systems, Inc.

Courtesy, Benson-Schlumberger Co.

A tabletop ink-jet, drop-on-demand plotter, the Benson Colorscan 800, provides high-resolution color graphics hard copy to mainframes and minicomputers. Because of its ability to mix colors and create subtle shading, the unit is used in applications such as solids modeling, advertising, and publishing.

Photo: Author

The resulting print, in shades of pinks for the car and greens for the background, has an airbrush appearance. From the Benson Colorscan 800.

Detail of above.

The family of Hewlett-Packard pen plotters covers almost every need. From top to bottom: the HP7550A automatic sheet feed plotter; the HP 7475A business professional plotter; the HP7470A personal computer plotter.

Courtesy: Hewlett-Packard Co.

of any other type. Pen plotters are the workhorses of the industry. Ink jet, electrostatic, and thermal transfer technologies are relatively new in plotter applications, and their procedures parallel the same technologies in printers.

The pen plotter produces images by controlling pens related to an X-Y coordinate system. They convert the raster output from the display to a vector output on the plotter. The pen colors are placed by the user so that plotted results are usually in color, although black pens are often used in varying tip widths. The pens can move or draw from point to point in a (seemingly) random manner, whereas a standard print procedure produces successive lines of output.

Small system plotters, with from one to eight pens, are popular in the small office and for a wide variety of business and mechanical drawing applications. Larger plotters are more frequently used in CAE and CAD/CAM work situations. Plotter speed is measured

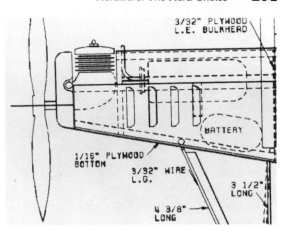

A dot matrix printed texture differs from that of an ink jet printer (page 269), and from the plotted line (right).

Detail of a line produced by a pen plotter illustrates slight stairstepping.

in DPI (dots per inch) and ips (inches per second). Resolution is expressed in fractions of an inch. These plotters can handle either cut or sheet-feed paper and are available in plotting "beds" of different widths. Pen plotters vary so widely in capabilities and features that it is not surprising that prices range from $500 to $100,000.

Pen plotters are usually driven by compatible software, but they can operate by controlling functions directly from a button panel on the plotter. In pen plotters, both the medium and the paper move in relation to each other. In the following technologies, there are no moving pens; paper feeds through the unit similar to the way it feeds through a printer.

Other plotter technology is coming onto the market rapidly and should be explored. Plotters promise high speeds and a variety of tonal and textured images.

In an electrostatic plotter only the paper moves across the plotter's head, which consists of addressable styli composed of thousands of tiny wires. The paper itself accepts a charge from the styli, using raster data. Next, the paper is subjected to a wet toning process, and wherever there is a charge on the paper, carbon particles adhere to it. The drawing is made the full width of the media. The next process is a toning solution, which removes any excess carbon, and the paper emerges dry.

Some electrostatic systems can mix color. This involves putting the paper through the toning bath five times: once for registration and four more times for color mixing and toning.

Everything except the media is stationary in a thermal transfer plotter. Pinheads are selectively heated and melt ink onto the media.

Products and Companies

The following are among the best-known manufacturers of a product; some representative items may be shown in this chapter. These are only a small number of the total manufacturers. For additional products in each category, refer to magazine ads and articles.

Input Devices—Mice, Digitizing Tablets, etc.

CalComp
2411 West LaPalma Ave.
Anaheim, CA 92801
714   821-2142

Electronic Arts
1810 Gateway Dr.
San Mateo, CA 94404
415   571-7171

Inset Systems (Software)
12 Mill Plain Rd.
Danbury, CT 06811
203   748-0844

Kurta Corp.
4610 S. 35th St.
Phoenix, AZ 85040
602   276-5533

Logitech, Inc.
6505 Kaiser Dr.
Fremont, CA 94555
415   795-8500

Microsoft
16011 N.E. 36th
Redman, WA 98073
206   882-8301

Mouse Systems Corp.
47505 Seabridge Dr.
Fremont, CA 94538
415   656-1117

MSC Technologies, Inc.
47505 Seabridge Dr.
Fremont, CA 94538
415   656-1117

Numonics Corp.
101 Commerce Dr.
Montgomeryville, PA 18936
215   362-2766

Summagraphics
777 State St. Extension
Fairfield, CT 06430
203   384-1344

Image Scanners

Apple Computer, Inc.
20525 Mariani Ave.
Cupertino, CA 95014
408   252-2775

Bell & Howell Co.
Document Management Products Div.
6800 N. McCormick Blvd.
Chicago, IL 60645
312   675-7600
312   673-3300

Canon U.S.A., Inc.
One Canon Plaza
Lake Success, NY 11042
516   488-6700

CompuScan, Inc.
3000 Broadacres Dr.
Bloomfield, NJ 07003
201   338-5000

Diamond Flower Electronic Instruments Co.
2544 Port St.
West Sacramento, CA 95691
916   373-1234

Howtek, Inc.
8500 Cameron Rd.
Austin, TX 78753
512   835-0900

Kye International Corp.
12675 Colony St.
Chino, CA 91710
714   590-3940
800   456-7KYE (in CA)
800   332-2KYE

Logitech International, Inc.
6505 Kaiser Dr.
Fremont, CA 94555
415   795-8500

Microtek Lab, Inc.
680 Knox St.
Torrance, CA 90502
213   795-8500

The Complete PC
521 Cottonwood Dr.
Milpitas, CA 95035
408   434-0145

Output Devices—Monitors

Amdek Corp.
1901 Zanker Rd.
San Jose, CA 95112
800   722-6335

Mitsubishi Electronics
991 Knox St.
Torrance, CA 90502
213   515-3993

NEC Home Electronics
1255 Michael Dr.
Wood Dale, IL 60191
708   860-9500

Princeton Graphics
601 Ewing St., Bldg. A
Princeton, NJ 08540
609   683-1660

Sony Corp.
Sony Drive
Park Ridge, NJ 07656
800   222-0878

Zenith Data Systems
1000 Milwaukee Ave.
Glenview, IL 60025
708   699-4800
800   842-9000

Printers/Plotters

Agfa Matrix
1 Ramland Rd.
Orangeburg, NY 10962
914   365-0190

Apple Computer (See above)

Benson, Schlumberger Co.
385 Ravendale Dr.
Mountain View, CA 94039
415   964-7900

CalComp (See above)

Enter Computer, Inc.
7710 Kenamar Court
San Diego, CA 92121
619   578-4070
800   356-2808 (outside California)

Epson America, Inc.
2728 Lomita Blvd.
Torrance, CA 90505
213   539-9140

Hewlett-Packard Co.
16399 W. Bernardo Dr.
San Diego, CA 92127
619   487-4100

Oasys—Office Automation Systems, Inc.
9940 Barnes Canyon Rd.
San Diego, CA 92121
619   436-4395
452-9400

Tektronix, Inc.
Box 500
Beaverton, OR 97077
503   627-1844

Workstations

Autographix
(See Chapter 14)

Genigraphics
(See Chapter 14)

Chyron Corp.
265 Spagnoli
Melville, NY 11747
516   249-3018

Crosfield-Dicomed
(See Chapter 14)

Pansophic Systems, Inc.
2400 Cabot Dr.
Lisle, IL 60532
708   505-6000
800   544-8309

Sun Microsystems
PO Box 13447
Research Triangle Park, NC 27709
919   469-8300

Superset, Inc.
11025 Roselle St.
San Diego, CA 92121
619   452-8665

The Big Picture: Projecting the Image

Ultimately, the visuals you create must be displayed on some type of device so an audience can view them. Whether the final image is seen on the computer terminal or on a floor-to-ceiling-size screen in an auditorium, a projection system is required.

Projectors usually fall into a small-screen or large-screen category. Many companies market a variety of units for different purposes.

Small-Screen CRT and Video Projectors

Small-screen projection would be a cathode-ray tube (CRT) such as your computer screen or a video terminal such as those used for videocassette recorders (VCRs). An average 12- or 14-inch computer screen can be viewed efficiently by a few people at one time. A few more can gather around a 19-inch screen. The same is true for VCR screens. Often, several small video units are placed around an auditorium so groups of 20 or 30 can view a tape.

There are four other small-screen CRT projection systems: Video-Show from General Parametrics, PC Emcee from Computer Support Corp., the VIP from Agfa Matrix, and Showmate 4 from Eiki/Bell & Howell.

VideoShow

VideoShow uses a proprietary technology that will project a high-resolution slide show from a floppy disk. The original disk can be made on any resolution system, and the files can be displayed on any CRT regardless of the resolution, or on any color TV, color monitor, or video projector. The resulting show will be high resolution because of the technology of VideoShow.

The unit is the size of a briefcase, so a presenter can carry it about easily, plug it into any compatible personal computer (MS DOS and Macintosh versions are available), insert the disk in the VideoShow unit's disk drive and make the presentation. No other software is required once the disk is prepared. The unit supports up to 1,000 colors (again, independent of the PC unit).

VideoShow business charts and graphs may be designed with

General Parametrics' compatible PictureIt software. Several other popular software packages have drivers that support VideoShow. The unit has a battery-powered, infrared, handheld remote control unit with 23 keys. The presenter can change screens from about 20 feet away and in line with the unit.

PC Emcee

PC Emcee, from Computer Support Corp., is a combination of software and playback equipment for your PC. An image can be captured from a software program and then inserted in a script using PC Emcee software. That image can be enhanced with a fully functional paint program and a variety of high-quality, well-designed fonts. The editor lets you arrange the sequence of graphics, alter the timing, and change the color of the elements. Then you play your script automatically or under manual control, but instead of appearing as one computer screen after another, the playback is like a videotaped sequence. You can program in 51 different special effects, animation, and sound. The inexpensive system includes software, a box, and a remote-control cordless hand piece. Three levels of the system are available; they range in price from $500 to $1,000.

VIP

The Agfa Matrix VIP electronic presentation system integrates graphics, animation, sound, video, and high-resolution output in one easy-to-use communication tool. Since it is compatible with popular

Courtesy, Mitsubishi Electronics

A monitor is the most obvious small-screen projection device. It's an efficient viewing system for only a few people at a time in a small area.

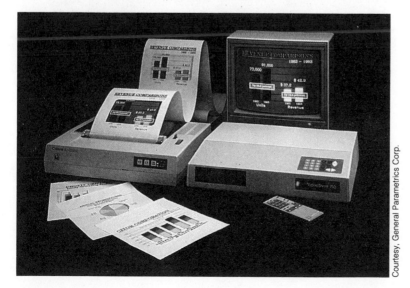

Courtesy, General Parametrics Corp.

The floppy disk is placed in the VideoShow unit, which outputs the image to the color monitor. The same image can be output to a printer for color and black and white hard copy.

Courtesy, Computer Support Corp.

PC Emcee consists of a software package and two presentation coprocessor hardware accessories. The IBM PC (or compatible) may be used to create and deliver a total business presentation quickly. The presentation may be automated or manually controlled, and images may be accessed randomly.

Courtesy, Agfa-Matrix Instruments, Inc.

The Agfa Matrix VIP is a total presentation system with which users can create animated presentations with input from a variety of electronic sources. The presentation can then be output to a computer terminal, a TV set, a VCR, or a large projection system. One can also send screen images to a film recorder for slide making.

PC Graphics software, the VIP allows users to create animated business graphics, integrate photos captured by a video digitizer, control a videodisk or VCR, and produce output to a VCR, TV set, computer monitor, various projection devices, and also to a film recorder if slides are desired.

Showmate 4

Eiki/Bell & Howell has a portable VCR system, the Showmate 4, that is lightweight and small enough to be stored beneath an airplane seat. The battery-operated unit lists for about $1,000, plus the rechargeable battery and carrying case. The screen is 7-inch diagonal.

Several other manufacturers have similar units or variations of the technology. They can be found in catalogs and in magazines that cater to the audio-visual industry.

Large-Screen Projection

35 mm Slide Projectors

A large-screen projection system is ideal when one has to address a large audience. The most popular systems are 35 mm slide projectors, which can project an image across a huge auditorium. Several models are available. In addition, there are 35 mm projectors designed for small-screen viewing, or they may be used for small- and large-screen images.

There are varying models of slide projectors with different capabilities, brightness, and features. Among new features are a built-in fade system; that means that one slide appears to fade off-screen as the next comes on-screen. Traditionally, one needs two machines and a special controller box to effect such a fade.

There are also slide projection systems for personal previewing to two or three people. Most have the option of presenting the image on the box itself or switching to a larger projection. These may be ample for a small group because lenses and light intensity are limited.

The presenter should watch for new utilities to use with projectors. Navitar, for example, has a unit that will replace the lamp housing

Eastman Kodak Ektagraphic units can play back a tape-recorded message timed with the displayed images on the self-contained screen. Slides may also be projected from the front of the unit onto a large screen.

The Bell & Howell RingMaster II is a microprocessor-controlled sound and slide projector with a hand-held remote control unit. The slides in the carousel on top are projected from behind the self-contained screen.

The OSRAM Diaster AV-Pro is a rear-projection slide viewer that folds into a compact unit for easy portability. The screen is 7 × 7 inches. Slides are mounted in a stack loader.

Courtesy, Eastman Kodak Co.

Courtesy, Bell & Howell Co.

Courtesy, Osram Sales Corp.

The Dukane PRO 150 sound/slide projector is compact enough to slide under an airline seat. It can project on its own built-in 6 × 9-inch high brilliance screen or be switched to a front screen projector for larger groups. It has a microphone and tape recorder system.

Courtesy, Dukane Corp.

A follow-focus power zoom 35 mm slide proctor, the Omni Zoom, allows for automatic zoom and automatic focus in the zoom mode so a still image can be projected in a wide variety of sizes, action, and special effects.

Courtesy, Elmo Mfg. Corp.

A twin projector unit with built-in special effect dissolve capability. The Royale system 150 also contains a stereo cassette tape system at the bottom of the unit. A pair of compact two-way speakers provides high-quality stereo. It closes into a compact transportable unit.

Courtesy, RMF Products, Inc.

in a Kodak Ektagraphic III projector and increase the unit's brightness by up to 50 percent. Look into cordless, remote-control slide changer units and pointers.

LCD Flat Panel Display Units

A group of projection devices is based on a liquid crystal display system (LCD) and the technology is advancing so rapidly it's difficult to keep up with who is doing what.

An LCD unit is a panel about 2½ inches thick and works with an overhead projection unit. The unit sits on the light stage of an overhead projector and is connected to the projector and to a computer. With this system, whatever is displayed on the computer screen is simultaneously displayed on a large screen in the same way an overhead transparency would be displayed. (See Chapter 10 for a full discussion on LCDs.)

Stand-Alone Monochrome Projectors

The Limelight, from Vivid Systems, is a monochrome projector that also takes images from the computer and instantly outputs them on a large screen. It works off standard composite video signals generated by an Apple II, Macintosh, or IBM color card, or from a VCR. The projected image is green.

Courtesy, Eastman-Kodak Co.

The Kodak DATASHOW Projection Pad is a liquid crystal display unit that is placed on an overhead projector (the Kodak Ektalite). This picture illustrates the hookup and projection using a Macintosh. In a real situation, the computer would face the speaker, not the audience, so he could see what is being shown. A hand control unit is used to advance the images; the keyboard may also be used when necessary.

The Vivid Limelight projector weighs only 15 pounds and projects monochrome images directly from the computer. It's aimed at small group presentations in an office, classroom, lecture hall, trade show exhibit, or for teleconferencing.

The Limelight, weighing 15 pounds, is also in the heavy portable category, compared to LCD systems used with overhead projectors. A Limelight projection works best on a special curved-foil screen, but the image may be projected on a conventional screen or matte wall. The unit must be placed close to the screen. It is quiet because it does not have a fan-cooling system as do conventional slide projectors.

Kodak Video Projectors for Large-Screen Presentations

The Kodak LC500 is a breakthrough in large-screen video because it can plug directly into a VCR, laser disk player, or computer. When the unit is interfaced into a computer, images can be played that are on disk, or the presenter can work interactively with a program. Videotape and computer graphics can be combined in a single presentation.

Computer/Video Projectors

If you've attended a football game or other major sporting event, it's possible that a large-screen projector at each end of the playing field was used to show a blowup of the live action or of an instant replay so it could be seen more readily by everyone in the stadium.

Large-screen color projectors aren't all aimed at vast stadium audiences. Nor are they all so gigantic. Businesses and organizations are becoming increasingly aware of the value of video as a communications medium. And computers are becoming increasingly capable of producing graphics that speed professional communications and decision making.

Where are such projectors used? In the growing number of corporate presentation rooms, large and small auditoriums and meeting rooms, at conventions, and in training centers. They're applicable wherever it's more practical to run a program directly from a computer screen, videotape, or camera, rather than use 35 mm slides.

Using a video projector system to display computer output makes good sense. One unit can replace several 19-inch monitors that must be placed around an auditorium for audience viewing. Monitors require coordinating and interfacing to a host computer or VCR. Even then, it's likely that one or more are not perfectly coordinated, or that color is not true. Wiring can pose a foot-traffic hazard.

The image size possible from a video projector ranges from about 5 feet to 15 feet diagonally, a vast improvement over 19-inch, and smaller, monitors. Units can be portable and placed on a rolling cart, or on a table, or they can be permanently mounted on a ceiling. Some units can project a sharp, bright image as far as 36 feet from the screen, though 5 to 25 feet is the average for mid-priced units.

What to Consider in Computer/Video Displays

Computer/video displays were traditionally heavy, bulky, and hard to use. Most units have separate lenses for each of three primary colors, red, green, and blue (RGB), so they require careful adjustment to get all three lenses aligned and focused, a process called "convergence." Systems installed in-house usually are ceiling-mounted and hard to get to. Those that have to be brought in from an AV source require careful readjustment each time they are transported.

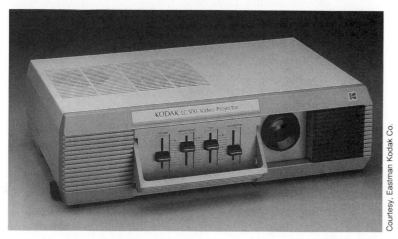

Courtesy, Eastman Kodak Co.

The Kodak LC500 video projector is smaller than a VCR and weighs only 13 pounds. It projects a video image up to 12 feet wide and is as easy to operate as a slide projector. In a medium-to-large-size room, using this projector would eliminate the need to set up several small VCR screens.

Manufacturers have addressed these problems and now have incorporated microprocessor control to automate conversion and diagnostics. They've added remote-control systems so the projectors are easier for the presenter to use. They've made the units lighter weight and more portable.

High image quality and setup are prime considerations, and these are improving, too. Now that convergence is not in the hands of an operator and one-time setups exist, image quality is retained. Generally, poor setups caused blurred lines or spots and failure to resolve fine details.

The Electrohome 2000 has only a single exterior lens to focus rather than the usual three lenses that have to be synchronized. The unit's three internal color lenses are prefocused so setup time should be no more than 15 minutes.

High resolution is important; computer displays are ahead of video in the use of higher scan rates for better resolution, and they keep improving. The problem is that large organizations that invest in video displays may have more than one generation of computer graphics in use. If they use computer-to-video display, the units may not be compatible. The answer is a system with multiscanning capabilities or an investment in a converter between projector and computer equipment.

Video color displays may not replicate a computer screen perfectly for the same reasons, already mentioned, that affect resolution. Display color and sharpness are also affected by the distance of the projector to the screen and by ambient room light. Generally, optimum rendition occurs using a 1½ to 1 ratio. That means for every foot of screen width, the projector should be 1½ feet from the screen. For a 10-foot screen, you should place the unit 15 feet away.

Units are designed for different room sizes and distances from projector to screen. Light intensity drops with the square of the distance, so the farther away and bigger the picture, the more throw light needed. Don't buy a low-brightness unit thinking you'll place it farther from the screen; that will cause sharpness and brightness to suffer.

Resolution, Scan Rate, and Brightness

Resolution and image quality depend on the horizontal scan rate of the CRT. The higher the operating frequency of the display, the higher the resolution and the quality of its signal. Video projectors have high horizontal scanning rates designed to support the range of resolutions that exist in graphics systems. Systems can generate images greater than the standard number of scan lines, depending on the graphics board used. Possibilities include the CGA (Color/Graphics Adapter), EGA (Enhanced Graphics Adapter), VGA

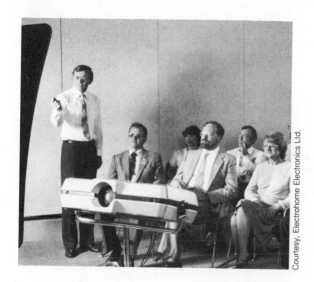

Courtesy, Electrohome Electronics Ltd.

Electrohome portable ECP1000 projects images directly from the computer or from videotapes to a large screen size. Color and monochrome units are available. With the addition of a special decoder, the image can be switched from videotape to computer output with the touch of a button. Images are bright and will show in subdued lighting when used with a curved high-brightness screen.

(Video Graphics Array), the Number 9 Board, AT&T Targa, and high-performance graphics workstations. High-resolution boards can produce images with as many as 1,024 lines compared to the low resolution of 512 lines.

Most have a scan rate between 15 and 27 kHz, which is the industry standard. The low end is 15.75 kHz; in some systems it's 50–60 kHz, even 100. Most units are in the 15–25 kHz range, which covers about 75 percent of users' needs. When you get above that you're getting into high-resolution CAD applications. A system developed to cater to high-resolution output is Electrohome's ECP CAD/CAM. This system has horizontal scan frequencies as high as 71 kHz, which will support a 1,280 × 1,024, 60 kHz, noninterlaced display for CAD workstations.

Resolution rating is often based on a 12-inch screen. When you blow the image up to 10 feet, the same 1,000 lines are now spread over 10 or more feet, so clarity is reduced. An image that is crystal sharp on a computer EGA or VGA monitor will still look good blown up large, but not nearly as sharp as it appears on the computer screen. Some units don't support EGA or VGA unless their scan rate goes up to 25 mHz.

All customers do not require high resolution, so many companies offer models with slower scan rates to achieve lower prices. Electrohome's model ECP 2000, with a 15 to 33 scan rate, is about half the price of its high-resolution ECP CAD/CAM unit, which has a 30 to 71 kHz scan rate.

Brightness differs by unit and the number of lumens output. (A lumen is a measure of light intensity.) Watch advertising claims of brightness carefully. Some manufacturers advertise brightness at peak level, but rarely will you operate a unit at peak all the

Courtesy, Electrohome Electronics Ltd.

The Electrohome ECP 3000 is a data/graphics and video projection system that uses a three-lens technology. Lens setting, convergence, and diagnostics are microprocessor controlled. The unit may be used on a base or suspended from a ceiling.

time because that would shorten the life of the tube. Also, as brightness is increased, contrast and sharpness decrease.

Some manufacturers cite specifications that are more conservative than others in their measure of brightness. A unit advertised as 400 lumens is not necessarily brighter than one that is advertised at 300 lumens. The same image viewed from these two units side by side appears the same.

There are other aspects of a machine and perceived brightness. GE's Talaria Multi-Standard Projector uses a light-valve technology that transmits or reflects light depending on the video signal. It can generate brightness of 3,800 lumens, compared to less than 600 lumens in other systems. That means that Talaria images can be seen well even in brightly lit rooms. The Talaria projector also uses a single lens. GE's Imager line generates 400 lumens.

When you consider purchase of a large-screen computer/video projector, research the market well before you make your decision. Renting rather than investing may make sense for individual presentations because you can familiarize yourself with a projector's capabilities and drawbacks in your environment. Look at the company's upgrade policies so you can stay up with technology at a reasonable cost. Evaluate your requirements realistically for the future, not just the present.

Projection Screens

Presenters usually walk into a room, set up their slides, and hope for the best possible lighting. Few presenters think about the type of screen used. Usually, they have little or no control over the conditions.

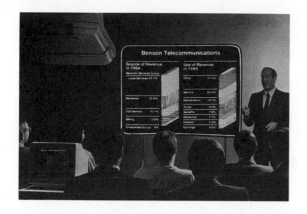

The Electrohome ECP 3000 (shown at left) suspended in a corporate auditorium. The system can take an image from a computer and display it, as shown. It can also be used for displaying video.

Anyone who buys a screen, from the individual who must drag it from place to place, to those who outfit corporate presentation theatres and large auditoriums, should know what they are installing and why. Screens differ in how they reflect light and the resulting image. The wrong screen could mean that everyone doesn't see the show, depending on where they are seated. It's sad when someone spends hundreds of hours and dollars preparing a presentation and finds that the image is sorely degraded when the screen is not appropriate for the room and the lighting.

Four types of surfaces are used for projection screens: matte, lenticular, beaded, and high-gain. They all do a good job of reflecting light thrown onto them, but each reflects light differently. One type reflects light within a narrow cone; another spreads it over a wide angle. The wider the angle of light spread, the dimmer the image. The object is to achieve the brightest image possible.

A *matte screen* produces the least bright screen; but it's the same brightness for all people viewing the screen regardless of their viewing angle. The color is excellent; it is the sharpest of all four types. It's the recommended screen when people are spread across a wide room. This screen is at optimum brightness when the room is completely dark.

A *lenticular screen* has a brighter image than a matte screen but has a more directional light pattern. It's a good choice when viewers will not be seated at extreme angles to the screen. The screen is composed of embossed patterns of rectangles, stripes, diamonds, or ribs that act like thousands of small mirrors or lenses to reflect the light. A lenticular screen can be used in a room that is only partially dark, because any stray light is reflected back onto the screen.

A *beaded screen* is a good choice for a long, narrow room. The screen is composed of clear glass beads bonded to a white backing. It reflects almost all the light back to the source. The image is about four times as a bright as that on a matte screen. However, brightness falls off quickly at wider angles. A beaded screen works best in a dark room where there is little or no stray light.

A *high-gain screen* is the choice when slides must be projected in a lighted room. The screens are made of thin sheets of specially processed aluminum foil, permanently laminated to a lightweight frame. The reflected image is about 12 times brighter than that on a matte screen. The audience must be seated within a 30 degree projection-to-screen axis; those sitting outside that viewing area may not see the image. These screens are relatively expensive and cannot be rolled up.

Consider the shape of a screen. Screens are horizontal, vertical, or square. The square is always a compromise because it will accommodate horizontal or vertical formats.

Products and Distributors/Manufacturers

35 mm Slide and Large-Screen Projectors

Contact the following companies for brochures and specification sheets about their units. Also see Chapters 9 and 10 for information on overhead projectors. See Chapter 11 for liquid crystal display (LCD) flat panel projectors.

Agfa Matrix Division
1 Ramland Rd.
Orangeburg, NY 10962
914 365-0190
800 828-6489

Arcturus, Inc.
50 Beharrell St.
West Concord, MA 01742
617 369-5360

Barco Industry, Inc.
195 Jefferson Dr.
Menlo Park, CA 94025
415 328-4380

Bell & Howell Video Systems
720 Landwehr Rd.
Northbrook, IL 60062
708 291-1150

Computer Support Corp.
15926 Midway Rd.
Dallas, TX 75244
214 661-8960

Dukane Corp.
2900 Dukane Dr.
St. Charles, IL 60174
708 584-2300
800 634-2800 (in IL); 800 356-6540

Eastman Kodak Co. (DATASHOW)
343 State St.
Rochester, NY 14650
716 724-3313
800 242-2424

Eiki/Bell & Howell AV Products
27882 Camino Capistrano
Laguna Niguel, CA 92677
714 582-2511
800 543-EIKI

Electrohome Electronics Ltd.
809 Wellington St.
N. Kitchener, Ontario, Canada N2G 4J6
519 744-7111

Electronic Systems Products (Esprit)
1301 Armstrong Dr.
Titusville, FL 32780
305 269-6680

Elmo Manufacturing Corp.
70 New Hyde Park Blvd.
New Hyde Park, NY 11040
516 775-3200

General Electric
Projection Display Products Operation
Electronics Park Building 6–295
Syracuse, NY 13221
315 456-2152

General Parametrics Corp.
1250 Ninth St.
Berkeley, CA 94710
415   524-3950
800   556-1234

Hughes Aircraft Co.
6155 El Camino Real
Carlsbad, CA 92009
619   931-3619

JBL Professional
8500 Balboa Blvd.
Northridge, CA 91329
818   893-8411

Kloss Video Corp.
640 Memorial Dr.
Cambridge, MA 02139
617   577-1000

Mitsubishi Electronics America, Inc.
991 Knox St.
Torrance, CA 90502
213   515-3993

Navitar/D.O. Industries, Inc.
200 Commerce Drive
Rochester, NY 14623
716   359-4000
800   828-6778

NEC Home Electronics (U.S.A.) Inc.
1255 Michael Dr.
Wood Dale, IL 60191
708   860-9500

Osram Sales Corp.
PO Box 7062
Newburgh, NY 12550
914   564-6300
800   431-9980

Panasonic Industrial Co.
1 Panasonic Way
Secaucus, NJ 07094
201   348-7000

RMF Products
1275 Paramount Pkwy.
PO Box 520
Batavia, IL 60510
708   879-0020

Sony Corporation
AV Products
213 N. Cedar Ave.
Inglewood, CA 90300
213   671-2636

Sony/Tektronix
Tektronix, Inc.
PO Box 500
Beaverton, OR 97077
800   225-5434

Toshiba America Inc.
One Parkway N., Suite 500
Deerfield, IL 60015
708   945-1500

Vivid Systems, Inc.
41752 Christy St.
Fremont, CA 94538
415   656-9965
800   331-2834

Projection Screens

Apollo Audio Visual
60 Trade Zone Court
Ronkonkoma, NY 11779
516   467-8033
800   777-3750

Brandons, Inc.
1819 Kings Ave.
Jacksonville, FL 32207
904   398-1591
800   874-5273

Da-Lite Screen Co.
3100 State Road 15 North
PO Box 137
Warsaw, IN 46580
219   372-1305

The Screen Works
3925 N. Pulaski Rd.
Chicago, IL 60641
312   588-8380

APPENDIX
A
Glossary

Addressable resolution A term that describes the number of pixels that are placed on each line of film by the film recorder's light source. The greater the number of pixels, the clearer will be the image on the finished film medium.

Airbrush A special effect in a paint program that simulates an airbrush texture.

Analog film recorder One that records the image as it comes from the computer screen and at the same resolution as the screen (see *Digital film recorder*).

Analog monitor Uses an analog signal; voltage varies continuously. Displays infinite number of shades of the primary colors, or a gray scale (see *Digital monitor*).

Animation A process in computer graphics of creating movement of images on-screen.

Anti-aliasing On a graphics display, any technique that will diminish the error that appears as a function of the graphics hardware. An example of this error is the common "stepped" or "jagged" appearance of a straight line when displayed on a raster system.

ASCII Acronym for American Standard Code for Information Interchange. This standard for data transmission assigns individual 7-bit codes to represent each of a specific set of 128 numerals, letters, and special controls.

Aspect ratio In computer graphics, the ratio of the horizontal to vertical dimensions of a frame or image. The ability to maintain or control this ratio is important in the transfer and reproduction of an image for various types of displays or for printed material.

Axes Plural of axis (see *Axis*).

Axis A line that is fixed, along which distances are measured or to which positions are referenced.

Axis label Either a number or name given to a position of an entry on the axis line.

Bar chart A pictorial representation by bars, horizontal or vertical, to show variations on one set of values and their relationship to variations in another set of values.

Bit map Each pixel (picture element) on a video screen is controlled by bits that set intensity and color. The full video screen with its grid of pixels is referred to as a bit map.

Build-up A method of presenting topics by adding one line at a time as the topic is presented (see *Reveal*).

Bullet In a text chart, the circle, star, or other symbol used to emphasize a line of type or word.

CAD Acronym for Computer-Aided Design. In graphics, the production of drawings and plans for architecture, engineering systems, and so on.

CAM Acronym for Computer-Aided Manufacture (see *CAD*).

CGA Acronym for Color/Graphics Adapter. The first color video interface standard established for IBM PCs. Resolution from 3,200 × 200 to 640 × 200.

Chart element Essential component of a chart or graph such as a bar, pie segment, line, grid element, legend, and so on.

Clustered bar graph Type of bar chart that compares two or three sets of data by grouping the elements together.

Column chart A chart consisting of vertical bars.

Convert utility A small program that allows the user to change one file format to another for output to different devices.

Coordinate Either of a pair of numbers used to specify the location of a point on a two-dimensional surface.

CP/M Control Program for Microprocessors. An operating system developed by Digital Research, Inc., for the Intel 8080 and ZILOG family of eight-bit word-size microprocessors.

Critical path A series of tasks that have a determined duration and how they appear in relation to the completion date of a project.

CRT Acronym for Cathode-Ray Tube. Type of display screen, video screen, or monitor used to display output such as text and graphics.

Curve fitting The automatic drawing of a smooth curved line between plotted points.

Default Standard specification, values, or settings given to a program or hardware, when no other specifications or conditions are given.

Diagram chart A pictorial representation of a subject with elements arranged in terms of the whole.

DIF Acronym for Data Interchange Format. A system that permits grabbing data from one program and bringing it into another.

Digital film recorder One that reads the files from the graphics software and converts the digital data into an analog signal. Resolution of final film is higher than screen resolution (see *Analog film recorder*).

Digital monitor Opposite of analog monitor. Smaller range of color choices compared to VGA or analog monitors (see *VGA* and *Analog monitors*).

DOS Acronym for Disk Operating System. A set of software instructions required to manage the hardware and logic resources of a computer.

Dot matrix printer A printer with several tiny projecting wires or needles that combine to form dotted representations of individual characters within a matrix. Dot matrix printers can produce graphics output because each pin is addressable.

Download To transfer programs and/or data files from a computer to another device or computer.

Driver Small programs used to control external devices or to run other programs. Driver software directs production, manipulation, and presentation of appropriate signals by the processor so that the device will perform as required. For example, a specific software driver is required to run each type of plotter or printer.

Dump To display, print, or store the contents of the computer's memory (also see *Screen dump*).

EGA Acronym for Enhanced Graphics Adapter. IBM standard developed after CGA. Maximum 640 × 350 resolution.

Enhance The act of altering a basic image to conform to better design standards and visual understanding.

Explode Style feature, usually used with pie charts, to move one slice of the pie out of the circle to give it emphasis.

Fat bit editing The ability to magnify a portion of a picture and edit it pixel by pixel.

Fill pattern Solid color or design provided in the software and used to fill in, or give texture and pattern to, elements of a chart or a drawing.

Font Style characteristics for alphabets and numbers such as roman, italic, Helvetica, bold, shadowed, and so on.

Gantt A chart used for project management that shows scheduling of steps required to complete a project during a given period of time.

Grab utility A small RAM resident program that allows the user to capture a screen from any program and bring it into a file for imaging or output through another program.

Graph area The area upon which a graph is plotted, located within the x- and y-axis ranges.

Grid Horizontal and vertical lines intersecting each other to form the graph area for line and bar charts. In a pie chart, lines that radiate from a point in degrees to form the graph area.

Hard copy The printed or plotted output on paper or other medium.

Host The computer or source of video signal that controls the graphics terminal.

Icon Symbolic images of software procedures that the user selects for carrying out a desired function.

Image processing The manipulation of picture elements. Usually two-dimensional images are entered into the computer, then enhanced into a form that has more meaning to the user. Examples are drawings, parts of drawings, photographs, or computer-aided designs.

Image recorder A peripheral device that records digital signals and graphics images for producing 35 mm slides or photographs.

Impact printer A printer in which a hammer or striking unit transfers ink from ribbon to paper. These include band, drum, chain, cylinder, typeball, daisy wheel, and thimble design printers.

Index chart Variation on a line chart used to show relative change; compares two or more series of data measured in different units.

Ink jet printer A type of printer in which dot matrix characters are formed by ink droplets electrostatically aimed at the paper surface. Some advantages are high resolution, color reproduction (if color is used), and quiet operation.

Input form In a business graphics program, the set of questions that the user must fill in to provide the program with data used to generate a chart.

Input/output The processes involved in transferring information into or out of a central processing unit.

Interlaced A method of scanning used in video transmission in which each picture (frame) is divided into two complete sets of interleaving lines to reduce flicker.

Interlaced fields A technique found in raster scan display systems to minimize flicker on the display screen.

Jaggies See *Stair-stepping*.

Joystick A vertical stick or lever that can be tilted in various directions to indicate direction of cursor movement on a screen. Most joysticks can move the cursor only vertically and/or horizontally.

Justification The position of type or print within an area so it begins flush left or ends flush right.

Keyboard An input device consisting of switches with marked keytops that, when pressed manually, generate a code representing individual characters.

Label The tag or explanation provided for a chart element.

Laser printers A printer technology that focuses laser beams to form images on photosensitive drums using a principle similar to that used in Xerographic office copiers. Laser printers used are high-speed, high-quality output devices for computers.

LCD Acronym for Liquid Crystal Display. A technology used in flat panel display systems.

Learning curve Refers to the speed and ease of acquiring facility with a program or hardware.

Legend Information attached to a chart.

Letter quality printer A printer that uses a ball, daisy wheel, or thimble element to produce one complete character representation with each stroke.

Letter quality printers are better adapted to text than graphics.

Light pen A stylus-shaped photosensitive pointing device that allows interactive communication between the computer user and a terminal screen. When the user touches the pen to a position on the screen, then that coordinate on the screen is input as data to the system.

Line chart Composed of connecting data points.

Line drawing Representation of an object's image by entering a solid-line outline of surfaces. The mass or shape of the form between the lines will be inferred by the viewer.

Line drawing, two-dimensional A method of display that represents line drawings on a flat image, such as a building floorplan, or a two-axis graph. No depth is suggested.

Line drawing, three-dimensional Describes a three-dimensional object's projection onto a two-dimensional display surface. Techniques of perspective projection are employed, similar to the projection of a real object through a lens onto the flat viewing glass of a camera.

Mainframe A large computer in both size and capacity.

Manipulation The act of changing or arranging data or their format to ease processing or arrive at a new image or problem solution.

Map chart A pictorial graph showing locations of a designated geographical area.

Mass storage Large-capacity (megabytes, gigabytes) secondary storage systems. Typical mass storage devices are recording tape and magnetic disks.

Menu A program-generated list of options, usually presented on the display screen, from which the user can select desired procedures for the computer to execute.

Mirror An effect where an image appears to be reflected but in reality is an upside-down or reverse drawing of the original image.

Modem Acronym for modulator-demodulator. A device that connects peripherals and that converts and reconverts digital signals from a computer into tone variations (in serial form) for a transmission over standard telephone communication lines.

Monochrome Producing only black and white images.

Mouse A cursor-positioning device, manipulated by hand, which moves the screen cursor in the same direction as the movement created when the mouse is rolled on a flat surface.

MS DOS Acronym for MicroSoft Disk Operating System, trademarked by MicroSoft Corp.

OEM Acronym for Original Equipment Manufacturer. One manufacturer sells equipment only slightly redesigned to several vendors. Each vendor puts its name on that equipment and sells it as its private brand. This applies to monitors, LCDs, scanners, printers, and many other items.

On-screen slide A graphic image projected directly from the computer terminal.

Orientation A feature of a chart program that permits the output to be plotted or printed horizontally or vertically on a page.

Overhead transparency A transparent film medium used for presentations with an overhead projector.

PC Acronym for personal computer.

PC DOS Acronym for Personal Computer Disk Operating System, trademarked by IBM.

Pell See *Pixel.*

Peripheral A device, usually for input/output such as storage or printing, connected to a computer and under its control to some degree. Examples are printers, plotters, mouse, disk drives, keyboards, and terminals.

PERT Acronym for Program Evaluation and Review Technique. A chart that identifies the major tasks of a project and specifies how the tasks depend on one another.

Picture library A predrawn set of images, designs, and elements that can be accessed and placed in a new picture.

Pie chart A graphic interpretation of data in which parts are compared in size or quantity to a whole.

Pixel Abbreviation for picture element (pix-el) (also "pell"). The basic rectangular element that, in combinations, forms the images on a raster-scan video screen.

Plotter A device for producing hard copy of graphic images by controlling pens or other drawing media. A plotter addresses points related to X and Y coordinate axes as contrasted with a printer that produces successive lines and columns of type.

Program A sequence of instructions given to the computer to perform specific functions or tasks. Programs are also referred to as "software."

Public domain software Software that is not copyrighted and that can be freely exchanged and copied.

RAM Acronym for Random Access Memory. It refers to Read/Write memory.

Raster The predetermined pattern of horizontal lines on the viewing screen of the cathode-ray tube. The lines are scanned by an electron beam and are spaced to aid uniform area coverage.

Raster-fill The process used by a graphics camera to fill in the spaces between the raster lines of the video image to result in an image that appears to have a finer, or higher, resolution.

Resolution The number of pixel positions and lines of pixels sent by the host computer to the video display.

Reveal A method of presenting topics by showing one line at a time.

RGB Acronym for Red/Green/Blue. The color signals transmitted from a monitor using RGB scanning guns.

RGB monitor A type of color monitor with separate inputs for red, green, and blue. It is required for high-resolution color images. Each color signal must be sent separately.

Rotation The turning of a computer-modeled object or image relative to an original point on a coordinate system.

Scale Refers to the series of spaces marked by lines or tic marks and given numerical values.

Scattergram A variation of a line chart that shows how two sets of data correlate. Plotted dots are used but may be connected by lines.

Screen dump To send to the printer the image currently displayed on the screen.

Semilog chart A variation on a line chart used to show a relative change between data expressed in different units.

SIG Acronym for Special Interest Group. People who meet to discuss and exchange information about specific computer-oriented topics such as graphics, business applications, robotics, and so on.

Slide A 35 mm transparency. An on-screen projected image (see *On-screen*).

Software Instructions and programs that tell the computer what operations to perform.

Solids modeling Geometric modeling of an object by construction of a computer model based on the measurements, properties, and relationships of points, lines, angles, and surfaces of the object.

Stacked bar chart Bars are placed on top of one another instead of adjacent to one another.

Stair-stepping Refers to the discontinuous nature of a line drawn by a raster display at any angle other than vertical, horizontal, or 45 degrees. The raster display must approximate the line because of the limitations of resolution. Also called "jaggies."

Stylus A penlike device used with a graphics tablet for inputting position information relative to a coordinate axis system employed by the tablet.

Support In computer practice, the promise by vendors of help and guidance in using purchased or leased software and hardware.

Surface chart Similar to a line chart, in which data points are connected, but the grid area enclosed is filled in or shaded.

Table chart (also *Tabular*) A listing of words or data with precise information.

Text chart A presentation using only or mainly words, messages, statements, and commentaries.

Thermal printer A nonimpact printer that forms characters by applying heat to special heat-sensitive papers.

Throughput The average amount of time for a film recorder to produce an image on a slide. The more complex the image, and the more colors it contains, the longer the throughput.

Tic (tick) marks Small lines that intersect the x-axis or y-axis at intervals that divide data into units. Major tic marks are slightly longer than minor tic marks.

TIFF Acronym for Tag Image File Format. The format used for transporting computerized versions of scanned images.

Trackball A device used mainly to enter data resulting from the movement of a ball which is set in a small box so that it rotates freely. The ball is manipulated by hand and the corresponding positions are shown on the screen.

Turnkey A system or installation that is complete and ready to run without further additions or modifications.

Tutorial (1) Lesson, classes, or demonstrations covering a subject area; (2) instructions about running hardware and/or software, usually in a manual or on disk.

Upload To receive data from another computer by direct interfacing or via a modem.

User interface The on-screen menu that is used to navigate through the program.

VGA Acronym for Video Graphics Array. The graphics standard for the IBM PS/2 compatible with EGA, with higher resolution. Supports analog monitors.

Viewgraph (also *Vugraph*) See *Overhead transparency.*

Window An isolated portion of a cathode-ray tube screen that is used to display information independently of the rest of the screen display.

Wire frame representation A three-dimensional representation of an object with hidden lines shown, giving the impression of a transparent object with only its structure visible.

WYSIWYG Acronym for What You See Is What You Get. The idea that what you see on your terminal is the same as what you get when the file is printed on paper or imaged on film.

X-axis The horizontal line of a chart.

Y-axis On a business chart, usually the vertical line containing the values for data points.

Zoom A feature in a software program that permits magnifying an area for pixel by pixel editing (see *Fat bit editing*).

APPENDIX
Software, Sources, and Company Lists

I. Software and Sources

The following list represents software for a variety of purposes. This is not meant to be a complete list; there are many more packages available. Inclusion does not indicate endorsement. Prices, systems supported, phone numbers, and addresses are subject to change. Each product and name is either a trademark or registered trademark of its company. For a cross-referenced list of companies and their products, see Part II of this appendix. Use it for locating a product by company name.

In the list, the system entry of MS DOS suggests that the program is for use on an IBM PC or is compatible with a PC DOS or MS DOS (Disk Operating System). Symbols used in the Feature(s) column of the list are given below. (Example: PR/CH/DR = PResentation, CHart, DRaw.)

Key to Symbols:

ACC = Accessory
ANI = Animation
Bridge = Connects program to a slide service
CAD = Computer-aided design
CH = Charting features
DE = Design features
DR = Draw features
Front = A front-end program for a specific slide service
PR = Presentation program
PT = Paint features
SLS = Slideshow capability

Software Company	System(s)	Price	Feature(s)
35 mm Express Business & Professional Software 143 Binney St. Cambridge, MA 02142 617 491-3377 800 342-5277	MS DOS	$495	PR/CH/DR/SLS

35 mm Express does much more than produce high-quality slides. Easy to use icon menu. Large symbol library, drawing tools, extensive print drivers, and links to major slide services.

Software Company	System(s)	Price	Feature(s)
Aldus Freehand	Macintosh	$495	PT/DR

Aldus Corp.
411 First Ave. South
Seattle, WA 98104
206 622-5500
800 333-2538

Considered among the top paint/draw packages for the Macintosh. Loaded with features.

Aldus Persuasion	Macintosh	$495	PR/CH/DR

Aldus Corp.
411 First Ave. South
Seattle, WA 98104
206 622-5500
800 333-2538

Complete set of tools and output compatibility for high-quality slides, overheads, prints. Uses outlining and direct application to on-screen chart.

Applause II (formerly DrawApplause)	MS DOS	$495	PR/DE/DR/CH/SLS

Ashton-Tate
20101 Hamilton Ave.
Torrance, CA 90502
213 329-8000

Impressive features for enhancing charts. Extensive clip-art library. Easy color palette customizing. Chart templates. Windows interface. Seamless connection to Ashton-Tate Slide Service.

Art Roundup	Macintosh	$39	ACC

Dubl-Click Software, Inc.
18201 Gresham St.
Northridge, CA 91325
818 349-2758

Opens any paint file, selects any part of a picture, and copies it to Clipboard for use with other programs.

Arts & Letters	MS DOS	$695	DR/DE

Computer Support Corp.
15926 Midway Rd.
Dallas, TX 75244
214 661-8960

A sophisticated, easy-to-use design program with over 3,700 clip-art images for the artist and nonartist.

AutoCAD	MS DOS/Macintosh	$3,000	CAD

Autodesk, Inc.
2658 Marinship Way
Sausalito, CA 94965
415 332-2344

CAD program with drivers to wide variety of peripherals including film recorders.

Autodesk Animator	MS DOS	$299	ANI/PT

Autodesk, Inc.
2658 Marinship Way
Sausalito, CA 94965
415 332-2344

A realtime desktop video program for sophisticated animated presentations.

Software Company	System(s)	Price	Feature(s)
Autographix AutoVisual	MS DOS	$695	Front

Autographix, Inc.
PO Box 9031
Waltham, MA 02154
617   890-8558

A front-end program to Autographix Imaging Centers and to their workstations. Other programs for MS DOS and Macintosh users are also supported.

Autumn
See **Mirage.**

Boardroom Graphics	MS DOS	$150	CH/DR

Analytical Software, Inc.
10939 McCree Rd.
Dallas, TX 75238
214   340-2564

Can include sound in presentations using additional software/hardware.

CA-Cricket Graph	Macintosh	$195	CH

Computer Associates
10505 Sorrento Valley Rd.
San Diego, CA 92121
800   531-5236

Graphs can be exported to Cricket Presents.

CA-Cricket Paint	Macintosh	$295	PT/DR

Computer Associates
10505 Sorrento Valley Rd.
San Diego, CA 92121
800   531-5236

A monochrome paint product for the Macintosh.

CA-Cricket Presents	Macintosh	$495	PR/CH/DR

Computer Associates
10505 Sorrento Valley Rd.
San Diego, CA 92121
800   531-5236

Templates with individualized frames that let you select portions of a slide. Wide choices of charts. Compatible with Cricket Graph and Cricket Stylist.

CA-Cricket Stylist	Macintosh	$295	DR/PT

Computer Associates
10505 Sorrento Valley Rd.
San Diego, CA 92121
800   531-5236

Uses object-oriented drawings that capitalize on the capability of PostScript printers.

CA-SuperImage VAX	MS DOS; Digital VMS	$495	CH/DR/PT

Computer Associates
10505 Sorrento Valley Rd.
San Diego, CA 92121
800   531-5236

A business graphics integration platform for use on a VAX workstation.

Software Company	System(s)	Price	Feature(s)
ChartMaster	MS DOS	*	PR/CH
See **Master Graphics Presentation Pack.**			
Colorix VGA Paint	MS DOS	$199	PT/DR

Rix Softworks, Inc.
18552 MacArthur Blvd.
Irvine, CA 92715
800 345-9059
800 233-5938 (CA)

Works only with VGA boards. High quality, high resolution. For screen output only.

Corel Draw!	MS DOS	$595	DE/DR/PR

Corel Systems Corp.
1600 Carling Ave.
Ottawa, Ontario, Canada KIZ 8R7
613   728-8200
FAX 613 728-9790

A feature-packed, incredibly versatile program.

Crystal 3D	MS DOS	$12,000	PT/DR/ANI

Time Arts
3436 Mendocino Ave.
Santa Rosa, CA 95401
707   576-7722

Solids modeling and animation software.

Dan Bricklin's Demo II	MS DOS	$195	ANI

Peter Norton Computing, Inc.
100 Wilshire Blvd.
Santa Monica, CA 90401
800   365-1010

Designed to develop animation and on-screen slide shows.

Dashboard	MS DOS	$150	CH/ANI

Bridgeway Publishing Corp.
2165 E. Francisco Blvd., Suite A1
San Rafael, CA 94901
415   485-0948

Software for developing on-screen slide shows.

DB Graphics	MS DOS	$295	CH

Microrim
3925 159th Ave. N.E.
Redmond, WA 98073
206   885-2000

A basic charting package with eight chart types.

Decision Graphics	MS DOS	$450	CH

Samna Corp.
270 NE Expressway
Atlanta, GA 30345
404   851-0007
800   241-2065

Well adapted to statistical analysis. Lacking good selection of drivers to film recorders/printers.

---

* No separate price.

Software Company	System(s)	Price	Feature(s)
DeluxePaint II	MS DOS/Amiga	$99	PT

Electronic Arts
1820 Gateway Dr.
San Mateo, CA 94404
415 571-7171
800 245-4525

Probably the most sophisticated group of painting tools in any inexpensive PC program.

DISSPLA & Telegraph	MS DOS/Work Station	$995 to	PR/CH/DR
	DEC/IBM	$120,000	

Computer Associates Intl.
711 Stewart Ave.
Garden City, NY 11530
516 227-3300

Both MS DOS and Workstation-based programs for high-quality visuals.

Dr. Halo III	MS DOS	$139.95	PT/CH/SLS

Media Cybernetics, Inc.
8484 Georgia Ave. #200
Silver Spring, MD 20910
301 495-3305

Paint and draw with a variety of tools. Some menus esoteric. But program is versatile. Includes program for screen capture and another for on-screen slide shows.

DrawPerfect	MS DOS	$495	PR/CH/SLS

WordPerfect Corp.
1555 Technology Way
Orem, UT 84057
801 225-5000

Five hundred formatted images for use with WordPerfect.

Easy Slider	Macintosh	$150	Bridge

Management Graphics, Inc.
1401 E. 79th St.
Minneapolis, MN 55425
612 854-1220

Works with several Macintosh draw/paint/chart and CAD packages to convert their formats to 35 mm slides or overheads. Seamless communications to independent Management Graphics centers.

Energraphics	MS DOS	$395	PR/CH/DR

Enertronics Research, Inc.
#5 Station Plaza
1910 Pine St.
St. Louis, MO 63103
314 421-2771
800 325-0174

General business graphics with extra emphasis on scientific and engineering applications.

Executive Picture Show	MS DOS	$245	PR/CH/DR/SLS

PC Software of San Diego
11627 Calamar Court
San Diego, CA 92124
619 571-0981

Comprehensive presentation with animation and sound.

Software Company	System(s)	Price	Feature(s)
Fontrix	MS DOS	$155	CH/DR/SLS

Data Transforms, Inc.
616 Washington St.
Denver, CO 80203
303   832-1501
Wide choice of fonts for print output.

Freelance Plus 3.0	MS DOS	$495	PR/CH/DR/SLS

Lotus Development Corp.
55 Cambridge Pkwy.
Cambridge, MA 02142
617   577-8500

A thorough program with charting, freehand drawing, object and symbol drawing. Outputs to a variety of devices. Extensive editing tools. Lotus-type menu.

GEM Graphics Presentation Team	MS DOS	$495	PR/CH/DR/SLS

Digital Research, Inc.
Box DRI
Monterey, CA 93942
800   443-4200

Gem Plus, Gem Draw, Word Chart, Business Library integrated under the Gem Windows environment. Objects are manipulated on screen.

Graftime	MS DOS	$395	Front

Genigraphics Corp.
4806 W. Taft Rd.
Liverpool, NY 13088
315   451-6600

A PC-based entry to Genigraphics' 26 regional service bureaus. Supports 14 basic business charts. Produces beautiful slides which can be further enhanced by the service center.

Graphics Express	Macintosh	$150	Bridge

Business and Professional Software
143 Binney St.
Cambridge, MA 02142
617   491-3377

Bundled with several Macintosh programs or used by slide-making companies to effect a bridge between program and film recorder.

Graphics Gallery Collection	MS DOS	$499	CH/DR

Hewlett-Packard Corp.
3410 Central Expressway
Santa Clara, CA 95051
408   773-6337

Three separate modules integrated in a multilayered user interface. A comprehensive selection of chart types and enhancement features helpful to the nonartist.

Graph-in-the-Box	MS DOS	$99	CH

New England Software
Greenwich Office Park #3
Greenwich, CT 06830
203   625-0062

A RAM resident program that will capture data information on screen from other programs. Good output options.

Software Company	System(s)	Price	Feature(s)
Grasp	MS DOS	$149	SLS

Paul Mace Software
123 N. First St.
Ashland, OR 97520
503   488-0224

For programming animated special effects, desktop presentations.

Harvard Graphics			

Software Publishing Corp.
1901 Landings Drive
Mountain View, CA 94039   MS DOS $495   PR/CH/DR/SLS
415   962-8910

Wide chart variety, templates, analysis capability, drawing and enhancement modules, macros, and drivers to many printers and film recorders. Spell checker and animated slide show features.

Hijaak	MS DOS	$149	ACC/GRAB

Inset Systems
12 Mill Plain Rd.
Danbury, CT 06811
203   775-5866

A RAM resident program that will grab screens for importing and converting to other formats.

HOTSHOT Graphics	MS DOS	$249	DR/PT

Symsoft, Inc.
444 First St.
Los Altos, CA 94022
415   941-1552

Works with image files brought in from other programs. Files can be enhanced and used in DTP and in presentation software.

HOTSHOT Presents	MS DOS	$349	PR/SLS

Symsoft, Inc.
PO BOX 4477
Mountain View, CA 94040
415   941-1552

For use with LCD projection devices using special effects and for overhead transparencies.

IBM Display Graphics	MS DOS	$682	PR/CH/DR

IBM Dealers
For local dealers, call:
800   426-3333

A charting program with an extensive clip-art library aimed mainly at overhead transparency output with a plotter.

IBM Storyboard Plus	MS DOS	$350	CH/PR/ANI/SLS

IBM
900 King Dr.
Rye, NY 10573
914   934-4488
800   IBM-2468

A dynamic program for creating on-screen slide shows with full animation effects. Some charting capability.

Software Company	System(s)	Price	Feature(s)
ImageBuilder	MS DOS	$99	PR/CH/DR

ImageBuilder, Inc.
7300 SW Hunziker #200
Tigard, OR 97223
503 684-5151

A low-cost, high-quality program specifically for slide making to the MAGICorp slide service, and for export to desktop publishing.

ImageStation	MS DOS	$1,800	GR/DE

Software Clearing House, Inc.
Three Centennial Plaza
895 Central Ave.
Cincinnati, Oh 45202
513 579-0455

AT&T Targa system support. Also has GraphStation at $795.

Impressionist	MS DOS	$995	PR/CH/DR

Execucom Systems Corp.
9442 Capital of Texas Hwy. N
Austin, TX 78766
512 346-4980

A package more for designers and design departments than for occasional users of PC software. Great output.

Kinetic Graphics System	MS DOS	$995	PR/CH/DR

Kinetic Presentations, Inc.
Distillery Commons 250
Louisville, KY 40206
502 583-1679

A complete system composed of individual units for chartmaking, slide making, word processing, art, which work seamlessly when all are installed. Templates. Many menu levels.

LaserKey	MS DOS	$100	CH

Arkwright, Inc.
538 Main St.
Fiskeville, RI 02823
401 821-1000

Specifically designed for output to a laser printer. For transparencies, labels, lettering decals, memos, and notices.

Lotus 1–2–3	MS DOS	$495	CH

Lotus Development Corp.
55 Cambridge Pkwy.
Cambridge, MA 02142
617 577-8500

A spreadsheet program with some charting capabilities.

Lotus Graphwriter II	MS DOS	$495	PR/CH

Lotus Development Corp.
55 Cambridge Pkwy.
Cambridge, MA 02142
617 577-8540

The program emphasizes chartmaking for an extensive number of chart styles. New data entered will automatically update charts. Charts can be exported to Lotus Freelance Plus for enhancements.

Software Company	System(s)	Price	Feature(s)
Lumina	MS DOS	$2,500	PT/DR

Time Arts
3436 Mendocino Ave.
Santa Rosa, CA 95401
707 576-7722

A high-end graphics program aimed at designers, fine artists. Optional add-on programs for film, print, video, fonts.

Software Company	System(s)	Price	Feature(s)
MacDraw*	Macintosh	$195	PN/DR

Claris Corp.
440 Clyde Ave.
Mountain View, CA 94043
415 962-8946

Software Company	System(s)	Price	Feature(s)
MacPaint*	Macintosh	$125	PT/DR

Claris Corp.
440 Clyde Ave.
Mountain View, CA 94043
415 962-8946

Software Company	System(s)	Price	Feature(s)
MacroMind Director, Animator	Macintosh	$695	SLS

Macromind, Inc.
410 Townsend
San Francisco, CA 94107
415 442-0200

Creates moving graphics, sound. Uses HyperCard data base.

Software Company	System(s)	Price	Feature(s)
Master Graphics Presentation Pack	MS DOS	$495	PR/CH/DR

Ashton-Tate
20101 Hamilton Ave.
Torrance, CA 90502
800 437-4329

Composed of three packages, ChartMaster, SignMaster, Diagram Master. ChartMaster has sophisticated calculating and analysis features and ability to combine one to four charts. Excellent output and seamless slide making to Ashton-Tate Slide Service.

Software Company	System(s)	Price	Feature(s)
Micrografx Designer	MS DOS	$695	DES/DR

Micrographx, Inc.
1303 Arapaho
Richardson, TX 75081
212 234-1769
800 272-3729

For the graphics designer, it combines drawing with design tools and excellent image libaries. It is used through Microsoft Windows. Twenty-four additional clip-art libraries available.

Software Company	System(s)	Price	Feature(s)
Micrografx Graph Plus	MS DOS	$495	CH/DR

Micrographx, Inc.
1303 Arapaho
Richardson, TX 75081
212 234-1769
800 272-3729

An excellent charting program used through Microsoft Windows with tools for enhancements. Ability to use extensive clip-art libraries and scanning devices.

---

* Both programs can be linked to slide-making software.

Software Company	System(s)	Price	Feature(s)
Micrografx Windows Draw	MS DOS	$395	DR/PT

Micrographx, Inc.
1303 Arapaho
Richardson, TX 75081
212   234-1769
800   272-3729

For the graphics designer; combines drawing with design tools and excellent image libraries used through Microsoft Windows.

Microsoft Chart	MS DOS	$395	CH

Microsoft Corp.
16011 NW 36th Way
PO Box 97017
Redmond, WA 98073
206   882-8080
800   426-9400

One of the first charting packages with extensive chart styles. New data will update chart. Minimal enhancement. Drivers to Polaroid and Matrix film recorders.

Microsoft Windows	MS DOS	$99	CH

Microsoft Corp.
16011 NW 36th Way
PO Box 97017
Redmond, WA 98073
206   882-8080
800   426-9400

An environment program for DOS systems that includes Windows Draw, Windows Write.

Mirage	MS DOS	$1,500	PR/CH/DR

Zenographics
19752 MacArthur Blvd.
Irvine, CA 92715
714   851-2266
800   423-3705

Popular and powerful program used by designers and in graphic arts departments.

MORE II	Macintosh	$395	PR/CH/DR/SLS

Symantec Corp.
117 Easy St.
Mountain View, CA 94043
415   964-6300
800   64THINK

A powerful outlining and presentation program; files can be imaged by several services.

Nimbus	MS DOS	$195	CH

Media Cybernetics Inc.
848 Georgia Ave.
Silver Spring, MD 20910
301   495-3305
800   446-HALO

Sold as modules within the HALO environment to be customized to user specifications.

Software Company	System(s)	Price	Feature(s)
Overhead Express	MS DOS	$95	PR/CH

Business & Professional Software
143 Binney St.
Cambridge, MA 02142
800   342-5277

Templates established for overhead transparencies.

Panorama	MS DOS	$595	Video

AT&T Graphics Software Lab.
10291 N. Meridian
Indianapolis, IN 46290
317   844-4364

For output to screen or to videotape via an encoder.

PC Chart	MS DOS	$495	Front

Aztek, Inc.
17 Thomas
Irvine, CA 92718
714   770-8406

Has predesigned formats for word slides and graphs. Can be transmitted to an Aztek Art center for enhancements and output.

PC Emcee	MS DOS	$295	DR

Computer Support Corp.
15926 Midway Rd.
Dallas, TX 75244
214   661-8960

PC-Key Draw	MS DOS	$100	DR/ANI

OEDware
PO BOx 595
Columbia, MD 21045
301   997-9333

Excellent draw features with special CAD/animation effects.

PC Paint	MS DOS	$99.95	PT/DR

Mouse Systems Corp.
47505 Seabridge Dr.
Fremont, CA 94538
415   656-1117

Paint and draw with advanced features for creating swirls, outlining, and other tools. Over 50 color combinations and 15 text styles, Capture program can take graphs from spreadsheets for enhancing.

PC Paint Plus	MS DOS	$149	PT

MSC Technologies, Inc.
47505 Seabridge Drive
Fremont, CA 94538
415   656-1117

An easy-to-use program that includes basic paint tools but lacks the sophisticated features of competitive programs. Bundled with an MSC (formerly Mouse Systems) mouse.

PC Paintbrush PLUS	MS DOS	$149	PT/DR

ZSoft Corp.
450 Franklin Rd., #100
Marietta, GA 30067
404   428-0008

Paint and freehand drawing. Includes Frieze for screen capture. A basic program for desktop publishing but files can be exported or grabbed for other programs.

Software Company	System(s)	Price	Feature(s)
Personal Business Slideware	MS DOS	$249	Front

Management Graphics, Inc.
1401 E. 79th St.
Minneapolis, MN 55420
612   854-1220

A basic charting program for sending files to an MCI image center for processing.

Perspective Jr.	MS DOS	$149	GR

Three D Graphics
860 Via de la Paz
Pacific Palisades, CA 90272
213   459-7949

True three-dimensional graphs.

Persuasion	Macintosh	$495	PR/CH/DR

Aldus Corp.
411 1st Ave. So.
Seattle, WA 98104
206   628-6674

Outlining and automatic template features. Updated entry feature for data and associated text.

PFS: First Graphics	MS DOS	$150	CH

Software Publishing Corp.
1901 Landings Dr.
PO Box 7210
Mountain View, CA 94039
415   962-8910

A low-price, powerful program with five fonts, and user-selectable features for legends, grids, etc. Good printer output. Export to Harvard Graphics for enhancement or output to film recorders.

PictureIt	MS DOS	$700	PR/CH

General Parametrics Corp.
1250 Ninth
Berkeley, CA 94710
415   524-3950
800   556-1234 (except California)

For use with General Parametrics Film Recorders.

Picture Perfect	MS DOS	$295	CH

Computer Support Corp.
2215 Midway Rd.
Carollton, TX 75006
214   661-8960

Easy-to-use basic charting program. Needs the company's Arts & Letters for enhancements. Good menu system and quick response.

Pinstripe Presenter	MS DOS	$200	PR/CH

Spinnaker Software
One Kendall Square
Cambridge, MA 02139
617   494-1200

Provides prestyled charts and expandable image library.

PixelPaint	Macintosh	$395	PT

SuperMac Software
295 N. Bernardo Ave.
Mountain Valley, CA 94043
415   964-8884

Software Company	System(s)	Price	Feature(s)
PixelPaint Professional	Macintosh	$595	PT

SuperMac Software
295 N. Bernardo Ave.
Mountain Valley, CA 94043
415   964-8884

Also see **PixelPaint.** "Professional" is better for printouts; "Paint" is better for on-screen viewing.

PixelPop	MS DOS	$128	ACC

ImageSet Corp.
555 19th St.
San Francisco, CA 94107
415   626-8366

Screen capture utility for converting screens into slides, transparencies, printing.

Pixie	MS DOS/Mac	$195	PR/CH/DR

Zenographics, Inc.
19752 MacArthur Blvd.
Irvine, CA 92715
714   851-6352
800   423-3705

Works in MS DOS under the Microsoft Windows environment as a limited, but innovative charting package. Clip-art can be easily added; some object drawing. Used as a front for Mirage and Autumn.

Powerpoint	Macintosh	$395	PR/CH/DR

Microsoft Corp.
16011 N.E. 36th Way
PO Box 97017
Redmond, WA 98073
206   882-8080

Powerful package with slide making to the Genigraphics system. Outlining, speaker notes, templates, drawing, a title sorter, and a slide sorter feature.

Present IT!	MS DOS	$80	PR

POWER UP!
2929 Campus Dr.
San Mateo, CA 94403
800   851-2917
800   223-1479 (CA)

Specially designed for making overhead transparencies on dot matrix and laser printers. Predesigned formats.

Presenter PC	MS DOS	$995	Front

Image Builder
11401 Rupp Rd.
PO Box 246
Minneapolis, MN 55440
612   895-3000

Chart, word, and drawing package with powerful controls. Seamless communication to Crosfield-Dicomed service centers.

Professional Image	Macintosh	$249	Bridge

Stokes Slide Services
PO Box 14277
Austin, TX 78761
512   458-2201

Software developed by 20/20 Data Systems for slide making.

Software Company	System(s)	Price	Feature(s)
Rio, Topas AT&T Graphics 10291 Meridian St., #275 Indianapolis, IN 46290 317 844-4364	MS DOS	$1,800 to $12,000	CH/PT/DR/ANI

A group of programs for use with the Targa Board for high-end graphics and animation.

| **SAS System**
SAS Institute, Inc.
Box 8000, SAS Circle
Cary, NC 27512
919 467-8000 | MS DOS | $1,995 | PR/CH/DR |

An integrated system for a variety of tasks including presentations, data management, statistical analysis. Integrates with mainframe and minicomputers.

| **ShowPartner F/X**
Brightbill-Roberts & Co. Ltd.
120 E. Washington St.
Syracuse, NY 13202
315 474-3400 | MS DOS | $395 | ANI/SLS |

A design package for creating animated slide shows and enhancing screens from other programs.

| **Slideworks**
Management Graphics, Inc.
1450 Lodestar Rd.
Downsview, Ontario, Canada M3J 3C1
416 638-8877 | MS DOS | $245 | Front |

Charts, and elegant geometric drawing capability, backgrounds, and drop shadow lettering. Basis of a larger graphic system with Management Graphics (Canada) slide centers.

| **SlideWrite Plus**
Advanced Graphics Software, Inc.
333 W. Maude Ave.
Sunnyvale, CA 94086
408 749-8620 | MS DOS | $345 | PR/CH/DR |

Exceptionally well suited to scientists and engineers, with calculation capability and data presentation beyond most charting packages. Fine nuances for using and displaying information.

| **SPSS GRAPHICS**
SPSS
444 N. Michigan Ave.
Chicago, IL 60611
312 329-3500 | Workstation
Mini/Mainframe | $3,000
$2,900
to
$6,900 | PR/CH/DR |

Part of an integrated set of high-end software.

| **StandOut!**
Letraset
40 Eisenhower Drive
Paramus, NJ 07652
201 845-6100 | Macintosh | $395 | PR/CH/DR/SLS |

Has all the top features of a Macintosh presentation program including sort, text handling, templates, and wide range of chart formats.

| **StarTime**
General Parametrics Corp.
1250 Ninth St.
Berkeley, CA 94710
415 524-3950 | Macintosh
VideoShow | $199 | PR |

Software Company	System(s)	Price	Feature(s)
StudioWorks Pansophic Systems, Inc. 709 Enterprise Dr. Oak Brook, IL 60521 312 572-6000 800 323-7335	MS DOS/Workstation	$39,000 to 46,900*	CH/PT/DR/PR

A complete workstation package. Separate modules for PCs.

SuperCard Silicon Beach Software, Inc. PO Box 261430 San Diego, CA 92126 619 695-6956	Macintosh	$200	SLS

An inexpensive, efficient way to develop animated color graphics and synchronized sound using HyperCard stacks.

SuperPaint Silicon Beach Software, Inc. PO Box 261430 San Diego, CA 92126 619 695-6956	Macintosh	$150	PT

A superior paint and drawing program for high-resolution output.

Trumpet 3M Audio-Visual Division 3M Center St. Paul, MN 55144 612 733-1110	MS DOS/Macintosh	$95	CH

Formats particularly adaptable to overhead transparencies. A subset of Overhead Express.

VCN Concorde Visual Communications Network 238 Main St. Cambridge, MA 02142 617 497-4000	MS DOS	$695	PR/CH/DR/SLS

An early entry in the presentation market that constantly updates. Now includes an animated slide show module along with EGA and VGA images in different professional categories.

Versacad Versacad 2124 Main St. Huntington Beach, CA 92648 714 960-7720	MS DOS/Macintosh	$1995	CAD

A comprehensive program for architectural drawing, mechanical design, and educational applications.

Video Works MacroMind, Inc. 1028 W. Worfram St. Chicago, IL 60657 312 871-0987	Macintosh	$195	PR/GR /SLS

A complete program for the Macintosh. Includes a slide show feature with sound and animation.

---

* With hardware.

Software Company	System(s)	Price	Feature(s)
Visual Business #5	Macintosh	$395	PR/CH

Visual Business Systems, Inc.
700 Lake St.
Ramsey, NJ 07446
301   327-2526
Offers unique 3–D features for Macintosh slides.

Windows Draw	MS DOS		DR

See **Microsoft Windows.**

Xerox Graph	MS DOS	$295	CH

Xerox Corp.
9745 Business Park Ave.
San Diego, CA 92067
800   822-8221

MS DOS version of Macintosh's Cricket Graph. Performs extensive data analysis. Intended for use by financial or statistical analysts, engineers, scientists, business users.

Xerox Presents	MS DOS	$495	PR/CH/DR

Xerox Corp.
9745 Business Park Ave.
San Diego, CA 92067
800   822-8221

MS DOS version of Macintosh's Cricket Presents, with advanced features. Microsoft Windows based.

II. Software by Company/Product Name

To locate a product by company: Find the company, then use the cross-referenced software and sources list in Part I of this Appendix.

Company	Product
3M Audio-Visual Division	Trumpet
Advanced Graphics Software, Inc.	SlideWrite Plus
Aldus Corp.	Aldus Freehand, Aldus Persuasion
Analytical Software Inc.	Boardroom Graphics
Arkwright, Inc.	LaserKey
Ashton-Tate	Applause II, Master Graphics
AT&T Graphics	Rio, Topas
AT&T Graphics Software Lab	Panorama
Autodesk, Inc.	AutoCAD, Autodesk Animator
Autographix, Inc.	Autographix AutoVisual
Aztek, Inc.	PC Chart
Bridgeway Publishing Corp.	Dashboard 2.0
Brightbill-Roberts & Co. Ltd.	ShowPartner F/X
Business & Professional Software	35 mm Express, Overhead Express, Graphics Express
Claris Corp.	MacDraw, MacPaint
Computer Associates	DISSPLA & Telegraph, SuperImage VAX, Cricket Graph, Cricket Paint, Cricket Presents, Cricket Stylist
Computer Support Corp.	Arts & Letters, Picture Perfect, PC Emcee
Corel Systems Corp.	Corel Draw!
Data Transforms Graphics Software, Inc.	Fontrix
Digital Research, Inc.	GEM Presentation Team

Company	Product
Dubl-Click Software, Inc.	Art Roundup
Electronic Arts	DeluxePaint II
Enertronics Research Inc.	Energraphics
Execucom Systems Corp.	Impressionist
General Parametrics Corp.	PictureIt, StarTime
Genigraphics Corp.	Graftime
Hewlett-Packard Corp.	Graphics Gallery Collection
IBM Corp.	IBM Storyboard Plus; Display Graphics
Image Builder, Inc.	Presenter PC, Image Builder
ImageSet Corp.	PixelPop
Inset Systems	Hijaak, Inset
Kinetic Presentations, Inc.	Kinetic Graphics System
Letraset	StandOut!
Lotus Development Corp.	Freelance Plus 3.0, Lotus Graphwriter II, Lotus 1–2–3
MacroMind, Inc.	VideoWorks II, MacroMind Director, Animator
Management Graphics, Inc. (Canada)	Slideworks
Management Graphics, Inc. (MN)	Personal Business Slideware, Easy Slider
Media Cybernetics, Inc.	Nimbus, Dr. Halo III
Micrographx, Inc.	Micrografx Designer, Graph Plus, Draw
Microrim	DB Graphics
Microsoft Corp.	Powerpoint, Chart, Windows
Mouse Systems Corp.	PC Paint
MSC Technologies, Inc.	PC Paint Plus
New England Software	Graph-in-the-Box
Norton, Peter	Dan Bricklin's Demo II
OEDware	PC-Key Draw
Pansophic Systems	StudioWorks
Paul Mace Software	Grasp
PC Software of San Diego	Executive Picture Show
POWER UP!	Present IT!
Rix Softworks, Inc.	Colorix VGA Paint
Samna Corp.	Decision Graphics
SAS Institute, Inc.	SAS System
Silicon Beach Software	SuperCard, SuperPaint
Software Clearing House, Inc.	ImageStation
Software Publishing Corp.	Harvard Graphics, PFS: First Graphics
Spinnaker Software	Pinstripe Presenter
SPSS	SPSS GRAPHICS
Stokes Slide Services	Professional Image
SuperMac Software	PixelPaint, PixelPaint Professional
Symantec Corp.	MORE II
Symsoft, Inc.	HOTSHOT Presents, HOTSHOT Graphics
Three D Graphics	Perspective Jr.
Time Arts	Crystal 3D, Time Arts, Lumina
Versacad	Versacad
Visual Business Systems, Inc.	Visual Business #5
Visual Communications Network	VCN Concorde
WordPerfect Corp.	DrawPerfect
Xerox Corp.	Xerox Graph, Xerox Presents
Zenographics, Inc.	Autumn, Mirage, Pixie
ZSoft Corp.	PC Paintbrush+

III. Sources for Hardware and Services

The following is a complete, alphabetical list of all the sources at
the end of each chapter. Refer to the chapter(s) for full addresses.

Company	Chapter	Company	Chapter
3M Audio-Visual Division	9	Enter Computer, Inc.	15
Agfa Matrix	9, 13, 15,16	Epson America, Inc.	15
Aldus Corp.	2	Express Slides	14
Amdek Corp.	15	Folex, Inc.	9
American Liquid Light	13	Fox Photo	14
Apollo Audio Visual	16	General Electric	16
Apple Computer, Inc.	15	General Parametrics Corp.	13, 16
Arcturus, Inc.	16	Genigraphics Corp.	9, 13, 14, 15
Arkwright, Inc.	9	Gepe, Inc.	13
Artronics, Inc.	14	Graftel	13
Ashton-Tate Graphics Service	14	Hewlett-Packard Co.	9, 15
Autographix	14, 15	Howtek, Inc.	15
AVL Inc.	14	Hughes Aircraft Company	16
Aztek, Inc.	13, 14	Ilford Photo Corp.	9, 14
Barco Industry, Inc.	16	Image Builder	13, 14
Bell & Howell/Eiki Intl.	9, 10, 13, 15, 16	In-Focus Systems	10
Benson, Schlumberger Co.	15	Inset Systems	15
Beseler Film Recorder	13	JBL Professional	16
Brandons, Inc.	16	Kinetics Presentations, Inc.	14
Brilliant Image, Inc.	14	Kloss Video Corp	16
Buhl Industries, Inc.	9, 10	Kurta Corp.	15
CalComp	15	Kye International Corp.	15
Camtron Electronics International Ltd.	13	Lasergraphics, Inc.	13
Canon U.S.A., Inc.	15	LogiTech International, Inc.	15
Celco	13	MAGICorp	14
Charles Mayer Studios, Inc.	2	Management Graphics, Inc., Canada	14
Chartmasters, Inc.	14	Management Graphics, Inc., MN	13, 14
Chisholm	10	Microsoft	15
Chyron Corp.	15	Microtek Lab, Inc.	15
Complete PC, The	15	Mirus Corporation	13
CompuScan, Inc.	15	Mitsubishi Electronics America, Inc.	15
Computer Accessories Corp.	10	Mouse Systems	15
Computer Support Corp.	16	MSC Technologies, Inc.	15
Cricket Software	2	Multiplex Display Fixture Co.	2
Da-Lite Screen Co.	16	Navitar/D.O. Industries, Inc.	16
Diamond Flower Elec. Industries	15	NEC Home Electronics	15
Dicomed	15	N.I.S.E., Inc.	13
Dukane Corp.	9, 10, 16	Noritsu America Corp.	9, 14
Eastman Kodak Company (DATASHOW)	10, 16	NPC Corp.	13
Eiki International	9, 10, 16	Numonics Corp.	15
Electrohome Electronics Ltd.	16	nView Corp.	10
Electronic Arts	15	Oasys-Office Automation Systems, Inc.	15
Electronic Systems Products (Esprit)	16	Osram Sales Corp.	16
Elmo Mgf. Corp.	16	Panasonic Industrial Co.	16

Company	Chapter	Company	Chapter
Photographic Sciences Corp.	13	Sun Microsystems	15
Pix Productions	14	Superset, Inc.	15
Polaroid Corp.	9, 13	Symantec Corp.	2
Presentation Technologies	13	Symsoft, Inc.	2
Princeton Graphics	15	Tektronix, Inc.	13, 15
Reactive Systems, Inc.	2	Telex Communications, Inc.	10
RMF Products	16	Toshiba America	10
Screen Works, The	16	Transilwrap Company, Inc.	9
Sharp Electronics Corp.	10	Tymlabs Corp.	2
Slide Express	14	Visual Horizons	9, 14
Slidecrafters, Inc.	14	Visualon, Inc.	10
Sony Corp.	15, 16	Vivid Systems, Inc.	16
Sony/Tektronix	16	Wilson & Lund	14
Stokes Slide Services	14	WordPerfect Corp.	2
Summagraphics	15	Zenith Data Systems	15

APPENDIX

C

Selected Bibliography

3M Audio-Visual Division. *Open Up to Brilliant Overhead Projection Transparencies.* St. Paul, Minn.: 3M, 1983.

3M Meeting Management Team. *How To Run Better Business Meetings.* 8th ed. New York: McGraw-Hill, 1979.

Anderson, Donald M. *Elements of Design.* New York: Holt, Rinehart & Winston, 1966.

Beatty, John C., and Kellogg S. Booth. *Tutorial: Computer Graphics.* 2d ed. Los Angeles, Calif.: IEEE Computer Society, 1984.

Bishop, Ann. *Slides-Planning and Producing Slide Programs.* Rochester, N.Y.: Eastman Kodak Co., 1984.

Blackburn, Bruce. *Design Standards Manuals.* Washington, D.C.: National Endowment for the Arts, 1976.

Bowman, William J. *Graphic Communication.* New York: John Wiley & Sons, 1968.

Carnegie, Dale, and Dorothy Carnegie. *The Quick and Easy Way to Effective Speaking.* New York: Association Press, 1962.

Dellinger, Susan, and Barbara Deane. *Communicating Effectively.* Radnor, Penn.: Chilton, 1980

Eastman Kodak. *Audiovisual Notes from Kodak* (periodical). Rochester, N.Y.: Eastman Kodak Co., 1982.

Eastman Kodak. *How to Be a Knockout with AV!* Rochester, N.Y.: Eastman Kodak Co., 1984.

Eastman Kodak, and Ernest Burden. *Visual Marketing.* Rochester, N.Y.: Eastman Kodak, Co., 1978.

Gill, Bob. *Forget All the Rules You Ever Learned about Graphic Design, Including the Ones in This Book.* New York: Watson-Guptill Publications, 1981.

Laroff, Gary P. *Choosing Hard Copy Devices.* San Diego, Calif.: ISSCO Graphics Co., 1984.

Leech, Thomas. *How to Prepare, Stage, and Deliver Winning Presentations.* New York: AMACOM, 1982.

Lotus Corp. *Creating Text Charts.* Cambridge, Mass.: Lotus Development Corp., 1988.

Lotus Corp. *Making Better Presentations.* Cambridge, Mass.: Lotus Development Corp., 1988.

Marcus, Aaron. *Managing Facts and Concepts.* Washington, D.C.: National Endowment for the Arts, 1979.

Matkowski, Betty S. *Steps to Effective Business Graphics.* San Diego, Calif.: Hewlett-Packard Co., 1983.

Meilach, Dona Z. *Better Business Presentations.* Torrance, Calif.: Ashton-Tate, 1988.

National Computer Graphics Association. *Proceedings of Computer Graphics Conferences, 1986–89.* Fairfax, Va.: National Computer Graphics Association, 1986, 1987, 1989.

O'Mara, R. Michael. *Effective Presentation Guide.* Louisville, Ky.: Kinetic Corporation, 1987.

Peoples, David. *Presentations Plus.* New York: John Wiley & Sons, 1988.

Ruder, Emil. *Typography: A Manual of Design.* Niederteufen, Switzerland: Verlag Arthur Niggli, 1977.

Sanders, Norman. *Photography for Graphic Designers.* Washington, D.C.: National Endowment for the Arts, 1979.

Sandler, Corey. *Desktop Graphics for the IBM PC.* Morris Plains, N.J.: Creative Computer Press, 1984.

Schmid, Colin F., and Stanton E. Schmid. *Handbook of Graphic Presentation.* New York: John Wiley & Sons, 1969.

Schmidt, Allan H., and Vernon Gorter. *The Computer Image: Applications of Computer Graphics.* Reading, Mass.: Addison-Wesley Publishing, 1982.

Stecker, Elinor. *Slide Showmanship.* New York: Amphoto, 1987.

Tufte, Edward R. *The Visual Display of Quantitative Information.* Cheshire, Conn.: Graphics Press, 1983.

Vignelli, Massimo. *Grids: Their Meaning and Use for Federal Designers.* Washington, D.C.: National Endowment for the Arts, 1976.

Walworth, Vivian, ed. *Neblettes Handbook of Photography and Reprography.* [8th ed.] New York: Van Nostrand Reinhold, 1989.

White, Jan V. *Graphic Idea Notebook.* New York: Watson-Guptill Publications. 1980.

White, Jan V. *Using Charts and Graphs.* New York: R. R. Bowker Co., 1984.

APPENDIX
D
Graphics Publications and Organizations

There are magazines devoted to computer graphics, presentations, architecture, audiovisual equipment, photography, filmmaking, computers, graphic design, and desktop publishing. Articles covering aspects of graphics appear in general computer publications that cover all systems: Workstations, PCs, Macintoshes, Amigas, and so on. The resources listed below cover computer graphics and design graphics. Magazines fold, merge, emerge, and return under new names and publishers. Many publications do not charge a subscription fee to readers who fill out their "qualify" forms. (Magazines are published monthly unless otherwise noted.)

For current articles, refer to a reader's guide or index that lists appropriate publications such as Ulrich's *International Periodicals Directory* (Oxbridge Communications); *Magazine Industry Market Place* (R. R. Bowker); *The Readers Guide to Business Magazines, The Readers Guide to Computer Literature,* and *The Art Index.* These are available at public and university libraries and often in corporate libraries.

Publications

ACM Transactions on Graphics
Association for Computing Machinery, Inc.
PO Box 12115 Church Street Station
New York, NY 10249
212 265-6300
  (Quarterly)

Advanced Imaging
PTN Publishing Co.
210 Crossways Park Dr.
Woodbury, NY 11797
516 496-8000
  (10 times a year)

The Anderson Report
Anderson Publishing Co.
Simi Valley Business Park
PO Box 3534
Simi Valley, CA 93063
805 581-1184

Audio Visual Communications
PTN Publishing Co.
210 Crossways Pk. Dr.
Woodbury, NY 11797
516 496-8000

AV Video
25550 Hawthorne Blvd., Suite 314
Torrance, CA 90505
213 373-9993

Color: Research and Application
John Wiley & Sons, Journal Dept.
605 Third Ave.
New York, NY 10158
212 850-6000
  (Quarterly)

Computer Graphics and Applications
IEEE Computer Society
10662 Los Vaqueros Circle
Los Alamitos, CA 90720
714   821-8380

Computer Graphics and Image Processing, "An International Journal"
Academic Press
111 Fifth Ave.
New York, NY 10002
212   741-6800

Computer Graphics for Management
The Management Roundtable, Inc.
824 Boylston St.
Chestnut Hill, MA 02167
617   232-8080

Computer Graphics Review
Intertec Publishing
PO Box 1291
Overland Park, KS 66212
913   888-4664

Computer Graphics Software News
Greg Passmore
910 Ashford Pkwy.
Houston, TX
713   493-5550

Computer Graphics World
Cygnus Publications, Inc.
54 Mint St.
San Francisco, CA 94103
415   543-0978

Computer Pictures
Knowledge Industry Publications, Inc.
701 Westchester Ave.
White Plains, NY 10604
914   328-9157
800 248-5474
   (Bimonthly)

Computers and Graphics
Pergamon Press, Inc.
Maxwell House, Fairview Park
Elmsford, NY 10523
914   592-7700
   (Quarterly)

Design Graphics World
Communication Channels, Inc.
6255 Barfield Rd.
Atlanta, GA 30328
404   256-9800

Desktop Presentations Report
253 Martens Ave., Suite 10
Mountain View, CA 94040
415   968-4105
   (Monthly Newsletter)

The S. Klein Newsletter on Computer Graphics
730 Boston Post Rd.
PO Box 89
Sudbury, MA 01776
617   443-4671
   (Biweekly)

PIXEL—The Computer Animation Newsletter
217 George St.
Toronto, Canada M5A 2M9
416   367-0088

Presentation Products Magazine
Pacific MagazineGroup, Inc.
513 Wilshire Blvd., Suite 344
Santa Monica, CA 90401
213   455-1414

Publish!
PCW Communications, Inc.
501 Second St.
San Francisco, CA 94107
800   525-0643 (Subscriptions)

True Imaging
Ariel Communications, Inc.
Box 203550
Austin, TX 78720
512   250-1700

Verbum
PO Box 15439
San Diego, CA 92115
619   436-4395
619   463-9977
   (Quarterly)

Video Manager
Montage Publishing Co.
25550 Hawthorne Blvd., Suite 314
Torrance, CA 90505
213   373-9993

Organizations

The following computer graphics organizations provide publications, annual conferences, and regional meetings. There are local groups in various cities. Write for membership information. Refer to the *Encyclopedia of Associations* (Gale Research Co.) for those related to other design disciplines (available at your library).

IEEE Computer Graphics and Applications
IEEE Computer Society
10662 Los Vaqueros Circle
Los Alamitos, CA 90720
714 821-8380
    (Membership includes a bimonthly magazine)

National Computer Graphics Association (NCGA)
2722 Merilee Dr., Suite 2000
Fairfax, VA 22031
703 698-2000
    (Monthly magazine included)

Special Interest Group on Computer Graphics (SIGGRAPH)
Association for Computing Machinery, Inc.
1133 Avenue of the Americas
New York, NY 10036
212 265-6300

APPENDIX
*Trademarks**

E

Product/Name	Company
35 mm Express	Business & Professional Software
3M	3M Corp.
Aldus, Aldus PageMaker	Aldus Corp.
Agfa Matrix	Agfa Matrix Corp.
Arts & Letters	Computer Support Corp.
Ashton-Tate, Applause II, Master Graphics	Ashton-Tate Corp.
AT&T Targa	AT&T
AutoCAD, Autodesk Animator	Autodesk, Inc.
Autographix	Autographix Corp.
Bell & Howell, RingMasterII	Bell & Howell Co.
BOSCH	Licensed by Robert Bosch Corp.
BRAVO!	Applicon, Inc.
Brilliant Image	Brilliant Image, Inc.
Byline	Ashton-Tate Corp.
CA-Cricket Stylist; CA-Cricket Graph; CA-Cricket Paint; CA-Cricket Presents	Computer Associates
CalComp	California Business Products, Inc.
Celco	Celco
ChartMaster	Ashton-Tate Corp.
Chyron	Chyron Corp.
Cibacopy Systems	Ilford Photo Corp.
Corel Draw!	Corel Systems Corp.
CP/M	Digital Research, Inc.
Crosfield-Dicomed D148S/A	Crosfield-Dicomed
Cycolor	Noritsu America Corp.
DATACAM	Photographic Sciences Corp.
DataShow	Eastman Kodak Co.
Diamond Scan	Mitsubishi Electronics America, Inc.
Dicomed	Crosfield-Dicomed
Digital Paintbrush System	The Computer Colorworks
DISSPLA	Computer Associates
Draw Applause	Ashton-Tate Corp.
DrawingBoard	CalComp

---

*Names of other products and companies mentioned in this book may also be trademarks or registered trademarks.

Product/Name	Company
Dukane PRO-150	Dukane Corp.
Easy Slider	Management Graphics, Inc.
Electrohome	Electrohome Electronics, Ltd.
Enter Computer	Enter Computer, Inc.
Epson	Epson Corp.
ExecuVision	VCN Communications Network, Inc.
Filevision	Telos Software Products
Fontrix	Data Transforms Graphics Software, Inc.
Framework	Ashton-Tate Corp.
Gem Presentations Team	Digital Research Corp.
Genigraphics	Genigraphics Corp.
Gold Express	Oasys Systems, Inc.
Graphics Gallery	Hewlett-Packard Co.
Hijaak	Inset Systems, Inc.
HOTSHOT Presents, HOTSHOT Graphics	Symsoft Corp.
IBM, IBM PC, IBM AT/OS2	International Business Machines
ImageStation	Software Clearing House, Inc.
Inset	Inset Systems, Inc.
Kodak DATASHOW HR, HR/M, LC500	Eastman Kodak Co.
Lasergraphics	Lasergraphics, Inc.
LaserPro	Oasys Systems
Limelight	Vivid Systems
Lotus 1–2–3, Graphwriter, Lotus Freelance Plus	Lotus Development Corp.
Macintosh, Macintosh II	Apple Computer, Inc.
MacPaint	Claris Corp.
MAGICorp	MAGICorp
Manager Mouse	Numonics Corp.
Masterpiece	Genigraphics Corp.
Matrix PCR, QCR, Pro-Color, VIP	Matrix Instruments, Inc.
Matrix VIP	Agfa Matrix
Metafile	Donald H. McNeil
Micrografx Draw, Windows, Designer	Micrografx, Inc.
Microsoft Windows, Microsoft	Microsoft Corp.
Mirus FilmPrinter, Mirus	Mirus Corp.
Montage FR 1	Presentation Technologies, Inc.
MORE II	Symantec Corp.
MS DOS	Microsoft Corp.
Multiplex	Multiplex Display Fixture Co.
MultiScan, MultiSync	NEC Electronics, Inc.
OSRAM Diaster AV-Pro	OSRAM Sales Corp.
PC Emcee	Computer Support Corp.
PERCEPTOR	Micro Control Systems
PolaChrome, PolaBlue, Palette, Palette Plus, AutoProcessor, Turbo Palette	Polaroid Corp.
PostScript	Adobe Systems, Inc.
PowerPoint	Microsoft Corp.
Rascol/II	Lasergraphics, Inc.
Royale System 150	RMF Products
ScreenShooter	NPC Corp.
ShowPartner F/X	Brightbill-Roberts

Product/Name	Company
SlideWrite	Advanced Graphics Software, Inc.
Solitaire	Management Graphics, Inc.
Springboard Publisher	Springboard
StarTime	General Parametrics Corp.
StudioWorks	Pansophic Systems, Inc.
SummaSketch Plus	Summagraphics Corp.
Sweet-P	Enter Computer, Inc.
Symantec	Symantec Corp.
Targa	AT&T
Tektronix	Tektronix, Inc.
ThinkTank	Symantec Corp.
UltraSync	Princeton Graphics Systems
Versacad	Versacad Corp.
VideoShow, Photomaker, PictureIt	General Parametrics Corp.
Visual Business #5	Visual Business Systems, Inc.
Visual Horizons	Visual Horizons
Visulite II	Multiplex
Wess Plastic	Wess Plastic
WordPerfect	Word Perfect Corp.
Xerox Presents, Graph, Ventura Publisher, XEROX	Xerox Corp.

Index

A

Analog film recorder, 218–19
Analytical graphs, rules for creating, 56–64
Animation, special effect, 134–35
Animation techniques, 159–63
Art and advertising designs
general discussion of, 172–73
illustrations of, 173–85
Audience, and planning, 11–12, 14–15
Audience readiness, and presentation, 25–26
Audiovisual services, location and directory, 253–54

B

Balance, and charts, 58–59
Barton, Ridgie, 14–15
Beginning, middle, and end of presentation, 15
Bibliography, 315–16
Bracketing, and photography, 234
Bravo Camera, 229
Budget, equipment, 18
Build-up slides, 39–40
Business graphics
analytical graphs, rules for creating, 56–64
bar charts, 65–76
chart appropriateness, 64–65
chart style consideration, 64
comparison charts, 83–88
diagram charts, 96–103
general discussion, 50–51
horizontal bar charts, 67–76
line and surface charts, 82–87
maps as charts, 91–95
pie charts, 77–81
poorly designed charts, 51–54
poorly designed software, 55
table, or tabular, charts, 88–91

Business graphics—*Cont.*
vertical bar charts, 65–67
well-designed software, 55–56

C

CAD/CAM and CAE applications, 104–5, 114, 257, 261
Camera on tripod, image photography, 234, 237
Cameras for film recorders, 217
CGM, standard for film recorder, 221
Characterized bar chart, 66
Chart and graph programs, 169–73, 201–4
Charts
analytical, rules for creating, 56–64, 204
appropriateness of, 64–65
bar, 203
column, 65–67
comparison, 83–88
critique of, 51–54
diagram, 96–103
double bar, 67
horizontal bar, 67–77
line and surface, 82–83, 204
maps as, 91–95
other graph types, 204
pie, 77–81, 203–4
poorly designed, 51–54
and poorly designed software, 55
style consideration, 64
table, or tabular, 88–90
vertical bar, 65–67
and well-designed software, 55–56
word, 202
Checklist, planning, 22–23
Click shop services, 243
Color, and text slides, 37–38
Color printers, 266
Color problems in slides, 250
Color schemes for overhead transparencies, 149–50
Column charts, 65–67

Combination special effects, 126
Companies and products, hardware, 272–74
Comparison charts, miscellaneous, 83–87
Computer generated slides, 216–21
Computer graphics
medium and message, 7–9
multimedia graphic support, need for, 5–6
overview, 2–3
savings, efficiency, tools, and techniques, 6–7
Wharton study on visuals, 3–4
Computer Graphics Metafile (CGM) (standard driver in software), 221, 245
Computer screen as display tool, 158–59
Computer/video projectors, 282–84
resolution, scan rate and brightness, 284–86
versatility of, 282–84
Confidentiality and security, 232
Correlation, and type of chart, 65
Creating picture library, 115–16
Custom shop services, 242–43
Custom slides, 242–43

D

Data and mark placement, and charts, 63
Deadline, for presentation, 13–14
Dempsey, Timothy, 136–37
Design considerations, pie charts, 78–79
Desktop film recorders, 227
Desktop slide shows, 158–70
software sources, 169–70
Deviation-column bar chart, 66–67
Diagram charts, 96–103
Differentiated divisions pie chart, 77
Digital film recorder, 210, 221

Digitizing and superimposition, 136–37
Direct computer terminal (on-line) viewing, 13
Directory of services, audiovisual, 253–54
Directory of slide services, 253–54
Distribution, and type of chart, 65
Divided-column bar chart, 66
Divisions, and type of chart, 65
Do's and don'ts
    planning, 20–21
    presentation, 24–27
Dot matrix printers, 266
Double bar chart, 67
Drawings, and text slides, 41–42
Dress, and presentation, 24

E

Efficiency and savings, computer graphics, 6
Emphasis, and charts, 57–58
Equipment and surroundings check, presentation, 27–29
Equipment sources, photographic, 238–40
Evaluation chart, graphics software, 212–15
Exploded segment pie chart, 77

F

Film, types of, 237–238
Film recorder
    analog, 218–19
    cameras used, 217
    companies, 239
    Computer Graphics Metafile, 221, 245
    controller, 218
    digital, 219, 221
    output quality, 221–222
    producing the image, 217–18
    and software compatibility, 221, 224
    throughput-time, 217
    wide range of, 225–230
Flip chart, 12
Floppy disk
    entire show stored on, 158
    input and output device, 263
Flowchart, 65, 97
Four-column stacked bar chart, 69–70
Frame preparation, overhead transparencies, 153–55
Freeform graphics programs, 204–6
Front-of-screen photography, hood devices for, 235–37
Full production companies, audiovisual services, 251

G

Gantt chart, 65, 97, 204
Glossary, 291–95

Glow or eclipse, special effects, 127
Goals, and planning, 11–12
Graphics publications and organizations, 317–19
Graphics resolution, and output, 221–22
Graphics software
    chart and graph programs, 201–4
    clip art, 206–209
    color selection, 206
    Data Import/Export, 209–10
    drawing tools, 204–6
    evaluation chart for, 211–15
    general discussion of, 188–89
    hardware requirements, 197–98
    keystroke testing, 194
    manual evaluation, 211
    need for care in selection, 183–94
    output devices, 210
    presentation program features worksheet for comparison, 211–215
    programs and purposes, 191–93
    protecting purchase, 189–90
    purchasing problems, 189
    requirements assessment, 194
    slide services, 210
    speed and, 198
    and technical support, 191
Graphics tablet, graphics input, 259
Graphics workstations, 257–58
Grid lines, and charts, 61–62
Grouped bar chart, 76
Guidelines, meeting room, 29–31

H

Hance, James, 150
Hard copy printouts, 13
    from customer files, 246–48
Hardware
    general discussion, 256
    graphics workstations, 257–58
    input devices, 258–59, 261
    output devices, 210, 263–70
    printers and plotters, 265–70
    products and companies, list of, 272–74
    projection devices, 276–86
    and software selection, 197–98
Histogram, 65, 67
Hood devices and front-of-screen photography, 235–37
Horizontal bar charts, 67–76
How things work and how much, and type of chart, 65

I–K

Image, text as, 42–47
Image projection, 276–84
Image recorder; *see* Film recorder
Image scanners, graphics input, 261–62

Index cards, and presentation, 16
Index chart, 65, 83, 87
In-house film recorder, key issues, 231–32
Ink jet printers, 267–68
Input devices, 258–61
Instant slides from hard copy, 229–30
Items in structure, and type of chart, 65
Joystick, and graphic input, 259
Keyboard, input device, 259
Keystroke testing, computer programs, 194

L

LCD (liquid crystal display) units, 165–71, 281
Large screen projection
    computer/video projectors and displays, 282–84
    Kodak video projector, 282
    LCD flat panel display units, 281
    projection screens, 286–87
    resolution, scan rate and brightness, 284–86
    stand-alone monochrome projectors, 281–82
    35 mm slide projectors, 279–81
Laser highlights, special effects, background effects, 130
Laser printers, 268
Lasky, Raymond J., 5
Layout
    overhead transparencies, 149
    text slides, 38–39
Learning and ease of use, computer programs, 188
Lettering, movement in, special effect, 132
Lettering and viewing distance, overhead transparencies, 155–56
Light pen, and graphic input, 259
Line and surface charts, 82–83
Line thickness, and charts, 62

M–N

Macintosh graphics capability, 257
Manual evaluation, computer programs, 211
Maps as charts, 91–95
Medium- and high-resolution cameras, 232–235
Meeting room guidelines, 29–31
Message and medium, 7–9
Mini-transparencies, 143–46
Mirrors, special effect, 129
Modem, sending slides by, 246–50
Modem problems in ordering, 250
Monitors, 263–65
Mouse, and graphic input, 259

Movement in lettering, special effect, 132
Multimedia graphic support, need for, 5–6
Multiuse visuals, 18–19
Neon lighting, special effect, 129
Numbers and labels placement, and charts, 63

O

One hundred percent bar chart, 66–67
On-time beginning and ending, presentation, 24, 27
Organization chart, 65, 97
Organizing visuals, theories on, 14–18
Output devices, 210, 263–70
Overhead and slide projection considerations, presentation, 30–31, 146–48
Overhead transparencies
 and computers, 138
 cautions concerning, 140–41
 color printers and plotters, 141–42
 color schemes, 149–50
 from files generated for slides, 138
 frame preparation, 153–55
 general discussion of, 138–42
 illustrations of preparation, 144–47
 and interaction with a projector, 156
 layout, 149
 lettering and viewing distance, 155
 mini-transparencies, 143–46
 photocopying on to film, 142
 projectors for, 146–48
 reveal and build techniques, 150–53
 rules for producing, 148–49
 slide service overheads, 139
 software, 142–43
 sources of information on, 156–57

P

Pacing, and presentation, 15, 26
Paired bar chart, 65, 67
Paller, Alan, 50–51
Percentage of change, and type of chart, 65
Peripheral hardware sources and service, services, 272
Personal computers and presentation graphics, 256
PERT chart, 65, 97, 102, 204
Photographic equipment sources, 239–40
Photography
 "bracketing," 234
 camera on tripod, 234, 237
 cameras and film, 234
 equipment sources, list of, 239–40
 front-of-screen shots, 232–35

Photography—*Cont.*
 images from screen, 191–93, 232–35
 kinds of film, 237–38
 medium- and high-resolution cameras, 232–35
 print and slide film, 238
 video image cameras, 261–62
Picture library
 creation of, 115–16
 general discussion of, 114
 illustrations of, 116–23
 stock slides, 116
Pie charts, 77–81
Pinwheel, special effect, 131
Planning
 budgets, 18
 checklist, 22–23
 deadline for presentation, 13–14
 do's and don'ts, 20–21
 establishing goals, 11–12
 importance of, 10
 means of accomplishment, 12–13
 multiple-use visuals, 18
 organizing visuals, theories on, 14–18
 presentation location, 14
 security considerations, 19–20
 targeting audience, 11
Plotters, 268, 270–71
Pointer, and presentation, 26
Polaroid Palette, analog film recorder, 218
Polaroid Palette camera, 201–2
Polaroid PolaBlue instant slide film, 232, 237
Poorly designed charts and software, 51–55
Posture, and presentation, 27
Precise data, and type of chart, 65
Presentation
 do's and don'ts of, 24–28
 environment, 14
 equipment and surroundings check, 27–29
 overhead and slide projection considerations, 30–31
Presentation graphics; *see also* Special effects
 and computers, 256–58
 and software, 158–60
Printed and plotted text handouts, 48–49
Printers, thermal and ink jet, 248
Printers and plotters, 265–70
Print film, 238
Prints made from slides, 248
Products and companies, hardware, 272–74
Products and distributors/manufacturers
 hood photographic devices, 239–40

Products and distributors/manufacturers—*Cont.*
 projectors and projection screens, 288–90
Projection, image, 276–90
Projectors, large screen; *see* Large screen projectors
Projectors, small screen; *see* Small screen projectors
Protecting purchase, graphics software, 189–90
Purchasing problems, graphics software, 189

Q

Quality and price variation, slides, 243–44
Quantity
 text per slide, 34
 and type of chart, 65
Questions, and presentation, 27

R

RAM resident software, 249
Range-column bar chart, 67
Rehearsal, for presentation, 25
Relationship chart, 65, 97
Requirements assessment, graphics software, 194
Reveal slides, 39–40

S

Savings and efficiency, computer graphics, 6
Scale, and charts, 59–60
Scattergram, 65, 83
Screen capture utilities, software input method, 262–63
Screen show design suggestions, 163
Security, and planning, 19–20
Semilog chart, 65, 83
Shade and color, and charts, 60
Showing how things work
 arrows and movement, 105–6
 and CAD/CAM and CAE applications, 104–5
 general discussion of, 104–5
 illustrating size, 107
 illustrations of, 107–14
Simple pie chart, 77
Simplicity, and charts, 56–57
Single bar chart, 67–68, 74
Single-column bar chart, 65
Slide and overhead projection considerations, presentation, 30–31
Slide film, 238
Slide prices, 243–44
Slide projectors, 35mm, 279–81
Slide quality
 depends on film recorder, 221

Slide quality—*Cont.*
    detecting differences, 222
    evaluating, 222–23
Slides, 13
    custom, 242–43
    from front of screen, 233–37
    from hardcopy, 237
    reveal, or build-up, 39–40
    software advances, 242
    stock, 116, 251–52
    and text, 33–40
Slide service resources
    custom slides, 242–43
    directory of services, 253–54
    full production companies, 251
    general discussion of, 242
    quality and price variation, 243–44
    stock slides, 251–52
    turnaround time, 243
    volume output and top quality equipment, 242
Small screen projectors, 276–79
    CRT (cathode-ray tube), 276
    video terminals, 276–79
Software
    choices for presentation, 159–60
    compatibility, 224–25
    creating overhead transparencies, 142–43
    graphics, 188–211
    and hardware selection, 197–98
    poorly designed, and presentation, 55
    sources, listed, 296–314
    used by slide services, 244–45
    well-designed, 55–56
Spacing, and charts, 59
Special effects
    animation, 134
    combinations of, 126

Special effects—*Cont.*
    general discussion of, 124–26
    glow or eclipse, 127
    incorporated into software, 159
    mirrors, vibrations, neon lighting, 129
    and mounts for cropping, 240
    movement in lettering, 132
    starburst, starbeam, laser highlights, 130
    superimposition, 136–37
    swirl, spin, pinwheel, 131
    tools for, 164
    zoom, 128
Speed, of computer programs, 180
Split bar chart, 66
Stacked adjacent bar chart, 67
Stacked-column bar chart, 66
Stacked-column chart, 72
Starburst and starbeam, special effect, 130
Stock slides, 116, 251–52
Storyboards, and presentation, 17–18
Superimposed photography, special effect, 136
Surface chart, 83, 86–87
Swirl and spin, special effect, 131

T

Table, or tabular, charts, 88–90
Targeting audience, and planning, 11
Technical support, and graphics software, 191
Text and titles
    color and, 37–38
    general discussion of, 32–33
    kinds of text slides, 33–40
    layout and, 38–39
    printed and plotted handouts, 48–49
    quantity of text, 34

Text and titles—*Cont.*
    reveal or build-up slides, 39–40
    text as image, 42–47
    text into drawings, interpretation, 41–42
    type styles, 35–37
Text slides, types of, 33–40
Texture and pattern, and charts, 61
Theories on organizing visuals, 14–18
Thermal printers, 266–67
Thought processing software, and presentation, 16–17
Three-dimensional bar chart, 69, 72
Three-dimensional surface chart, 87
Three-pie chart, 78
Title and legends, and charts, 64
Touchpad, graphics input, 217
Trackball, graphic input, 259
Trademarks, listed, 320–22
Two- and three-column bar chart, 66
Two-column bar chart, 66
Two-pie chart, 77
Type styles, text slides, 35–37

U–V

Unity, and charts, 58
Vertical bar charts, 65–67
Vibration, special effect, 129
Video cameras, 261–62
Video capture systems, 261–62
Videotape, 13

W–Z

Well-designed software, 55–56
Wharton Business School study on visuals, 3–4
Writing style, and speaking situation, 26
Zoom, special effect, 128